❖

My Journey
from Godavari in Rajahmundry to
Mississippi in Greenville, USA

Upadhyayule Family in 1953

From left: Standing (in shorts): Pedda Babu, Sitting: Father; Sitting: Mother; Standing between the two: Me; sitting: Baby Indira; Standing behind: Bhanumati; Sitting: Manikyam; Sitting: Chinna Babu

❖

My Journey
from Godavari in Rajahmundry to
Mississippi in Greenville, USA

Sarvamangala Ganti

authorHOUSE®

AuthorHouse™ LLC
1663 Liberty Drive
Bloomington, IN 47403
www.authorhouse.com
Phone: 1-800-839-8640

Published by AuthorHouse   09/23/2013

ISBN: 978-1-4918-1340-9 (sc)
ISBN: 978-1-4918-1343-0 (e)

Library of Congress Control Number: 2013916087

CONTENTS

FOREWORD

I have been interested in learning about people and their back grounds and life they lived. I first thought about this when I migrated to the USA in 1998 to live with our daughter Gnanu in Dover, Pennsylvania. Chenulu's parents had also come for a visit at the same time and I spent many pleasant afternoons with his father Ayyalasomayajula Peravadhanulu garu reminiscing about his past. His memory was so good that he remembered all the incidents in his life and the dates of each event. I was impressed with his phenomenal recollection power and suggested to him that he should pick up his pen and begin writing his story. He did not write, nor did he live long after also and so to me this piece of family history was lost. Same thing I had noticed in Chenulu's maternal uncle Vedula Narayana Murty garu and he too did not consider writing his memoirs. I met my mentor and boss Dr. Ashok Karande and he was telling me of all the small incidents that happened in his childhood and he was publishing a book in Marathi. He was also reluctant to write his memoirs and so also another colleague of mine Dr. Kelkar. Each one of the persons above was endowed with such excellent recall powers but they would not like to write about themselves. I realized that in such a work one is likely to hurt some ones feeling. Sarvamangala was also hesitant for the same reasons. I encouraged her that those who are upset with her are not going to change their mind so why worry and write about your family as you remember even today.

I was sure she will write in Telugu our native Indian language Telugu. But she insisted that any work in Telugu will be lost as many in the next generations may not know Telugu. She wanted it to be written in English only but she could not. This prompted me to pick up the pen and I began noting incidents in her life when she moved with me to New Jersey in 2007. We had the opportunity of working on the memoirs together. Sarvamangala is blessed with excellent memory but that is not so with me and any discrepancies in dates etc. are mine and so also mention about some of the parallels in American novels etc which are my own thoughts drawing a parallel on those incidents narrated by her. If the book is successful, I would also ride on the success, sort of riding piggy back on her fame.

Satyanarayana Ganti (Chitti Ganti)

PROLOGUE

My story began on the banks of Godavari in Innispeta in Rajahmundry, but I moved a lot in all these years and one such place that has parallel to Godavari is the river Mississippi in the USA where I lived for a short period in Greenville along with Chitti my husband of 50 years.

I am writing this story about my family along with the history of my father as I owe everything to my parents. Reason for these memoirs is that with globalization we are losing touch with every one near and dear and most of the relations have spread far and wide both nationally and internationally. People do not remember their ancestors today since no one is there to tell about them. Joint family system may not exist as a phrase in the dictionary now. I have been told these incidences about my family by my father, mother, and grandmother and so on. Thus it is not a written history, but one that has been passed to me through the word of mouth. I was a curious child from birth and so my curiosity of those days has resulted into this small work. I would like to pass on this to all of the future generation who at one time or other would also be curious like me and would like to find out about their roots and their ancestors and I am hoping this will help them. Unlike an ancestral chart this is not a list of names but an effort to capture some incidents in my life during my childhood and adult period.

I value my father dearly but I have lasting memories of my mother who did not live long enough to guide me and I missed her. This book is dedicated to her since I did not have the opportunity her guidance and support in my fights for justice all throughout my life. I was not mature enough to seek her advice in the 13 years of my life that she lived after my birth. There were only few instances where she advised me or guided me and probably all were childish feeling of hurt. Still I have lasting impressions of my mother and have always missed her company and this in itself tells you about the saddest event in my life. Do you know what I miss most all these years? Not meeting her even in my dreams though I remember to have dreamt almost every one after their death. She was the only person who understood me so well and she was snatched away from me when I needed her most. The book is also dedicated to my father who was like a Rock of Gibraltar to all of us siblings. My mother was supportive in my early formative years, but my father was there to lead me all through his life till he died in 1984.

I am blessed with the number "Seven" as I am the seventh child. Seven is considered to be a powerful magical number in numerology and I am not complaining. But these astrological laws stopped short for me as if I am some one very special! Number seven translates to Yedu in Telugu my own Indian language which literally means to "Weep". Shop keepers in Andhra Pradesh, India would not say for an item costing seven (Yedu) but will say six plus one to save embarrassment to their customers. But my life has been Yedu and not six plus one in this respect. My periods of happiness have been very short and I have witnessed so many incidences of injustice done to me that often times I feel bitter about all these occurrences. I have no feelings of ill will or vindictiveness for all those who have contributed to my sadness, but only a feeling of frustration for my destiny. I have no intention to hurt any one since all these people in my life are related to me directly or indirectly. My reason of writing this memoir is only to record a mini family saga with me and my brothers and sisters as the center of the history.

I am the seventh child of my parents Upadhyayula Narasimha Murthy and Kamala Devi and this is the beginning of seven in my life. I was born in Rajahmundry on 16th (another Seven numerologically) October, 1944. According to our Telugu calendar I was born in the month of Aswijam, the seventh month. True I was not born at 7.00 am but at 10.00 am in the morning with the ringing of clock bells in our rental house in Rajahmundry. My maternal grandfather Nookala Agastya Sastry was working up his anger that my birth was being delayed as two hours later according to the Telugu calendar date or tithi will change to "Amavasya" or New Moon, an inauspicious day for everything. But I was not born on Amavasya though I may have inherited the bad signs of New Moon such as my color in particular. People stop working on a new moon day to avoid any dark influences of Amavasya. Fortunately, I came to this earth just a short time before Amavasya avoiding being notorious. I was born on one of the most auspicious of days in Indian calendar, on "Naraka Chaturdasi day" that falls one day before "Deepavali" or the festival of lights. Deepavali is celebrated with pomp and fanfare all over India. It is also celebrated by Indians every where in this world including in the White House in the USA.

My grandfather immediately opened his astrological almanac and calculated the future of this new born me and declared that I was going to be very fortunate throughout my life and will experience wealth and prosperity. He called me "Gantala Lakshmi" or 'ringing Goddess of wealth' as the bell of the wall clock were chiming when I was born. Everyone in the house was jubilant that I was born on this most auspicious day. My birthday is thus celebrated by the Indian population with cheer, joy and with fire crackers wherever they live. I was the first child in my family who was born in Rajahmundry and coincidentally my daughter Gnanu was the last child in our family that was borne in this city. You don't have to guess but she was born on 7th May another "Seven" in my life.

I am the ugly duckling in a family where all other children were very fair. In fact I am like the ray of light that did not pass through a prism showing all the seven colors in grandeur but a single color dark. Someone even recommended that I should be placed next to my older brother who was very bonny and fair so that the black magic or "dishti" of visitors to our family and neighbors is warded off. Let me begin at the beginning and introduce you briefly to all my other siblings as this is their story too. I have devoted one chapter to each of my siblings as they were my life then and even now.

1. **Sarva Lakshmi:** Oldest in our family was Sarva Lakshmi who lived only for a short period and died at the age of 2 years due to unknown causes.

2. **Manikyam:** Manikyam was the second child and we all looked up to her for advice as she was the oldest. She was married to Vedula Kashihpati Chayanulu of Anakapalle, a neighboring town near Visakhapatnam and had four children three daughters followed by one son Yagneshwar who died at a very young age of 20 years due to sunstroke. She is survived now by three daughters and she had the good fortune of seeing her grand son Vamshi born to her eldest daughter Gouthami. She died 15 days after birth of her grand daughter Deepthi due to brain hemorrhage when she was just fifty! I will write more about her later.

3. **Annapoorna:** I do not know anything about Annapoorna since she died early.

4. **Bhanumati:** Bhanumati born on April 19th, 1940 is the second oldest sister to me and she gave strong support to me even till her death on 30th March, 2013. She has four children, three sons and one daughter Durgasree all of whom are healthy and all have grown up children, four of whom are studying abroad; all three sons of Durgasree have

completed their masters in England and children of both Murty and Sekhar. Her husband Ganti Umamaheshwara Rao died in 2009. In 2010 her youngest son Kamalakar died and in 2013 she died. There will be more about them in later chapters.

5. **Sastry:** Sastry, my brother again did not live to celebrate his first birthday. This is the only photograph available so I have reproduced below.

6. **Lakshminarayana (Pedda Babu):** My brother named after my grandfather Abbayi Tata Garu on father's side, he was born in 1943 at the peak of World War II when there was an economic down turn and life became very difficult. Black marketing was rampant and most of the items of necessity were not available in the regular grocery stores. In addition to mother's milk, he was also supplemented with condensed milk that was not available in the market, but my father did not spare any cost to get the tins of condensed milk. As a child he was very active and fearless and would climb roof of our house to see people coming over to our house and particularly as a lookout for my father who would go for short trips to visit our lands. My mother would worry endlessly. He became a medical doctor and contrary to wishes of my father, he did not settle in Rajahmundry near our lands to help local village folks but went to Bangalore, a very important city in the neighboring state of Karnataka. He has two daughters and one son all very intelligent and the second daughter Aparna became a District Collector after competing successfully in the Public Service Examination, a first in our family.

7. **Sarvamangala:** Me. The "seventh" child and this is my story and these are events as I remember and recollect.

8. **Agastya Sastry (Chinna Babu):** Eighth sibling was a brother named after my maternal grandfather Nookala Agastya Sastry, he was born in 1946 and as I was more than one year older to him, my father decided that I should study in his class only so that he has company and would concentrate in his studies and so he reduced my age by one year in school records with little concern to my future and now my official date of birth is 16th July 1945 and see now even the month of western calendar is matching **Seven**. My grandfather Agastya Sastry was a very well known civil engineer participated in designing Life Insurance Corporation building in the city of Madras (now Chennai) and even today his name is engraved inside the main hall of the building. So my brother was also made to study engineering and he did this with reluctance. He became a television star and produced his own shows on local channels. He died in 2012 of brain tumor and his son Sriram came back to India from the USA to give support to his mother and brother Lakshminarayana.

9. **Indira:** She was born when we had plentiful in the family and there appeared to be total happiness all around us. Our front yard and backyard had such wonderful flowering plants that the whole house would be full of fragrant smell. She was the prettiest baby of the family and every one would shower their love to her. She had a rocking horse that was very colorful and she would not share with any one. She is very close to me even today and I would like to talk more about her in detail later. She is sitting wide eyed in the front in the family picture.

10. **Trivikram:** He is five years younger than Indira and was a very beautiful child with curly hair and big eyes. Our mother died before he was one year old and the entire responsibility of looking after him virtually fell on me as both Manikyam and Bhanumati were married and I was just 12 years old. It is for this reason that both Trivikram and Indira are very close to me and they call me "Akka" or older sister but not Manikyam

or Bhanumati who were older than all of us. My father never married again. He was just 42 years when my mother died and he took the responsibility of bringing the large family all by himself. Trivikram married Durgasree, and is blessed with three sons all of them presently living in the UK. He is not seen in the family picture as he was not born at that time.

I am no historian and although I was quite young to understand all the family intricacies and politics, I certainly absorbed many incidents about my family both near and extended and I would like to recapture these as I remember. I have no ill will for any of my family members who I believe may have done injustice to me and my family, but it is necessary for me to bring out all these incidents since they confirm the sadness in my memoirs. My father always quoted that events in every one's life are governed by three factors namely Deshamu (place), Kaalamu (time) and Paristhiti (circumstances) and he never harbored any grudge against any one.

My main purpose of writing the details of all my family members including my grandfathers and all those who were responsible for the subsequent development of our Upadhyayula history is to let those related or otherwise know about these facts. I have been told so many stories about my grandparents by my father and also some by my mother that I want to capture these incidents for the posterity. I was surprised to know that my mother was married not by her parents, but by her uncle. I have written about this also. My life and that of my father is so intermixed with the life of Rajananna that writing about him as a separate chapter does full justice to his role in our family history. I hope Ganti clan is not angry. I would have liked the story to be completed in seven chapters, but when you add all these details, the story became longer.

Sarvamangala Ganti

June 1st 2013

I dedicate this book to
My mother Kamala Devi and
My father Upadhyayula Narasimha Murty, Landlord

CHAPTER 1
ABBAYI TATA GARU: ENTREPRENEUR

My grandfather Abbayi Tatagaru was interested in doing any type of business and believed in free enterprise. This was not a common trait for a Brahmin in those days. He was an entrepreneur and entrepreneurship is an individual trait and quality that is found as a spark only in one or two members of a family in a generation. I believe it is not considered hereditary. Contrary to what science says, I believe that Entrepreneurship is hereditary or if not genetical it is an acquired character passed on from generation to generation. My grandfather however, did not show any success in his ventures and did not come anywhere near being a Birla or a Tata. He did not pass on the business to the next one in our family. But still, generations later also children in our family show a tendency to enter into free enterprise. In my family even today I see the same trait. My son Dinkar who is the 4th generation of my grandfather Abbayi Tata garu shows the same trait. I wish to forward this question to the scientific community and I know they too are divided on this subject.

My grandfather Upadhyayula Lakshminarayana was popularly known by his pet name Abbayi and many also knew him as Jhai (short for Upa-jhyayula) and interestingly he was the only one known by this short family name of Upadhyayula. He was probably the first known entrepreneur in my family. He would not hesitate selling any product to achieve the objective and that included selling grinding stones from door to door. I do not know how an entrepreneur should look like or what should be his mental strength to make him one but from his description I always thought that such a person would be almost 6 feet tall with good and strong shoulders and a strong physique just like my grandfather. He should be tallest among tall, should be strong willed and should have the ability of weathering any type of a storm in life. Abbayi Tata garu wore simple clothes and was less fussy about tidiness unlike his father Narasimha Murty who was known for his neatness and keeping things spotlessly clean in his house. My grandfather was a very private person and had a very cool temperament and he was not known to become angry.

His strength was always his quiet personality and one who never lost his temper. I know of an incident that was related time and again to highlight this point. Two of his nephews, both named Lakshminarayana, both Ganti and one was Pedda Tammu and the second Chinna Tammu were bent on finding ways to make him angry. One day they spread thorns along with flowers on the road and some thorns pricked his feet but he coolly removed thorns from his feet and laughed and said you will always find thorns among beautiful flowers and looked at his nephews.

Just being a good person does not make one a man of business but he should also have good communicating skills. Of course I did not know my grandfather but when I enquired, I was told he was a fairly talkative person and would share news and gossip with every one including ladies. He was so good in his language skills that he could make the discussions more interesting by interspersing sentences with proverbs and homilies. I would like to humbly mention here that even I have imbibed that art of using proverbs and homilies during conversations but then I have never been a very popular person. Same thing may have happened to him also and even he was not popular and I know this for certain that he was not successful. Why, what went wrong? No one knows.

Let us go back to his brief life story to know him better. His father, Narasimham was a rich farmer in Aduru and was married to the oldest daughter Mahalakshmi of Ganti Narasimham garu and Visalakshi or Vichamma of Peruru. Mahalakshmi was more commonly known as Reddamma. Narasimham is very common name being the name of village deity of Peruru Lord Narasimha Swami and so the name became very common in families living in Peruru or in nearby villages. They were happily married well settled in Aduru and were blessed with one son they named as Lakshminarayana who was fondly called Abbayi meaning 'boy' a pet name in Telugu. Aduru being in the delta region of river Godavari, the lands are fertile where cash crops like coconuts, rice, jack fruits are produced all through the year. I have never been to

3

Aduru but since Indira had recently gone to Aduru, she sent some photos of the fertility of the land for my information.

We have a very special protocol of naming children in our family, a tradition that is not practiced now. The normal custom is to name the first son after father's oldest brother and if it is a daughter she is named after father's oldest sister and so on and so forth. It was easy to determine the genealogy and a child new to the village would be immediately identified with his/her ancestral relations and the exact identity is immediately established. In western society also a similar practice is seen and parents name children after father with a suffix of two (II) or three (III) and so on till the oldest member is dead and the oldest living one promoted as one and three becomes two. People would identify the native place of the person just by his name and in some cases even by some of the mannerisms inherited by the person. Everyone knew each other and the boundaries were very small. It is for this reason that you will find similar names in many of my relatives, not because they did not know of better names, but more so because they were following a tradition. Every person belongs to a Gotram and marriages are decided on the basis of Gotram. It is considered to be a sin to marry in the same Gotram. Each Gotram is believed to have been set up by three Rishi (Sages) or one could say was based on the gene pool from these three very learned men. Marriage between members of the same gene pool is prohibited even though the family names are different. Thus Ganti cannot marry a Vadlamani since they both have the same common gene pool or Gotram even though their last name is different.

Coming back to the story, my great grandfather Narasimham died very early and so his brother-in-law Subbarayudu Ganti took upon himself to support his sister and her only son my grandfather Lakshminarayana or Abbayi. Subbarayudu was an attorney-at-law and practiced in Kakinada a small town near Konaseema in Andhra Pradesh so that he could take care of his nephew. He then moved to Rajahmundry and supported his sister and my grandfather. He would call his sister very respectfully Akka and this name remained till she died at the age of ninety six. He was popularly known as "Rajananna" Nanna or father from Rajahmundry and he remained Rajananna even to his grandchildren and great grandchildren. His sister or my father's grandmother was known as Akka or elder sister of Rajananna to us all as she lived with my father in our house in Rajahmundry and we too respected like my father who always respected her.

My Grandfather Abbayi Tata garu was married Sarvamangala, beautiful daughter of Adibhotla Ayyababu Garu, a rich family in Eastern Part of Andhra Pradesh in a village of Karivalasa near Vizianagaram and bordering the present state of Orissa. Although I am named after her, I have not inherited her beauty or her attractive features. The Karivalasa village was owned by my grandmother's Adibhotla family as this was gifted to them by the King of Vizianagaram who was pleased with their knowledge of Vedic scriptures and religious support they gave to the king and the people of Vizianagaram. He was greatly respected by the king and whenever the head of the Adibhotla family visited the king or go out on any official duty, he would be carried in a palanquin on the shoulders of 4 carriers or you could call it a Staff Car of the olden days. The front door of their ancestral house was lit by torches mounted on silver holders and were lit even during the day as a mark of great honor and respect. My grandmother came from her parental home after a delivery of a child and was accompanied with a large contingent of maids and plenty of traditional gifts such as turmeric powder, kumkum, aritha (soap nut) and other powders for beauticare along with sweets, fruits and dry fruits like cashew etc. befitting to her status. Some of the quantities were so large that it would last our family for almost one year!

The village was owned by Ayyababu garu and all the produce belonged to them and they wisely distributed to the people in the village in an amicable manner many of whom were their farm hands. They were affluent and my grandmother never had to work with her hands at any time during her early life before marriage as they had many maids to do all the domestic chores and she lived a life of luxury. However, she acted like an ordinary person when she came to join my grandfather as he was not as wealthy as her parents. She had to do everything with her own hands but she did not complain and they both lived a happy life. My grandfather began to search for job and found one outside the state of Andhra Pradesh and he accepted a position in the Kingdom of Jamnagar in Gujarat in Western India and was very much respected there. They had spacious quarters and they were very happy. Abbayi Tata garu was the first in our family to emigrate for the purpose of a job, but then his experience of independent job in a far off place was short lived and he returned back shortly because of very peculiar circumstances.

One day my grandmother was lighting oil lamps in the house as those days there was no electricity and she stepped over some rubber like substance and she pushed it away with her foot without giving it a second thought. When the room was lit, she did not see anything on the floor and forgot the incident. In the morning when she was trying to step down from her bed, she saw a very large King Cobra snake with its hood fanned out and in a threatening posture. After a few minutes the snake went away and she realized that the object she had pushed away previous evening was probably the snake and now the snake was seeking vengeance. It is believed in India that a Cobra has a very long memory and he would never forget the aggressor or attacker. The snake would follow the person wherever he or she would go till either the cobra or the other person is dead. In my grandmothers' case the snake would appear every morning to remind my grandmother of the hurt she had given to the animal and would go away. No one would dare hurt the cobra bent on vengeance because Cobra is considered a very pious animal by Hindus as it adorns the neck of Lord Shiva. Why the cobra did not kill my grandmother is a mystery. They then decided to leave Jamnagar and so my grandfather and grandmother left Jamnagar for good and returned back to Rajahmundry and hoped the snake would not follow them there. The snake did not follow them or I would not be here to write this chronicle. Was moving back to Rajahmundry a wise decision?

Sarvamangala gave birth to three children two sons and one daughter. My father Narasimha Murty is the oldest son followed by my aunt Gnanaprasunamba or Gnanamba Attayya (Auntie) and the youngest son Venkateshwara Chenulu or Babayya. My grandfather had two pet names Abbayi and Jhai and over the years people would call him by either of the names. Almost everyone I knew had some form of nick name but surprisingly my father was always known as Narasimha Murty. He did not have any pet name. My father was a strong support for his mother and she would tell everyone that if Narasimha Murty was at her side, she was safe. My grandmother was carrying fourth child so she went to her father's place in Karivalasa for delivery when she was suddenly taken ill and she died shortly afterwards along with the unborn child. The story goes that my grandmother was standing at the doorway with her long dark beautiful hair rippling on her beautiful fair body looking so radiant and beautiful that evil eyes (dishti) fell on this beautiful person. She became very ill almost immediately and was declared dead a short time later. My uncle Venkateshwara Chenulu or Babayya was then 3 years old and my father just 8 years old.

I was born in a Brahmin family so we are expected to serve the community by reading scriptures written in Sanskrit or perform religious rites that only a Brahmin is authorized to perform. My forefathers on father's side may even have been working as priest performing various religious functions in the village, but somewhere along the way the situation changed. My grandfather Abbayi Tata garu began his road to service that ended suddenly and he returned back to Rajahmundry and began to dream of a successful business ventures in his fertile mind. In those days, business was carried out in India by members of Vaisya or commerce community commonly known as Banias since they have resources and support of all their family members and relatives in setting up their businesses including financial assistance when needed. They believed in money and generating more money including lending money at high interest rates that a Brahmin is not expected to do. Members of Vaisya community would not serve under a master and so he would set up his own mom and pop shop such as a grocery store, a jewelry shop or become loan sharks. My grandfather was bitten by the business bug and began to explore diverse areas and was always teeming with new ideas but none succeeded. Success depends mostly on the support an entrepreneur receives from his own family as demonstrated by the Vaisya community and most other businesses die prematurely if not supported by their own family members or community. Generally when starting a new business or a venture an entrepreneur is prompted to borrow first from his own family as this will show strong relationships within their own family. But this is the first drawback for a Brahmin beginning his own venture. A Brahmin is expected to perform religious rites, read Vedas or spread religious thoughts by giving discourses and not indulge in commerce as laid down by the laws of Manu. So naturally other members of the clan would not support such an activity and same thing may have happened to my grandfather.

My grandfather was a very upright person but he failed to get the support of his own family members. He did not know the wheeling and dealing that goes on in doing a business and believed that quality governs the business. His business was generally a low investment one and more often involved buying a good product and selling the same at a reasonable profit like any commission agent. His customers were known to him; mostly our relatives and they would not stoop so low to pay him for his material and services. How can they insult him! So they did not pay him. He was too soft with all the people and would not like to be tough on any one in collecting his dues and people took advantage of his good nature.

Getting back to my story, my grandfather was now busy looking after his children after sudden demise of his lovely wife Sarvamangala. He was supported in this task by his mother Akka and his uncle Rajananna; in fact my grandfather with his three children lived with Rajananna. But over a period of time, Akka felt she could not cope up with bringing up small children and insisted that my grandfather should marry once again. She even threatened to end her life if he did not do so. He was left with no choice but to consider a second marriage simultaneously realizing he may be taking a risk and that his other children may not receive love and care from their step mother. He was finally persuaded to marry Ratnalu, daughter of Ganti Suryanarayana garu from Visakhapatnam. She was then just twelve years old and about four years older than my father. She was very fair, beautiful and sported very long and thick dark black hair reaching almost to her knees. But this image of her beauty remained short lived as my grandfather did not live long and she had to shave her head once she was widowed. I heard my father and other elders in our family talk about her maiden beauty.

My grandfather acquired two large pieces of lands one in Gurraja Peta a sandy land supporting casuarina trees, coconut and other cash crops. The casuarina trees were grown for five years and once the trees grow to a fairly large size they were auctioned off and hence the yield was never annual but yielded cash after these auctions. These plantations did not require much supervision and so could be managed even from Rajahmundry which was far away and one had to travel more than 100 miles by train. My grandfather began bringing different crops and began planting coconut trees which would give him regular yield once the tree reached a fruiting stage. He loved agriculture and he tried to improve the fertility of the land with good practices.

Second plot of land was an agricultural farm near Rajahmundry in Diwancheruvu. Here the land was suitable for fruits namely oranges, cashew nuts, mangoes and Sapotas. Here too maintenance was bare minimum and since these plants required less water they grew well in these types of soils. The crop was auctioned off every year and the income would offset the costs of inputs. Akka would always say that if you invest 100 rupees in the land you would get a return of more than double or more than 200 rupees but you invest 100 rupees in house, the return on investment is zero. My grandfather thus invested in land and not in houses. He invested in his land by way of manure and fertilizers, and in return he harvested a rich produce that would meet the household expenses in addition to meeting the expenses incurred towards the maintenance. Diwancheruvu was almost eight miles from where my grandfather lived and he would walk down to the field almost on a daily basis and supervise planting seedlings of good variety of horticultural plants. Even Akka went to Diwancheruvu on foot. My grandfathers' land produced fruits that were best in the area and so he would always get good offer during auction. But again he would borrow more money to invest in fertilizers for the next crop and this increased a hole in his pocket and he was perpetually in debt like every farmer even today.

Somehow, he found time to consider and implement many of his other ventures. He set up a shop on the banks of Godavari selling best quality mango fruits to a frugal community which did not have cash available and even though people appreciated the quality of the fruits they would be reluctant to purchase them. Very few people had the purchasing power and much of the business was conducted through a barter system. Since my grandfather was busy in managing both the farms he would seek the help of his two nephews' one younger son of Rajananna Chinna Tammu and his cousin Pedda Tammu who were at home because of summer vacation. They were very considerate and regarded that eating one or two of these fruits was OK as they did not charge any salary. They also believed that since mangoes were a perishable commodity they helped in reducing the loss by their eating as they did not throw fruits into trash when they became rotten. With such helping sales people it was no surprise that the entire venture was a total loss and my grandfather became a laughing stock. In fact some would even come to the shop when my grandfather was there to indulge in local gossip and pick up one or two mangoes promising they would pay later and that later would never come. That is why I said he had good business acumen but not good business sense or practices.

In those days he was probably the first few who became interested in Homeopathic medicines as an alternative medicine in place of either home based medicines or allopathic medicines. He learnt many treatments for common health problems and even today some descendants of his time remember receiving medicines from him that helped them or members of their family. He was a pioneer in this field of medicine in these parts of Andhra, but did not become a successful practitioner and did not make any money just like his earlier enterprise in selling excellent mango fruits. His mind would always work on finding new ideas of new ventures but from his history of failures he would be reluctant to put into practice these new ideas nor would he share them with anyone else for being mocked at. He probably shared these with my father who was very mature for his age and he was very resourceful and supportive.

My grandfather was having a very happy time in spite of nagging by his mother for his string of failures. His friends and relatives also did not understand the greatness of this person and made fun at him or mocked him all the time and so he was virtually all alone. He would probably spend his time in going from one farm property to another both being so far away from our home. He was very hard working and unfortunately for him his hard work failed to give him success he so much deserved. He was living with Rajananna so that he could attend to plantation in his farm at Diwancheruvu and family was taken care of with minimum worry for support. His wife Ratnalu gave birth to three daughters Jagadamba, Suryamba and Lakshmi and they too began growing along with my father and other children. The house was now full with the chatter of children and clamor of cooking by his mother Akka and Ratnalu. However, in 1932 when Lakshmi was six months old my grandfather died suddenly at a very young age of 42 and as there was no medical report available, the cause of death is not known. My father was then just eighteen and he was too young to face these encumbrances and liabilities but he did so with courage and integrity and this will be narrated in later chapters. Akka remembered this event of premature death of my grandfather and was always worried and hoped that the early death is not hereditary and she would constantly inquire my father about his health once he reached 40. I will briefly mention about my father's siblings below.

Gnanamba Attayya:

Gnanamba Attayya or Gnanaprasunamba was born in October 1915 at Karivalasa my grandmother's parental place. From her very childhood, she was very sharp and protected her brother and though she had a very short temper she was a reasonable person. She was skilled in pinching technique for getting things done without anyone noticing and so most people regarded her as a very quiet person. Young girls in those times would keep some vows or other and one such was a vow where she would not speak or remain silent (maunam) and yet she must invite young girls for the function. She took my father as an escort to invite neighboring ladies and girls of her age for the function and my father would invite everyone on her behalf and to her satisfaction. However, if he did not invite correctly as per her instructions, she would pinch him hard leaving red marks on his skin and no one would know about it. She was very close to my father and she never did anything without consulting him. She was so neat and maintained her clothes so well that she was regarded a well-dressed person whether in the day or at night and that too without a wardrobe of expensive clothes. She appeared as if she dressed just then looked ever ready even after she was married or living in a far off place called Billimora in Gujarat. My father noticed similar characteristics in my daughter Gnanu who has been named after my aunt Gnanamba Attayya.

Attayya was married when she was eight years old to Rajananna's second son Sita Ramiah or Ramam Mavayya who was then eighteen years old. A few hours before the wedding, Ramam Mavayya fainted and this upset Rajananna and he immediately declared that he would not allow this weak son of his to marry Gnanamba Attayya and wanted to call off the wedding. But my grandfather Abbayi Tata garu was firm about the wedding and he insisted that the marriage should be concluded as Ramam may be nervous. He argued that if this was known after the marriage what could we have done? I can positively say Ramam Mavayya who became my father-in-law enjoyed a long healthy life and lived till he was over ninety. The marriage was thus concluded in spite of the objection from Rajananna. My father always maintained that Rajananna was one of the highly principled people and he applied the same yard stick for every one including his own son. No wonder my father held him in highest respect.

First child Mahalakshmi was born on 3rd November, 1931 when Gnanamba Attayya was just sixteen years old. The good news that Gnanamba Attayya was pregnant was conveyed to my grandfather Abbayi Tata garu who was extremely happy; but he did not live to see the birth of the child as he died just a few days before.

My uncle Ramam Mavayya had studied in Victoria Jubilee Technical Institute (VJTI), Bombay (Mumbai) and became a chemical technologist for a textile mill in Bombay specializing in the bleaching processes for the cotton yarn. Sometime during 1930's Ramam Mavayya contracted pneumonia that spread to both his lungs culminating into double pneumonia because of his constant working with chlorine. He was hovering between life and death and was being treated by his doctor brother Satyanarayana but Gnanamba Attayya wanted my father also to be there. My father traveled to Bombay to take care of Ramam Mavayya and support his sister Gnanamba Attayya. Ramam Mavayya was in a delirious state and there was always a concern that he may jump from the balcony as he was not conscious of his actions and my father was there to restrain him. Fortunately treatment from his brother Dr. Satyanarayana and support from my father allowed him to recover very fast and he became normal. He accepted a job in Ahmedabad in another textile mill and moved away from Bombay. Gnanamba Attayya thus moved from place to place in Gujarat, then home of the textile industry. Not much is known about his experiences in Ahmedabad except that in later years after my marriage to Chitti his youngest son, he would often reminisce about owner of Vadilal Ice Cream, a brand that has become very famous over the years. It seems during his stint at Ahmedabad, he would often go over to the ice cream parlor run by the same Vadilal and he felt very happy that the same became a famous ice cream company over time. Vadilal Ice Cream is even today a very popular brand in Western India and is also available in some parts of the USA.

Five years later on 8th January, 1936 she gave birth to Subbarayudu or Babu at Bombay in her brother-in-law Satyanarayana's nursing home in Dadar. This was probably first delivery in our family that had not taken place in parental house. Babu was liked by his doctor uncle and he would often chat with him and play. There was one serious incident in Babu's early life that needs to be mentioned here. Ramam Mavayya was recuperating from double pneumonia and during this time he used to keep all his medicines on table top within easy reach. One day, the nurse had left a bottle of tincture iodine on the table near the bottle of food supplement medicine Babu used to take every night after his meals. Both the bottles looked similar and even the color of medicine was similar. As per his habit, Babu drank table spoon full of iodine instead of his own medicine. The situation became very serious and even after emptying the stomach content some of the iodine entered in the blood stream and Babu was in a critical state. At about the same time, the doctor received a call from his client, an owner of a nearby Broadway movie theatre that his son of almost same age as Babu had swallowed another type of poison namely the fire cracker powder and he too was in a serious condition. The doctor rushed to treat this son of the then famous movie theater in Dadar and warned Ramam Mavayya and Gnanamba Attayya not to allow Babu to fall asleep since sleep would be fatal.

He treated the other boy in the same manner and once his pulse was stabilized he instructed his client that his own nephew had the similar accident and he will have to go back to his home to monitor the progress of recovery. He warned these parents also that at no time should they allow the boy to sleep as that will be disastrous. The parents agreed and the good doctor returned home. Babu was weeping loudly since both Ramam Mavayya and Gnanamba Attayya would not allow him to sleep and kept him awake the rest of the night by either spraying cold water on his face or occasionally slapping. Doctor Satyanarayana told his brother that he was tired and will rest now as things appeared to be under control and that they are following his instruction. He called the owner of the movie theater to confirm that his son was awake and so he told the client that he is now going to retire as it had been a very trying day and to call him if needed.

Next day morning Babu became his normal active self and he was playing with his doctor uncle and so he inquired about his other patient the son of the movie theater. The owner was very happy about the progress and told the doctor that his son was not having any problem and in fact he was sleeping peacefully. Dr. Satyanarayana was known for his very short temper and he flew into rage and fired his client and rushed over to see the second patient of his and try as he did he could not save the boy and the boy died. With a great pain in his heart, he told the owner that his son is no more and he could not bear to see the grief of this bereaved family. The whole incident looks like a story now when I repeat it but then it actually happened and my father would always repeat to us to impress upon us that there is a very thin line between life and death and how a simple act of negligence by the parents resulted in a tragedy.

Ramam Mavayya's mother Sitamma or Ammamma for us all would tell me the same story when I came to Bombay after my marriage that her doctor son would always sit by her side in the night after day's work "Mom, see there is always life in my hands and these are 'miracle hands' and I can even bring to life those who are almost dead. My hands gave life and none have died because of me or my treatment." He was a very emotional person and liked to hear every one in his family talk about his success but unfortunately for him it did not happen.

Gnanamba Attayya traveled to Rajahmundry and delivered a daughter on 28th August 1938, just one day before Vinayaka Chaturthi or Lord Ganesh's birthday. She was named Sarvamangala after our grandmother. After a gap of another two years on 1st June, 1940 she delivered a son in Bombay in the same nursing home and he was named Satyanarayana (Chitti) after his uncle or the famous Dr. Ganti of Dadar. I am married to this Chitti and so the story of my life became more entangled with that of Ganti family. I know as many details of my in-laws as I know of my own family. Gnanamba Attayya and Ramam Mavayya had only four children and all of them are living in good health.

One year after birth of Babu, my uncle joined Gaikwad Mills in Billimora, a small town about 200 miles west of Bombay. Gnanamba Attayya along with Lakshmi and Babu went to live in Billimora after he found appropriate accommodation. The first one was in a private home of one Mr. Chaganlal Mistry and the house was just one block away from the only movie theater in Billimora. Gnanamba Attayya became very friendly with the ladies in the house and my uncle Ramam Mavayya was very well received by the men folk of the family and they became our family friends for many years even after he left Billimora. After about a year, they moved to the company accommodation located just outside the mill gate. It was the longest stay for them and lived happily till 1952 and their four children received all their education in Gujarati, a language of the State of Gujarat. All of them studied in the local school Jamshedji Tata Secondary High School. Not only her children learnt Gujarati but even Gnanamba Attayya became very proficient in Gujarati. She would receive classics in Gujarati from the school library and read them thoroughly. She read such authors like K. M. Munshi the founder of Bharatiya Vidya Bhavan, Jhaverchand Meghani and so on and would even discuss merits of each. She did not like the book 'Prithvi Vallabh" written by K. M. Munshi as she felt the author did not do justice to the Dravidian culture and in fact showed them inferior to Aryans. She was very proud of our culture as we are Dravidian Brahmins.

It is true that my aunt and my cousins visited us every summer or whenever they have holidays in the school to be with my father. My father had once given her 100 rupees when she was going to Bombay for the first time and instead of buying clothes etc. she invested the amount in a bank and continued to add to her account every so often. My cousins would be wearing either long shorts or white pajamas normally worn by Muslims in Rajahmundry and hence it was unusual for us and we would call them 'saheb' to make fun of them and that would make them angry and resulted in war between the kids. The period of her happiness continued till 1953 when Ramam Mavayya was afflicted once again with pneumonia and the consulting specialist doctor told him "quit the job if you want to live" and so Ramam Mavayya left his job and left Billimora for good and returned to Bombay. I have always wondered why he chose Bombay and not Rajahmundry as that would have also given him a good healthy life while overlooking their properties. But who can change the course of history and so they moved to Bombay.

Doctor Satyanarayana died early in 1942 but their younger brother Lakshminarayana or Chinna Tammu Mavayya began his medical practice in the same Dadar area. The old dispensary and house were surrendered after Satyanarayana died as Chinna Tammu Mavayya was still in Indian Military Medical Corp so he did not inherit the practice. Once the war was over and at the end of his tenure of short commission, he left the army and began his practice in Dadar just around the corner of the road where his late brother's dispensary was located. The road on which Dr. Satyanarayana had his thriving practice was named after him by the Municipal

Corporation of Bombay as 'Dr. Ghanti Road' spelt wrongly even today in honor of this doctor who had given a lot to the local community. In 1947 Chinna Tammu Mavayya set up his dispensary at the corner of Dr. Ghanti Road and Parsi Colony Road No. 4 and a few years later he bought an apartment in Deep Mala at the other end of the road in a newly constructed building. Gnanamba Attayya and Ramam Mavayya with their children came to live with them in this apartment after leaving Billimora.

My uncle Ramam Mavayya returned from Billimora with all the retirement benefits along with his boss one Mr. Giridharilal Bhatt who also left the service along with Ramam Mavayya and following the advice of Mr. Bhatt, he was on the lookout to purchase an apartment near Dadar close to his brother Chinna Tammu and he selected an apartment in Shankar Niwas near Shivaji Park beach in a fairly peaceful locality. The apartment house is located next to famous Brahman Sahayak Sangh, a marriage hall. According to my father, my aunt Gnanamba Attayya did not want to move in rainy season since it was inauspicious month of Ashadha but then they could not have lived in his brother's house which was too small an apartment for two families.

Once they moved to the new apartment house 10, Shankar Niwas, Shivaji Park Road # 3, Gnanamba Attayya was very happy since all the neighbors were very good. Their immediate neighbor opposite to the apartment was a widow Prabhavati Gokhale and next to that apartment were a Mr. and Mrs. Joshi who lived along with their only son Pradeep. Next to Joshi was a doctor of Homeopathy Doctor Menon. Next apartment was owned CKG Pithawala, a contractor who lived in Gujarat and used the apartment for his occasional visit and for his staff when they visited Bombay on company duty. Every floor had thus five apartments. Both Gnanamba Attayya and Ramam Mavayya were very extrovert people and they became very friendly with all the neighbors and were warmly accepted by other apartment owners. Gnanamba Attayya demonstrated her progressive nature there though she was not formally educated in regular schools. It so happened that the widow Prabhavati Gokhale had a relationship with one Mr. Mohan Sohail and this made other conservative families in the building to boycott her. Mrs. Gokhale was planning to marry him under Hindu rites and no one supported her for the remarriage. Only Gnanamba Attayya stood up and gave her full support in re-marriage of widowed Prabhavati Gokhale at the cost of her relations with other neighbors. Prabhavati Gokhale or Sohail after marriage would not forget this support given by Gnanamba Attayya and told me the details of her relationship as long as she lived. She is survived by her son who is married happily and she was happy to see her grandchildren but she died very unexpectedly when she was on a pilgrimage at a very young age.

In May, Gnanamba Attayya's oldest daughter Lakshmi came to visit her parents in their new house along with her two children Annapoorna and Bhaskar and the house was full of fun and laughter. One day she along with Chinna Tammu Mavayya's family planned to go for a Telugu movie when Ramam Mavayya was called by one of his close friend and the program was cancelled. So Gnanamba Attayya was busy in cooking for all the kids in the kitchen. The kitchen was a cooking area raised over the floor and she was cooking on a kerosene stove. She tried to reach for some spices from the shelf above the stove and her saree caught fire. Although everyone was in the house except of course Ramam Mavayya, they were stunned and did not know what should be done in this situation till another neighbor Professor Rao saheb living diagonally opposite above their apartment saw the flames and rushed with a blanket and extinguished the flames, but the knots of her silk saree on her stomach remained and she suffered third degree burns and lived for just one week before she succumbed to burns on 7th May 1954. She was conscious in the hospital after being admitted and gave a statement to the police about the nature of her accident and removed any doubts of suspicious or foul play on the part of any one in her family. My husband Chitti was fourteen years old, Sarvamangala or Baby was 16 years and Babu was 18 years old and was preparing for his studies in engineering. Ramam Mavayya was not even fifty years when this happened. He did not marry again and observed a celibate life devoted to religious activities.

His parents Rajananna and Ammamma came to Bombay to be with him in this hour of grief. Coincidently and sadly Rajananna lost his oldest daughter Chinnamanna the same day in Vakkalanka in Andhra Pradesh on 7th May 1954. It was noon and all of them were at the crematorium and remains of Gnanamba Attayya were in the final stage of burning when a telegram was delivered to Rajananna in the funeral parlor and Rajananna thus suffered a double whammy. But always a great philosopher Rajananna just waved his hands to indicate that one could do nothing and went on to participate in the proceedings in front of him.

Venkateshwara Chenulu (Babayya):

Venkateshwarulu Chenulu was born in 1917 at Karivalasa at my grandmother's parental home and this time my father was old enough to make friendship and obtain affection from his maternal grandfather and her brothers. Babayya was named after the maternal grandfather Ayyababu garu and was often known by the shortened name of Venkanna. He was protected by his older brother my father, Sister Gnanamba Attayya, mother Sarvamangala and father Abbayi. But this affection remained very short lived. Even before celebrating his second birthday he lost his mother Sarvamangala and all three children led a life without mothers' love and affection. Is this hereditary? Even Gnanamba Attayya died early leaving her children behind to be cared by others. My father too lost his wife when he was in his forties. Akka always believed this to be so and so when my father reached forty she would constantly inquire about his health and notice any difference in his cough or sneezing with grave concern. She kept a sharp eye on his health.

My father and others were brought up by their grandmother Akka in Rajananna's house in Rajahmundry along with children of Rajananna. Rajananna's wife Sitamma had plenty of love for all the children and she showed no difference between her own and those of my grandfather's and she was very fondly called Ammamma by everyone. She loved my father as much as she loved her own sons Satyanarayana or Ramam or Chinna Tammu.

Babayya was pampered by both older siblings and the loving parents to a fault. He was very fussy and all his requests would be fulfilled by older siblings even if that spoiled him. In one famous instance he received a gift of clothes from his uncle when he was not even five years old and he liked these so much that he wore the same clothes from morning till night for almost a week. Clothes became dirty from over usage and were given for washing one morning when the washer man came for collecting clothes. In the evening Babayya asked for the same clothes and when he was told that the clothes were sent for washing he threw tantrums and began to cry. Every one tried to calm him or divert his mind away from the clothes but he would not budge and so my grandfather went over to the washer man in the night and requested him to return those clothes without even ironing so that my uncle is pacified. Once my son Dinkar also fussed about his one set of clothes that were given for washing and I remembered Babayya. My father loved him so much that he would not mind his tantrums and supported them and did not make him study hard. He was the pet of the family. My grandfather died when he was 11 years old and so there may have been a fair degree of set back to his studies. My father did not let him feel the loss of their father and gave him all the support and facilities for him to study hard and become a doctor.

By the time Babayya reached his matriculation, my father had moved to Diwancheruvu so that they lived near to their agricultural farms. They bought a small house and Akka and my father with his brother moved there. Looking around the conditions in the village with the nearest doctor more than 5 miles away and all the villagers suffering from various types of illnesses my father was keen that his brother became a doctor and set up his practice over there and both would manage their respective profession and live together and help the local community. My uncle was admitted to the medical college as at that time there were more opportunities for studying but he did not join and instead joined a graduate course in Agricultural Science. He explained to my father that study of medicine was expensive and requires almost 8 years before he is allowed to practice whereas he would join my father immediately after completing his graduation in Agricultural Science in just three years. My father could only agree with him and thought at least he will come to support him in managing the two farms but he did not do so.

He was married to Venkata Lakshmi or Venkayamma (Tocchhi for us) daughter of Karra Lakshminarayana garu of Amalapuram and they both lived with us in Rajahmundry till the birth of their fifth child, a son Narasimha Murty named after my father and only then they set up their independent family in Bangalore. He had a very large family like ours and we knew each one of my cousin very well as they lived with us early on and later they would visit us in Rajahmundry almost every year. He too loved his children very dearly just like my father. He started his career by working in some private agricultural research station in Tuni before he was selected for a government job. He was appointed as a plant quarantine officer in ports and air ports and was posted to various ports and air ports every three years or less and at no time lived near his brother to the disappointment of my father. We never had any opportunity to visit my uncle and their family at any of those places they lived as most of the time they would come to our house every year for vacation and looking back now, I do not think we ever received any invitation from Babayya. My father had so much love for his brother and would have gone to his house with lots of fruits and other crops but I do not think my uncle realized his loss.

It is unfortunate that my father did not receive any invitation from all those whom he loved dearly even during later years of his life.

Gnanamba the oldest daughter of Babayya was born in March, 1937 and was named after my auntie as per the tradition and she was followed by second daughter Sita born in January, 1941; followed by Subhadra or Papa in September, 1942 and Sarvamangala in August, 1945. They were blessed with Son who was born in September, 1947 and was named after my father Narasimha Murty. He was then followed by Aruna in November, 1949; Jayasree in August, 1952 and Kalpakam in October, 1954. Ramalila was born in May 1957 followed by another son Kashinath, who was born in Calcutta in November, 1959. The last child a daughter Padmasree was born in June 1961. Babayya had a very full and happy family.

Although my father had a great love for my uncle it was mostly one way. It started with sharing the debt of Abbayi Tata garu and my uncle disowned his responsibility as the decision to pay off their father's debt was taken by my father and so it was his liability. My father married all his three step sisters to good families and spent large sums of money on their weddings and was hoping that his brother would also share these but again he disagreed. Every issue was contested by him. My father was a very good person and went out of his way to help every one of his relative who accepted his support but they soon forgot about it. Why would this happen to good people and why are they never appreciated? Sometimes I feel dejected thinking about everything my father passed through and feel there is no God or if there is one he did not care for good people. Same is true even in our scriptures. Rama spent all his life in forests or without his wife Sita, but Ravana enjoyed all the pleasures of the world. What did Krishna get out of his life, nothing and he was shot by a hunter when he was sleeping in a forest! What did Gandhi or Nehru get out of life for all their sacrifices? Nothing and they too were good people. I think there is an element of injustice there.

Mamma: Mamma gave birth to three daughters before my grandfather died. The first child was Jagadamba and she was born in 1926, Suryamba in 1928 and Lakshmi in 1930. My grandfather did not celebrate her first birthday and died in 1931. I do not know more about my aunts as they were all married and were well settled before I became curious and somehow I did not make any long term relationship with their children. Jagadamba Attayya was married to Ganti Surya Prakash Rao garu of Visakhapatnam and lived there most of her life, Suryamba Attayya was married to Pappu Suryanarayana garu in Bombay till he retired and moved to Visakhapatnam. Third daughter Lakshmi Attayya was married to Anuppindi Someshwara Rao garu who was well positioned in State Public Works Department of Andhra Pradesh and they moved from one place to another place on frequent transfers. I met their children also and have known them time to time but did not have any long term friendship with them to write more about them in this volume.

We all had a close attachment with Mamma but we did not visit her often in Visakhapatnam where she lived. Only Vikram took time out and visited her more frequently after my Father's death and continued to support her expenses jointly with his brothers. I do not remember if either Pedda Babu or Chinna Babu ever visited her in Visakhapatnam. From Babayya's family, Kashinath shared expenses with Vikram and supported her every time she needed. Baby from Attayya's side visited Mamma whenever she had an opportunity and twice she accompanied me to Visakhapatnam. I feel blessed that I could visit her in 2010 when I visited India in anticipation of many marriages but attended only one wedding of Deepthi, daughter of Gouthami. Baby came with me to visit Mamma in Visakhapatnam and we both went by plane. Baby's son Prabhakar arranged for a car for our movement in Visakhapatnam and I could visit many places there. We took this opportunity for taking some pictures with Mamma and my aunts Suryamba Attayya and Lakshmi Attayya who took care of Mamma till her death.

Mamma celebrated her 100th birth anniversary in 2009 and she died on March, 23 of 2011 in Visakhapatnam at the age of 102 years. According to Telugu calendar, she died at the age of 106 years including all the additional months (adhik masam). I was so happy that I had the opportunity of visiting her before she died and spend some time with her. She was very frail and was looked after so well by her two daughters who themselves were more than seventy years of age.

Parental Care

At my age, I have become more conscious of parental care and I realize how difficult it is for children to care for their parents. I would like to mention those that have impressed me with their service to their parents and this is not the complete list but I believe they signify the best in our family systems.

My Father: My Father believed in Lord Rama and his philosophy of life and so he believed in serving parents and other elders in the family. He inherited family responsibilities at a very young age and so too his parental duties. Rajananna Akka or my father's grandmother lived to a ripe age of 92 and was afflicted with paralysis and lived a virtual cripple for 10 years in our house. Both my mother and father looked after all her needs without ever disrespecting her. We were all instructed to see that we gave full respect to her though she could not walk and nor could she see. She lived in vasara (extension of room) outside of father's bedroom so that he kept constant vigil on her needs. She too was watchful of my father's health and would inquire from us all if he was feeling OK.

Father also looked after Mamma and Ammamma with respect. In addition to these two, father also looked after Rajananna and Ammamma who lived in Peruru. Almost six months in a year they would spend their time with us in Rajahmundry and as Rajananna always interfered with our programs, we would argue with father why should we look after them. He would chide us that when our family needed a support Rajananna stood like a rock behind my father and grandfather Abbayi Tata garu. It is now our payback time. We should always remember any good done to us by any one since it is very easy to forget their good deed over a period of time.

Suryamba and Lakshmi Attayya: I have just seen my aunts Suryamba Attayya and Lakshmi Attayya who served their mother till her death. Lakshmi was so attached to her mother that she would come to visit her every day and nurse her. When Mamma had a fracture of her hip, she nursed her most of the time since they could not afford a professional nurse. I have photos of my aunts along with me and Baby and I cherish these moments of my stay with them. We visited all the temples in Visakhapatnam with them and we had a very good darshanam of Narasimham Swami the deity of Simhachalam. All this was not possible without the car and driver given to us by Prabhakar. Mamma did not have any sons but these two daughters spared no effort to make her life comfortable even though they were neither wealthy nor healthy. Lakshmi Attayya became so depressed after Mamma's death that she too became ill and could not participate in Suryamba Attayya's grandson Ravi's marriage on 26th June, 2011 at Hyderabad.

Upadhyayula Brothers: I consider my two aunts as an example of showing parental care on par with that shown by Suryanarayana brothers. My father's clerks Upadhyayula Suryanarayana and Satyanarayana cared for their mother till she died and the same loving care were given by their spouses also. She was addicted to opium that was common in those days and these two illustrious sons spared no efforts in getting required quantities of the drug from black market even though they were not rich. Their mother would beg them not to spend any money on her, but these two brothers continued to serve her all through her life. My father quoted them as examples of ideal sons. Upadhyayula brothers are an example of the second type of service.

Vadlamani Subba Rao garu: He is older brother of Babi, my sister Indira's husband and he looked after his parents with care and respect difficult to find in many others. This is not to say his wife Kamakshi garu did not look after her in-laws, since she too was very devoted to them and did not allow any lapse from her side too. In fact both husband and wife were one where it came to serving his parents. He held senior management position and had to move on transfer to various metro cities in India. His father Vadlamani Someshwara Rao garu and mother moved with them to all these places and were looked after by them till their death. They received the same degree of comfort wherever they went. Normally when you find a son serving his parents you praise him. It is common not to consider the contribution of his wife. But what can a son do if his wife does not cooperate? I give more credit to Kamakshi garu in the parental care.

Interestingly Indira's husband Babi died just 6 months after his brother Subba Rao garu died. Kamakshi garu was leading a healthy life in Delhi at her second son's house. Dinkar had the opportunity of meeting her in 2011 at Indira's house and receive her blessings to Mythili, Dinkar's adopted child. She died in 2012 of cancer after a short period of suffering.

Karra Brothers: When we lived in Kakinada we were visited by Karra Gopalam garu about whom I have mentioned elsewhere in the memoirs. He was known for his speed of questions and his disinterest in answers and Chinna Babu would never fail to comment. As soon as he entered the house, Gopalam garu would ask every one hello how you are and would move to the next person in the house. He was known by Chinna Babu as "Prashnala Rao (Mr. Questions)". He retired as a school teacher with a very small pension and his brother Pantulu garu retired as a clerk but they both looked after their parents so fondly and without a murmur with the low salary of school teachers that there is no parallel. It would surprise the readers to know that their parents died on the same day, a most unusual event.

Kanchinadham Family: Chitti's sister Baby is living in Hyderabad with her husband Kanchinadham Ramam garu with all her children living nearby. She has been very fortunate of receiving best treatment from her daughters-in-law Sujata and Suhasini both always ready to satisfy any request from her. After we returned from Visakhapatnam in 2010 we returned back to Hyderabad and I came to US in November. In early 2011, Baby developed a crack in her hip bone and had to undergo surgery and when she returned from hospital she was virtually bed ridden for a very long time or till doctors allowed her movement in the house. Indira went to see her and she told me it is rare to see such daughters-in-law as they both took turns in serving Baby. Her daughter Bhanu also lives nearby and sends tiffin to her mother and shares chores with her sisters-in-law. All of them live independently, but are so united in their concern for their parents.

Babu and family: This is a family very near to me since it belongs to Chitti's brother Babu and my cousin Papa. On 18th February, 2011 Babu's son Aditya was married and they returned to Bombay. Babu had a relapse of acute asthma leading to Pneumonia and was admitted to an Intensive Care Unit for more than two weeks. Babu needed complete bed rest and someone to look after his needs. He needed oxygen almost twenty four hours a day. Our apartment in Shivaji Park, Mumbai was too small to give these comforts and so Vani and her husband Surya Mantha took him along with Papa to their home in Sion. They looked after Babu who was totally dependent on bottled air and was on liquid diet. They nursed him back to a good health and he took his first steps after discharge on 24th April, 2011. When Leena, Babu's second daughter was there she would follow the hospital routines and also look after her own two babies. Aditya would sleep in the hospital and his wife Gouri would cook for everyone. It was a demonstration of a full family support in giving parental care since Papa who is older to me also showed signs of deteriorating health.

Vikram and Family: My father had an ideal son in Trivikram who looked after him till he died. He looked after his daily needs including his quota of opium and other drugs he needed to overcome his acute bouts of asthma. Durga helped Vikram in his parental duties and gave full support and that is what mattered most. Vikram was at his bedside till he died. In my view Vikram is the example of Sravana Kumar in my own family.

Chitti: Talking about my husband in this book may sound like bragging by me and so I will make a brief mention. He looked after his grandparents Rajananna and Ammamma till they died and he also nursed his father almost till his death and was respectful to all.

Sravana Kumar: While most profess themselves to be followers of Rama, how many are Sravana Kumar? When it comes to parental care and love people quote Rama as an ideal, but Rama never looked after his parents and in fact he was away when his father died. Real meaning of parental care is shown by Sravana Kumar, who carried his aged blind parents on his shoulders for a pilgrimage to famous temples and was killed by an arrow from Rama's father Dasharatha when he was filling a water jug at the river. King Dasharatha heard the sound of burping of water and shot the animal in dark with one single arrow not realizing that it was not a forest animal but a human. He rushed to the scene and there he saw Sravana Kumar dying with the shot. King was very much upset with his action and inquired how he could help him. Sravana Kumar told the story of his blind parents waiting for water and he begged the King not to reveal that he was killed by him to his parents as that would kill them instantly. Please give them this water as they are very thirsty. But when King Dasharatha went to the blind parents, they realized something was wrong and when King Dasharatha told him the incident they died then and there and cursing the King. I have heard most commenting that they followed the example of Rama in respecting parents but how many would declare they followed Sravana Kumar?

The above examples show that there are some who would even today go beyond the call of duty. Sravana Kumar carried his parents on his shoulders in Kavidi (shoulder supported baskets) to various places of pilgrimage till his life was shortened by the arrow of King Dasharatha. The story goes further that pleased with his service to his parents, Sravana Kumar was accorded the highest honor of placing him as a star. Even today one can see the star of Sravana Kumar with two stars representing his parents in a curved formation like a Kavidi.

Mamma's died in 2011 under the constant care of her two living daughters. I can now finally close the Chapter of Abbayi Tata garu spanning two centuries.

CHAPTER 2

RAJANANNA: MY FATHER'S MENTOR

My story of Rajananna is a very important element in my memoirs as he was closely intertwined with my family in many many ways. He was living in Rajahmundry and so he acquired the famous title Rajananna meaning Nanna (father) from Rajahmundry to everyone in his family and our family. He too had a very difficult life as a child and his story thus becomes part of our Upadhyayula history. His story starts with my great grandfather Narasimha Murty garu and ends with me in my house in Bombay. I had a close contact with almost all the children and grandchildren of Rajananna and his family and hence my story is incomplete without writing about him.

Rajananna advised my father from the day he picked up the reins of his father's business after his early and premature death when my father was just sixteen. He advised my father every step of the difficult way and allowed my father to use his discretion and personal integrity to govern his decisions. In spite of a wide difference in their ages, Rajananna respected every decision taken by my father even though my father did not always follow his advice. Like Mamma Rajananna too trusted my father in doing the correct thing and he treated my father more like his son.

Rajananna: The Background

Rajananna or Subbarayudu Ganti was fourth and the youngest son of Ganti Lakshminarayana and Vichamma (Visalakshi) garu of Peruru in Godavari Delta. Rajananna lost his father even before he was born and the family was supported by their widowed mother. Oldest child was daughter Mahalakshmi or popularly known as Reddamma, followed by Polamba, then Simham short for Narasimham and finally Subbarayudu. After marriage of Reddamma, her husband Upadhyayula Narasimha Murty garu of Aduru or my great grandfather undertook the responsibility of supporting education of Rajananna who had shown a spark of brilliance from a very young age. He became very much attached to Rajananna and together both husband and wife Reddamma showered their love and affection on this youngest child of Vichamma. He was in fact brought up by his two older sisters. The deep love and affection among the three Reddamma, Polamba and Subbarayudu was so strong that it remained unwavering till their death. I do not know much about Vichamma and nor about her life as a widow nor her death and so cannot give more details. Reddamma and Narasimham garu were proud parents of their only son Lakshminarayana or Abbayi Tata garu and they simultaneously educated and supported Rajananna. Rajananna became a well-known attorney through hard work and perseverance and began his practice in Rajahmundry. I will briefly mention about his other siblings and their family details below to complete the story.

Simham (Narasimham) garu family:

Simham garu was older to Rajananna but he was afflicted with diabetes and asthma at an early age and was of weak constitution and his poor eye sight did not help him and it became a handicap. He remained in Peruru looking after ancestral properties after completing his schooling. He married Peramma daughter of Peri family of Bhandarlanka, a nearby village. They had two sons the oldest was Lakshminarayana or Pedda Tammu to identify him from Rajananna's son Lakshminarayana or Chinna Tammu and the second son Ramam was nick named as Chilaka Ramam as his nose was like beak of a parrot to identify him from his other cousin Ramam garu or my father-in-law. Rajananna supported Simham garu once he became a successful attorney in Rajahmundry and left the property in Peruru to his brother and his children. Simham garu lived almost all his life in Peruru and may not have come to Rajahmundry to the best of my knowledge and I am not aware of these incidents or mentioned by my father or anyone else in our family. But we were closely connected with his sons Pedda Tammu and Chilaka Ramam.

Pedda Tammu: Pedda Tammu Mavayya lived for a long time with his uncle Rajananna and was very close to my father and also Grandfather Abbayi Tata garu. He was often a custodian of my grandfathers' business ventures along with his cousin Chinna Tammu. They both studied in the school in the same grade and while Pedda Tammu would study hard, Chinna Tammu would apparently hardly study but was always in the top ten students in his class. Pedda Tammu Mavayya concluded his studies after graduating. Soon he got a posting at a paper mill in Sirpur about 150 miles away from Rajahmundry and is served by train services going to Nagpur from Vijayawada. He was a very dynamic person in his work place and became active in labor politics and worked to find better deal for his colleagues. He came to Rajahmundry very often and talked about his connections with political leaders like Neelam Sanjiva Reddy of Congress Party and my father would joke about it saying that Neelam (meaning Blue in Telugu) or Red will not help you in your career so why not be like other employees in your company? Interestingly Sanjiva Reddy became President of India during 1980's and if he had clicked correctly Pedda Tammu Mavayya would certainly be in some senior political position but this did not happen. He was given company quarters and he brought up his family in that small house. He also had the bug of entrepreneurship probably acquired from my grandfather Abbayi Tata Garu and he set up a small grinding mill to make wheat flour for local residents in Sirpur. But it did not show good promise since very few in Andhra ate chapatti as most of the community is rice eating. But he continued to pursue in this venture and I believe my father also helped him in this but I cannot claim positively.

He married Subbalakshmi, the oldest daughter of Chinnamanna and Mantha Subrahmanyam garu of Vakkalanka and they lived happily in Sirpur within their meager means. They had four sons and one daughter and all of them are well settled and I am touching briefly about each whatever little I know.

Oldest son Narasimha Murty was born in 1941 in Vakkalanka at his grandparent's house and was a very hard working and studious person just like his father. After completing his matriculation Pedda Tammu Mavayya requested my father to allow him to study under his supervision in Rajahmundry and my father readily agreed and Narasimham stayed with us in Rajahmundry till he got accommodation in a college hostel and thus he became very close to us. He was very naïve as a teen and did not understand the intricacies of world. In one incident, one of our neighbors daughter eloped with a student in his college and since he was also living in student hostel, my father asked him if he knew of the affair. He innocently replied that she used to come to hostel to his friend's room and he thought they were studying together and did not give it another thought! I remember another incident when after we sat down for our dinner, father asked Narasimham to go out and look at the sky and see if it was likely to rain. He returned to tell us all that the sky was clear and even before he completed his sentence, it rained cats and dogs. My father asked him what he meant when he said the sky was clear; he replied the sky was clear of such things like stars and constellations. Nobody asked him if the sky was cloudy so he did not venture extra information and everyone laughed and this became a common quote in our family. Another time, Pappu Bhyranna garu was staying in our house and he was criticizing the then Prime Minister Mrs. Indira Gandhi for her policies and Narasimham told us when he was not around 'maybe he wants the position of Indira Gandhi' and we all burst into laughter.

Narasimham completed his graduation in chemistry and then joined in the quality control department of a public sector steel mill in Bhilai. He married Prabhavati in 1967 and their first daughter Phani Kumari was born on November, 19th 1969 and second daughter was born five years later in 1974. He remembers our association even today after so many years of separation and in 2009 he sought out Trivikram and got addresses of all my brothers and sisters in Hyderabad and invited them to the wedding of his second daughter, of course I was in the US at that time so I missed the event. Even as late as in October, 2010, he was here in the US at his daughter Phani Kumari's place and he sought out to meet me but I was in India this time and so missed meeting him again. I could meet him in 2012 when he came with his wife and daughter Phani Kumari to participate in the wedding reception of Vikram's oldest son Bhanu or Babloo. He had not changed at all in all these years and for me it was a pleasant and a happy reunion.

Pedda Tammu Mavayya had three more sons and one daughter and since I know very little about each of them, I will mention them briefly. Narasimham was followed by Mahadev Sastry, Bhaskar Rao, and Subba Rao and daughter Prasanna Lakshmi. Mahadev Sastry lives in Hyderabad and after a stint as a sales representative for a compressor manufacturing company of Bombay; he set up his own company and became one more victim of entrepreneurship in our family but most certainly a successful one. Bhaskar was not very successful and led a very short life. Interesting fact about him is that he was born in 1949 and died in 1994 or reverse of 49. Only daughter Prasanna Lakshmi was born in 1950 and is currently living in Visakhapatnam with her husband Nookala Satyanarayana.

Chilaka Ramam: He is the second son of Simham garu and was nick named Chilaka Ramam as his nose is slightly curved like the beak of a parrot. He did his graduation in ceramic engineering from the Benares Hindu University, a prestigious University of the time. He was married to Shanta Lakshmi, the only daughter of his cousin Visalakshi and Pappu Bhyranna garu. He was employed by Moravi Potteries in Gujarat and he thought he was fairly settled and was planning to set up his family. But his father-in-law Pappu Bhyranna garu had a different plan. Bhyranna garu worked in a Government Ordinance Factory in Kanpur and he used his position to get a posting in the Ordinance factory so that his daughter lived close to him. Chilaka Ramam garu did not appreciate this interference from his father-in-law and this remained a bone of contention between the two. All these incidents added to his woes and reflected on his married life and it remained a very sad one. His wife Shanta divorced him and began to live alone in Rajahmundry while he lived in Sirpur after his retirement with his brother till he died. He did not enjoy married life with his frequent quarrels at home and began to devote his time in clubs playing contract bridge where he excelled. He played for his company and also for his state of Uttar Pradesh. Chilaka Ramam Mavayya had five daughters, four living and all of them are in the USA. Shanta did not bear any sons and this was translated in his dislike for his daughters. His children did not love him and blamed him for the difficulties of their mother and continued to feel that way even after his death. After he died the family ties remained broken and his children did not acknowledge his existence and began to harbor an enmity for the entire Ganti clan. My father-in-law Ramam Mavayya was in the Intensive Care Unit of Susrusha Bhavan a hospital near our house in Shivaji Park when Chilaka Ramam died. I went from Ghatkopar where we were living at that time to see him during visiting hours and before I went I asked Kalpakam Tocchhi whether to convey this information to Ramam Mavayya. She told me to give the news to him as he may feel bad otherwise. I told him of Chilaka Ramam garu's death and for the first time I saw a very grown up elderly person crying like a child with tears streaming from both sides of his face. I became very worried thinking that I may have aggravated his illness so he looked up to me and said "Sarvamangala, we all did injustice to Chilaka

Ramam and did not let him live in peace. Let me mourn his death by not eating my meals today and observe fast."

Their oldest daughter Prabhavati is married to Maruvada Suryanarayana Murty of Visakhapatnam. I met Chilaka Ramam Mavayya's children first time when they all attended one of my cousin's wedding in Rajahmundry and Prabhavati was very curious about every aspect of the ritual and inquired about all the ceremonial events of the weddings. She would ask me so many things in Hindi as they were more used to Hindi, being brought up in Kanpur and I tried to answer them in Telugu. After her marriage she settled in Bombay and used to visit us in Koliwada where we lived for a short period from 1976 to 1979. I went to the nursing home where her daughter Shubha was born and she felt very much at home with us. She would visit us when we were living in Koliwada in Bombay and became close to me but they migrated to the US soon after. I met her in US after a very long time when I visited US for the first time in 1994 to visit my daughter Gnanu after birth of my second grandson Kartik. Prabhavati visited us when she came to know about my visit as she too was living in Pennsylvania and I felt very happy to meet her again.

Second daughter Bujji was known to my husband Chitti since she had come to their house for her treatment for cancer. She died of cancer before she reached the age of sixteen. The third daughter is Prema and I met her when she was doing her masters in Visakhapatnam when we were living there. I hardly know their fourth and fifth daughters and now I believe they do not like to keep in touch with us.

Chilaka Ramam Mavayya was very close to my father and he would come to Rajahmundry whenever he could and spend time with us. He was a very pleasant person and I remember him always smiling and have never seen him angry. He would share all his problems with my father freely and he was particularly very angry with his father-in-law Pappu Bhyranna garu and my father would admonish him. He never had a day of peace and happiness and died in his brother's out-house in virtual poverty as his pension was going to his wife. Even today very few may remember him or think about him.

Polamba family:

Polamba was the third daughter of Ganti Lakshminarayana after Simham garu. She was married to Karra Jogayya garu and had three sons before she was widowed. She also showered her love to Rajananna from the time when he was young and she continued to shower her affection even after she married Jogayya garu. But Polamba could not give the same degree of support to her brother openly and every time he visited her she would give him a packet of money to meet incidental expenses without letting anyone see this transaction. It is said that every time her brother visited, she would keep a bundle of money under a tumbler or a chembu so that nobody would notice her giving him money. No one knew how much money she gave in this manner but Rajananna remembered all these acts of generosity and supported her after she was widowed. She was afflicted with hearing disability and was not able to hear and was virtually deaf but she was highly intelligent. It is said that when Rajananna along with everyone in the family visited Benares on a pilgrimage and while others were busy in setting up their luggage in the room and busy with their bath etc. Polamba attayya was busy scouting the place. They were in a land of a different language where everyone spoke Hindi and she did not know any Hindi. Rajananna was worried when he did not see her that she would be lost in the floating population of pilgrims and devotees. But she returned back within an hour with all the groceries and food items and also information on shops nearest to them where they could get items that would be needed during their stay and all information about shops and shop keepers.

It is unfortunate but this deafness of hers was the cause of her death. Polamba Attayya lived with her brother Rajananna in

Rajahmundry. She would walk to river Godavari every morning to take bath in the river and return back home to do her other chores. One day she was walking along the rail line to go over to the river for her bath and a goods/freight train came and hit her from behind killing her almost instantly. The driver of the train was weeping all the time after the accident saying that he was blowing the whistle and did not expect this fatal accident to blemish his career. It is a normal practice that people would move away from the track as soon as the train comes near and he expected her to move away. But the driver did not know that Polamba attayya was deaf and could not hear the whistle or else he would have stopped the train when it reached near her and he was grief stricken over this incident in his life.

In her short life, Polamba brought up her three sons Jogayya or Abbulu Tatayya, Annaji Rao or Annappa Tatayya and Sheshadri Tatayya two of them brilliant engineers and successful in their respective professions. Each of them became very successful by virtue of their intelligence and hard work. The oldest son Jogayya or Abbulu was a city engineer in Madras and he settled in Madras, I do not know much about him nor his family. The second son Annappa Tatayya was a traveling sales man selling small perfume bottles to major perfume companies and he also settled in Madras. He too was bitten by the bug of entrepreneurship like my grandfather and soon he left his job and set up a factory for making bark corks for the perfume industries. He set up his factory in Visakhapatnam in an Industrial Estate and he was joined by his cousin and my father-in-law Ramam Mavayya.

Sheshadri Tatayya, the youngest son of Polamba was a character by himself. He was a merit student and was admitted to a prestigious engineering college in Benares, famous in those days for the high quality of education. But he dropped off when he fell in bad company by participating in betting and horse racing and he lost his money and so he dropped off and did not continue his studies. He realized his mistake after a lapse of seven years and so he came back to the University of Benares and took permission to complete final examination and his request was granted. He was so brilliant in his studies that he was awarded gold medal in his final examination as he topped the University. Imagine if he had continued his studies without any distraction would he not have been a very successful engineer? He began working on different civil projects in India and he was part of the engineering team that built the famous Hirakud Dam in Orissa. But he never held a permanent position and would flit from job to job and left his wife in Peruru at her parental home and would come there in between jobs. He had five children three daughters and two sons. His two daughters are now living in the USA and his one son Venkata Rao continued to live in India working in a printing ink factory set up by his own uncle in Hyderabad and died there. Second son Nageshwara Rao became a chartered account and was working in Ahmedabad before he moved to the USA where he died in 2009. Oldest daughter Mahalakshmi continues to live in Peruru in the ancestral home and second daughter Polamba and the youngest daughter Surya Kumari live in the USA. Polamba's sons became very close to my son Dinkar in US and I will mention about them in another book.

Peddamanna family

Rajananna's oldest daughter was known as Peddamanna and I do not know of any other details about her except that she was married to another Karra Jogayya garu of Amalapuram who died very early and she was widowed without any children. In Ganti family or rather in my father-in-law's family marriage to a boy belonging to Karra family was a taboo as both Polamba and Peddamanna were widowed early and so it was believed that a daughter from Ganti family would suffer the same fate if she married a boy from Karra. I know this very well because, Ganti Ramam Mavayya's second daughter Sarvamangala or Baby was liked by Satyam son of Karra Annaji Rao Tatayya but remembering sister Gnanamba's words, my father changed the direction by stopping the suggestion midway and within a month after her mother's death anniversary, Baby was married to Kanchinadham Sri Ramchandra Murty of Amalapuram in our house in Rajahmundry almost immediately following my sister Bhanumati's wedding in 1955. I would like to record an interesting coincidence that in the year 1955 my grandmother Sarvamangala's three grandchildren were married; my Uncle Babayya's oldest daughter Gnanamba, my sister Bhanumati and my aunt Gnanamba's daughter Sarvamangala. I do not know if there is any significance in this.

Lakshmi Narasamma (Chinnamanna) family

Sitamma and Rajananna had one more daughter who was named Lakshmi Narasamma but was known as Chinnamanna to all. She was born in 1907 and was married to Mantha Subrahmanya Sastry of Vakkalanka who was a Hindi teacher in Amalapuram high school. He would travel to his school on bicycle though the distance was almost 5 miles and continued to live in Vakkalanka in his ancestral house. He had a farm of about 10 acres of fertile land where they grew paddy/rice and coconuts and managed to bring up his family on this income in addition to his monthly teacher's salary. They had four children two daughters and two sons. The oldest daughter Subba Lakshmi was married to Pedda Tammu oldest son of Ganti Simham garu of Peruru or her uncle from mother's side. I have given her details above in describing Pedda Tammu Mavayya above.

Second daughter Sundari was born in 1931 and was married to Nookala Ramam garu of the nearby village of Anathavaram who managed his ancestral agricultural property in the village. They had four children; their first daughter is Nagamani followed by son Ammanna, daughter Aggi Lakshmi and the fourth daughter is Kameshwari. I knew Sundari very well as they would be coming to our house for all the weddings and I also met her when she came to visit us in Bombay. I thought she was a very courageous person when she came to Bombay all by herself. She came to us from Pune after visiting her daughter Nagamani there and no one went to the railway station to receive her as we did not receive telegram sent by her son-in-law. She got off at Dadar railway station and got into a cab driven by a Sardarji or one belonging to Sikh community. She gave him the address of our house in Shivaji Park and he brought her directly to our house early in the morning when we were having our first cup of tea. I opened the door and we all stood looking at her in surprise. She did not know Hindi or Marathi yet she managed to locate the address without any help by trusting a taxi cab driven by Sardarji! Of course in Bombay even today cabs driven by Sardarji are considered safe.

Chinnamanna's oldest son Venkateshwarulu was not well educated and he got into some bad company during his early life, but then he changed direction of his life and joined Khadi and Village Industries an organization known to follow the footsteps of Gandhiji for some time and then settled in Vakkalanka looking after his ancestral properties till his death. Her Second son Surya Prakash Sastry or Suri on the other hand became a commerce graduate and joined a defense establishment in Hyderabad and is leading a happy retired life there. Both of them used to come to our house and talk to my father whom they called Annayya or elder brother and used to give good company to us all. Every time we passed through Hyderabad, we used to have one visit to Suri's house where Ganga his wife would prepare a hearty meal and I cannot forget her hospitality even today. He came to live with us during his short stay in New Jersey and we all went over to Dover, PA to visit Gnanu over a week end.

Chinnamanna lost her husband Subrahmanya Sastry in 1953 due to Tuberculosis and before the end of one year Chinnamanna too died of Jaundice. According to our philosophy she was not considered widowed since she died within one year of her husband's death. Coincidently she died on the same day when my aunt Gnanamba died in Bombay earlier.

42

Satyanarayana family

Rajananna's oldest son Satyanarayana was born after Chinnamanna and was so named after the famous deity Lord Satyanarayana of Annavaram. He like many young students of his time participated in the Independence struggle and dropped out of his studies. He was married to Annapoorna, daughter of Tata Kamanna Dora a very rich farmer landlord of Gangala Kurra Agraharam a village near Amalapuram. Satyanarayana realized that it was a blunder dropping his studies and since his father Subbarayudu himself was an ardent supporter of the freedom struggle felt he will not be able to complete his education and will be wasting away his time here. He mortgaged all his wife's jewelry and ran away to Bombay along with his cousin Karra Abbulu garu oldest son of Polamba Attayya, and with that money he joined Topiwala Medical College now known as Nair Medical College near Bombay Central Station in Central Bombay. He became a medical practitioner and set up his practice in Dadar. Of course Abbulu garu went back to his parents place and completed his engineering

Satyanarayana garu now a medical doctor started his practice very humbly and he would visit people on his bicycle and dispense medicines. This impressed the local residents and he earned their confidence and people came to him with a belief that he was gifted with a skill to save lives of his patients. He rented an apartment at the corner house in Parsi Colony in Dadar and set up his practice there and rented upstairs apartment and invited his wife to join him there and set up their home. They did not have a good family life as his wife did not support him as he desired and was suspicious. They had two children both daughters one died at a very early age and the second daughter Lakshmi lived for almost 10 years and she was an apple of his eye. He had an Alsatian dog named Blackie and everyday he would come in his car and take Blackie out for a drive and even before he would start his car, Blackie would jump into the car and off they would go. This was the happiest period of his life. He became very well-known because of his very friendly and compassionate nature and this attracted many famous personalities who became his patients and that included many movie personalities who lived in a nearby suburb Matunga. The list included the first family of the movie industry the Kapoor clan with Prithviraj Kapoor the patriarch leading them and the superstar singer actor Kundan Lal Saigal. Saigal would come to his home late in the evening and together would share their drinks and spend their time with melodious singing by the famous singing hero Saigal. However, this happiness was short lived and in 1941, he lost his daughter Pedda Lakshmi after contracting Typhoid fever and this left a very lasting effect on him and in less than two years he too died. His dog Blackie did not drink or eat after his death and he too died a short time later and this event became a talk of the town. His wife Annapurna garu went back to her parental house and lived there till her death.

Sitaramiah family

Rajananna's second son was named after Ammamma's father Tata Sitaramiah garu and was known as Ramam and he too followed the footsteps of his older brother Satyanarayana and dropped his studies even before completing his matriculation. He also joined the freedom struggle and was going about in that direction when his brother in Bombay realized that Ramam will be wasted living in Rajahmundry so he called him to Bombay and enrolled him in the same Nair Medical College to follow his footsteps and become a doctor. The very first day of the laboratory during dissection of a body looking at all the blood he fainted on the spot and thus convincingly proved to his brother that medicine was not for him. He joined an industrial training institution the famous Victoria Jubilee Technical Institute or VJTI and received his diploma in Dyeing and Bleaching of textiles. He had a meritorious record during all the four years of the studies and he topped the class and was awarded a gold medal for his performance. He worked in Prahlad Mills near Parel and lived with his brother Dr. Ganti. He has four children two sons and two daughters. His oldest daughter Lakshmi was followed by son Subbarayudu or Babu and the third one is Sarvamangala named after our grandmother and youngest Satyanarayana or Chitti after his brother and also the deity of Annavaram Lord Satyanarayana. Our families became so intertwined that this would be unbelievable in the present days; both brothers married daughters of two Upadhyayula brothers Babu to Babayya's daughter Subhadra and I was married to Chitti.

Visalakshi family:

Rajananna had one more daughter and she was named Visalakshi after his mother and she had a great influence on him and was regarded as his pet child. She was a strong willed woman and would not allow anyone to cross her path and this created considerable friction between my father and Visalakshi and since both knew their position with Rajananna but they would not complain to him so their quarrels would always be subtle. She was married to Pappu Bhyranna garu who was employed in defense ordinance factory in Kanpur till he retired. They then settled near Peruru in Peramma Agraharam and lived a life of partial isolation living frugally.

They had five children; the oldest one was Shanta or Pappu Lakshmi, followed by Kamesh, Suryanarayana Murty or Suri, Subbarayudu or Raja and Prabhakar or Papa. Pappu Lakshmi was married to Chilaka Ramam and I have given a brief description of her unhappy marriage. She lived for a short period of time in Rajahmundry after divorce and brought up her two daughters and married them happily. All her daughters are well settled in the US and she too migrated to the US and lived there for a very long time on the West Coast but I had no opportunity to meet her in the US.

Kamesh became an engineer and was married to Papa, the daughter of Karra Dakshinarayana Murty garu of Rajahmundry. Interestingly my father was involved in their post marriage relationships. The marriage was performed in Tirupati under the auspices of Lord

Venkateshwara and soon after Kamesh left for Germany for higher studies. But as soon as he left for Germany, Bhyranna garu and Visalakshi were disenchanted with their choice of daughter-in-law Papa and were trying to motivate Kamesh to leave his wife by writing letters to that effect. Kamesh refused to divorce Papa and the two are living happily even today. Kamesh is a very common name in Pappu clan and during this period there were three boys named Kamesh in the Pappu family. Each was identified by pet names and son of Visalakshi is known as German Kamesh since he returned from Germany after completing his Masters in Engineering.

Second son Suri became a doctor and he also went over to Germany for advanced studies but did not return. He migrated to the US and from US to Canada and did not marry any one in our family. It is believed that he was disgusted with the girls of India after hearing stories about wife of his older brother Kamesh. He began to believe that every Indian girl and particularly those in our Telugu family were bad or characterless so why invite trouble? I never met him and do not know anything about him to write here.

Third son Subbarayudu or Raja became a very senior officer in Indian Military after graduating from Indian Military Academy (IMA) in Dehradun in U.P. He was married to the granddaughter of then Vice President of India V. V. Giri who later became the President of India. Mr. Giri was a special invitee and was an attraction and was very much a part of the entire wedding function of course we did not participate in the wedding. I only remember Raja when he visited us on the way to Peramma Agraharam with his parents. For reasons not known to me Bhyranna garu did not prefer staying at our house and would have left by boat the same day but for the fact the ferry service was stopped since the river Godavari was flooded. His Telugu was not very good as he lived all his life in Kanpur and he looked different from the locals with the ruggedness of a military officer and his long dark moustache. Our house was almost in downtown and we could get a cycle rickshaw for short distance travels at our door step. He would call Rickshaw pullers in a less formal manner appearing to be very rude and disrespectful. My father advised him that the rickshaw pullers would like to be shown some respect. He felt sorry for his earlier behavior and believe me he would virtually call every one with so much respect and address them "garu" equivalent to 'Sir'. The rickshaw pullers were always happy to come when he called because he was liberal with tips and in Rajahmundry giving tips to a rickshaw puller was unknown. He has one son and one daughter and both are living in the US and he had come to visit us once at New Jersey and he died one year later in Hyderabad.

The youngest son Prabhakar or Papa became a doctor from Army Medical College, Pune. I still do not know why but Bhyranna garu had a liking for military service and he wanted his second son Suri also to join the force but he was not selected. After completing his contract with the military Prabhakar began his own practice in Hyderabad. He went for higher studies in England and joined some well-known hospitals in Hyderabad as a specialist in gastro enteric diseases. I do not know much about him and met him probably twice when I went over to their house to pay a visit to his ailing mother Visalakshi. He has two daughters and both of them are in the US and I have no contact with their family to mention any more details about them.

My Father and Rajananna:

'Rajananna and my father's grandfather were closely related and he helped Rajananna during his formative years. Subbarayudu or Rajananna became a practicing advocate but my great grandfather Narasimham garu died prematurely at a very young age of 42 and did not live to see the success of his brother-in-law. Subbarayudu brought his sister Reddamma and nephew, my grandfather Abbayi Tata garu to Rajahmundry where he took care of his education and career. Subbarayudu was married to Sitamma daughter of Tata Sitaramiah garu of Amalapuram. She was just 12 years old when she was married as in those days most marriages were performed before the girl reached the age of puberty and are popularly known as child marriages. Her parents were quite progressive and so when British wanted girls also to be educated she was sent to a school. In those days girls were not allowed to join schools by parents hence the Government offered girl students' a silk petticoat and a blouse piece when they joined the school in order to motivate more girls join the school. Sitamma was one of those recipients of gifts and she went to school regularly before she got married and she was very proud of this part of her life whenever she told me. One could see similar thing being shown in the movie "Swadesh" and this was shown to happen in twenty first century! She was a very frail person and was probably less than 5 feet in height whereas Rajananna stood almost six feet tall with very fair skin and healthy personality. Rajananna was the sole bread earner for the entire family and the management of the house was dominated by his two sisters Reddamma and Polamba both were widowed early. They both managed the house with iron discipline and Sitamma was so much afraid of them that she would never dare talk back. My father always compared her to Sita wife of Lord Rama surrounded by demons of Ravana in famous Ashok Vatika gardens. Rajananna never involved himself with domestic matters. Although much is known about everyone else very little is known about Sitamma except that she was a most loving and compassionate person. I can say this with confidence because of my close association with her in Bombay after my marriage to Chitti.

Sitamma was very docile and so everyone dominated her and she was made to work like a slave. Since my father called her Ammamma (mother's mother) she was known to all as Ammamma except her own children. I am reminded of a very funny anecdote. My daughter Gnanu was about three years old and we were living in Bombay and one day Ramam Mavayya called her Amma and went on to ask something. Gnanu closed her mouth and came to me running and said in astonishment "Amma, Tata garu called Ammamma Amma! I told her even older persons have mother and they call her Amma so do not laugh." She was responsible for many of the chores in the house as she was greatly afraid of Akka or her husband's sister. Rajananna's house was thus full with family and extended family members and every one lived there for days with no one to challenge them.

Rajananna was very much respected by the community of lawyers and bench. If a particular case was handled by Rajananna, the judge would not hesitate in issuing judgment in favor of his clients because of his reputation that he supported only truth. He received invitation to participate in the reception function held in the honor of the King George the Fifth in Delhi when the King visited India in 1915. He was presented with a black long coat given to all invitees and he cherished this gift and kept it well preserved for wearing during winter months.

Rajananna was known to have a horse driven carriage with an attendant standing behind the carriage as customary for Landlords or British Royalty similar to one seen in old English movies. He bought a motor car later, the first car in those days in these regions. He lived the life of a rich and famous. Nobody knew his exact income because his secretary Vadlamani Veeranna garu who handled the clients was not good in accounting and much of the money remained unaccounted due to the expenses of the large household. He made one investment in his life time and that was purchase of a plot of land in Bommuru near Rajahmundry. The land was not fertile for crops like paddy or coconut but was good for some horticultural plants. He was very busy most of the time hence he did not spend more time on development of the farmland. Fruit plants like the Sapota, Custard apple or Sitaphal, mangoes, cashew, Guava or Jamakaya and even aritha or soap nut was grown in Bommuru. He trusted the person who sold him the land and he trusted the farm hand that looked after the land and would often spend money on it without consulting anyone. His sister Akka loved any fruit coming from Bommuru as it was coming from her brother's farm and felt it had a special taste when compared to the fruits coming from our farm in Diwancheruvu or her own grandson's farm. When I was a young child, we would often kid Akka and tell her that the fruits had come from Bommuru though we had received from our other farm lands just to hear her tell us that the fruits were delicious. This only goes to show that even at that ripe age a woman cherishes her association to her family on her parent's side and values gifts she receives from them.

Rajananna loved fruits and it would be wrong to believe that he did not get the type of land that he desired since it produced many types of fruits he loved. He loved plantains or Banana but these could not be grown in Bommuru. He would therefore purchase choicest variety of bananas from the market and banana has remained a staple fruit through generations of Ganti and most of them love Banana to a fault. I remember his passion for a variety of yellow Bananas known as Amrutpani or Manna from heaven. They had golden skin and a very sweet taste typical of this variety and that probably is the reason for the name. These are grown at plantations in Kovvuru near Rajahmundry and he would buy clusters of raw Amrutpani and ripen them at our home in his room. The fruits were allowed to ripen in stages so that a new tier of ripe bananas was available every day. Rajananna would not eat them unless the skin became dark and fruit becomes soft; he would then give it to us all saying the fruits tasted sweet like Amrutam or Manna but we would hate to touch the very soft fruit and complain to my father. This would bring a sort of discussion between my father and Rajananna and my father would suggest softly since children like the fruits to be eaten early why not give them when they are near ripe and Rajananna would agree and my father would normally prevail. At times like this I would regard my father as the bravest person as everyone else was scared stiff of Rajananna. Most of the fruits would be kept in his room and no one was allowed to get to them without his permission and so most of the fruits would remain in the room till they were overripe.

His sense of responsibility to the country became a passion for him and he joined the freedom movement of Mahatma Gandhiji or Father of Nation very actively. He was standing for elections for the position of mayor of Kakinada Municipality and he was certain to win, but Gandhiji called for a Non-cooperation movement against the ruling British in 1921 and this call was enough for him to withdraw from the race since according to him becoming a part of municipality is equal to joining hands with the British rulers. He not only quit his contest but he also resigned from the Bar and quit practicing law. He changed his lifestyle and instead of wearing expensive clothes he was used to, he began to wear Khadi or hand woven clothes as a part of his non-cooperation movement. He continued to wear Khadi till the day he died.

He lived frugally and lived mostly on light food and fruits and followed a strict routine and dietary practice. He was a very healthy person and walked miles at a time and was used to long distance swimming in flowing river. He would go to Godavari River and swim more than a mile every day morning as a regular practice for several years. But one day he developed cramps in his leg and would have drowned but for timely help he received from another person swimming alongside. He left his swimming from that day. But his practice of walking continued till he was bed ridden towards the end of his life. He was a voracious reader of books in English and Telugu the only two languages he knew. When he lived with his son Ramam Mavayya in Bombay, he virtually finished books in the United States Library Ramam garu brought almost every week. He knew all 18 chapters of Bhagvad Gita or popularly known as Gita by heart and he would recite all chapters while walking. There were no good parks for him to walk so he developed a habit of walking in the home and recite till all the chapters are done. He had a very powerful but melodious voice and it was always a pleasure hearing him every morning.

He was very forward for his times and a sincere follower of the thoughts of Mahatma Gandhi. Gandhiji called for removal of caste barriers and invite people of lower caste in homes of upper castes and so Rajananna arranged a community meal for the backward community in Peruru in his home. Although he was a devout Brahmin he felt no qualms of inviting them to his home and did not care about what others in the village would feel about his action. His two sons also joined the freedom movement and were school drop outs in order to spread the message to the masses. Contributions from the Ganti family to the Indian freedom struggle remained unsung since no one ever took credit for any of their action; they were just silent practitioners. Neither government nor local community remembered these sacrifices but Rajananna was least concerned and he continued his routine of walk twice a day and reciting all 18 chapters of Bhagvad Gita and manage his land in Peruru along with his brother Simham and after his premature death he supported his widowed wife. He lived most of the time either in Peruru or in our house at Rajahmundry and I remember he spent more time with us than in Peruru from the time I began remembering.

Rajananna was against purchases on the door step by the women of the house so all the vendors were asked to come in the back entrance when he was in our house and by chance if someone stopped at the front door to sell his wares he would face Rajananna's wrath and listen to his outburst along with a sample of his choice words. I could never understand why he should be so angry for everything but it could be hereditary in Ganti family. My father would patiently nudge him and ask him if 'you were to drive away all the vendors from the door step, how are you going to get your vegetables for your lunch and dinner?' and he will laugh and say 'yeah, that is true, Narasimham but I do not know why I get angry when I see them at the front door. Next time I will not be angry' and that next time would never come. My path always clashed with his and since I was the darkest in the family, he almost always disliked seeing me. It has been my love and hobby to collect all fragrant flowers in the garden and put them together in a string or 'mala' so that we all sisters would adorn their hair before going to school. Every time I stepped in the front yard in the flower garden for cutting the flowers, he would shout at me and I would run away in fear and once again my father would come to my rescue and chide Rajananna not to scare children away. At these times I would feel once again that my father was the bravest person in the world and he has always been my hero. Rajananna's life can be divided in two parts one when he lived in Peruru/Rajahmundry and the second when he and Ammamma moved to Bombay after he lost his daughter-in-law or my aunt Gnanamba in 1954. I joined the family as a daughter-in-law to Ramam garu. But now he was friendlier towards me may be because he may not have associated me to my old frail dark form.

He came to Rajahmundry once in 1955 and performed Upanayanam ceremony for Babu so that he could perform the final rites for his mother Gnanamba Attayya. Baby's wedding and Kanyadanam to Kanchinadham Ramam garu was also performed by Rajananna in the same year since Ramam Mavayya, a widower, could not perform the Kanyadanam or give away the bride. He next came in 1961 for Babu's wedding and was very much reserved. He somehow did not remember my father correctly and mistook him to my father's uncle Aatakeshwarudu in Karivalasa. He did not see my mother and this also mislead him to believe that he was in a different house. Every morning he would go into the kitchen presumably looking for my mother who had died earlier but did not see her and my father had put on weight beyond his recognition so he virtually lost his bearings. He and Ammamma performed Snatakamu for Babu, a function that is supposed to be performed by mother and father, but after death of Gnanamba Attayya, these ceremonies were performed by Rajananna and Ammamma. This was the last time he visited us as he did not come for my wedding due to ill health. He died in 1965 in Bombay and Ammamma died in 1969 and I looked after both of them and learned many good things. Ammamma would tell Gnanu my daughter stories from Ramayana and every time she would tell her that the King of demons Ravana kidnapped Sita, tears would swell in the big eyes of Gnanu and Ammamma would then change the story without mentioning the kidnapping. Ammamma was my biggest support and she trained me in many intricate culinary arts. I felt blessed to have had the opportunity of serving these two stalwarts. Today when I look at my granddaughter Mythili, I feel as if Ammamma or her namesake has returned back to look after us and Dinkar and Kiranmai. On March 2, 2013 Dinkar and Kiranmai are blessed with a daughter Mahati and her middle name is Shanmukhi nearly meaning Subbarayudu. Now I feel relieved that not only Ammamma is in our midst, but Rajananna too has come to join her.

CHAPTER 3

MY FATHER NARASIMHAM: THE LION

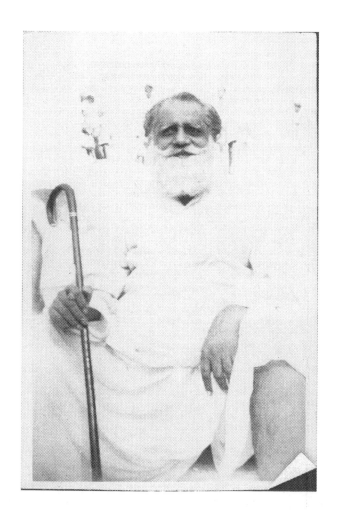

My grandfather Abbayi had died prematurely leaving behind a huge debt. The drawing room in Rajananna's house in Rajahmundry was filled with these debtors who had come after final rites were formally completed. My grandfather's sudden death put the burden of the entire family on my father's young shoulders as the oldest son. Rajananna was an attorney and was wise with the worldly knowledge. He advised my father to take the easy course of declaring bankruptcy and since he was still a minor, the properties would not be attached and the courts would accept the petition and he can begin his life with a clean slate. My father had to support education of his younger brother Babayya and marry three step sisters and the last one Lakshmi was not even one year old! This was a tall order for any one and certainly more so for one who has just completed his school. Rajananna was convinced that my father even though the oldest son in the family should not take the responsibility of clearing the debt he inherited in addition to supporting the large family. Filing for bankruptcy was the best course according to Rajananna. But Rajananna trusted my father's maturity and responsible thinking even at that young age.

The lenders were also resigned to accept bankruptcy as the option and were prepared to accept the fact that they have lost all their money with the untimely death of my grandfather. My father entered the room full of people more than twice his age and greeted them. The debtors did not know how they should respond to this young boy. My father sat at the table next to Rajananna and told everyone that since he was so young he would like the seniors in the community to bear with him. He told them that he has been advised by his attorney, Rajananna that he should file for bankruptcy but he was not in favor of the idea. Every one sat upright in their chairs to hear what this young man was saying. "My father has taken loan from you with the full intention of repaying and I would like to fulfill his obligation to you all. However, at the present time we do not have any means of repaying the same. I would like to work out a payment plan and see that all the debts are cleared over time as this is what is my father would have expected from me as his son. But I need time. Are you prepared to give me this opportunity?"

Everyone was surprised by the statement of this young boy barely twenty years old and they were more than ready to work out a payment plan. Rajananna was totally against this whole madness of my father and told him he was making a grave mistake. He warned him that he cannot take it for granted that his younger brother will support this decision once he is old and self-supporting? According to Rajananna he will most probably say no to share this debt and all the debt cleared by my father would be debited from his own share of the property when the time for dividing the property came. It happened exactly as he described and Babayya did not agree to share this burden at the time of partition of the property. My father was not naïve but was confident his younger brother would be different from others and will share the liabilities. Even if he did not, he had to do what is right and morally correct. This is what his hero Lord Rama of Ramayana fame would do in such a situation.

My father had appeared for his matriculation examination that year and was surprised that he failed in the examination and so he dropped out from the school. But the principal of the school, a British teacher did not accept the results and he applied for recount of the marks of my father. My father and Rajananna had told the principal that it was OK and they were not interested in pursuing the petition. But the principal was firm in his resolve. Finally 2 months later results were corrected and my father was declared pass in first class, but by then things had already taken a different turn and he left the studies for good. He immersed himself in managing the properties, the finances and paying off his father's debtors as per his promise. My father was a very religious person and Lord Rama was his role model. He would follow his father's wishes as if he was there alive and his first task was to clear all the debts so that his soul would rest in peace. Like Rama he was the oldest son and so he took upon himself the responsibility to look after the welfare of his brother and sisters and respectfully carry out the wishes of his step mother who was incidentally just a few years older than him.

His step mother Ratnalu or Mamma went back to her parents place after she was widowed and her brothers hoped they could get a part of my grandfather's property if she lived separate. But partition of the property could not be done unless all the debts were cleared. Mamma along with her three daughters went over to her parent's house happily but after living for about five years she realized that she was not respected in her parental home since their primary interest was her share of the property. Rajananna was again correct and he did not allow my father to consider division of the property at that time. Mamma had seen the responsible manner in which my father had acted after death of her husband and she trusted my father more than anyone else in doing everything justly and correctly. She realized her place was with my father and so she requested my father if she could come back. Rajananna told my father that it would be a mistake to let her come back as that would only add to his burden and he should not expect any return of gratitude from his step mother nor should he hope that his brother will share these additional expenses. But since his role model Rama of Ramayana would support his step mother in this situation, so my father would also do same and he gladly invited her and his step sisters to his house disregarding Rajananna's advice. He believed in the three principles of Rama one word, one arrow and one wife (Oke Maata, Oke Baanamu, and Oke Bharya). He hated liars and he never resorted to untruth throughout his life. I idolized him for this character of his and most of my life I too spoke the truth but this has not helped me and often hurt me. I realized early on that it is not easy to follow the beliefs of my father or those of Rama my father idolized and so I can understand the difficulties my father experienced during his life time.

Valentine's Day Baby

My father was born on Saturday 14th February, 1914 on a full moon day in Karivalasa my grandmothers' parental home or Adibhotla Ayyababu garu's house. The day was a very auspicious day and since it was Magha Purnima (Maha Maghi in Hindi), most of the devotees take bath in the sea or a river on this day. He was born on a Valentine's Day according to the western beliefs in the year 1914 did this have any significance! Imagine we never realized it! I do not think anyone followed Valentine's Day in India at that time and least of all anyone in my family who were living in Rajahmundry far away from civilization. I will be surprised if someone in my family believes in Valentine's Day even today as we are still conservative. He was named Narasimha Murty after his grandfather Upadhyayula Narasimham garu. He was very much loved by all his uncles and grandparents on his mother's side and was a healthy baby who was not known to cry even as a child. His mother Sarvamangala returned to Rajahmundry to Rajananna's house and became a part of the joint family. She was a hard worker and even Reddamma or Akka or my grandfather's mother did not find any lapse in her work ethics. My grandmother never shirked her duties and met the standards of the family and satisfied every one of her in-laws. That was a real tough task.

I would like to mention here that it is customary in our community and in most of the southern India for a woman to go over to her parental home for delivery and she would thus be away for almost six months living with her parents. This results in strong bonds with her family and children having a second home away from their own. This is not a custom in Northern part of India where once married the daughter was not expected to return to her parental home.

My grandmother Sarvamangala again left Rajahmundry to Karivalasa for delivery of her second child and this time she gave birth to a girl named as Gnanaprasunamba or Gnanamba named after my grandmothers own mother Prasunamba. Gnanamba was the favorite of the family being the first girl in the house. Again after another two years my grandmother returned to her father's house to deliver another son Venkateshwarulu and came back with all her three children to take care of her responsibilities in the large household and look after her husband after a lapse of six months of maternity leave. She left Rajahmundry again went to her parent's home for delivery of another child. This time my father who was just eight years old escorted her to Karivalasa looking after his other siblings. As soon as she reached her house Ayyababu Garu inquired how come she came without an escort, she told her father Ayyababu garu that she did not need one now "as my son Narasimham is my right hand and he will look after me". These words of his mother remained imprinted on my father's mind for years to come. But she died during child birth and the new born child also did not survive and I do not know if the child was a male or a female. It is believed that my beautiful grandmother looked even more beautiful and radiant during her pregnancy and someone may have cast an evil eye on her as she died suddenly. Even today these beliefs are prevalent in India and I too believe in them. I try to remove such a spell from my grown up daughter Gnanu who does not mind or my daughter-in-law Kiranmai who occasionally allows me to do so.

My grandfather was grief stricken and heart broken and began to live a life of a widower and looked after his three children and their needs. My father helped my grandfather in his filial support of other siblings. My aunt Gnanamba was very sharp and intelligent and was able to fend for herself and her two brothers. But then they were all living in his uncle Rajananna's house where they were not given equal status. My grandfather married again and had three children all daughters through Ratnalu (Mamma) before he died in 1931. My father always had a maturity beyond his age and he understood the situation so well that he gave the same degree of love and affection he gave to his own sister Gnanamba.

Early Years

My father kept company of people of different avocations. My father was very much interested in body building and maintained good health in the company of his good friend one Dr. Nath. They concentrated on body building with Indian exercise protocol and together they wrote a manual of Indian exercises. Dr. Nath subsequently became a senior officer in the British administrative services and left Rajahmundry and my father became fully engrossed in his work and additional responsibilities. The manual remained unpublished and was in the custody of my father as long as we were in Rajahmundry. I do not know what happened to the manual after he moved to Hyderabad. My father was afflicted with asthma at a very young age and this restricted physical activity including his body building activities. One more associate of my father was Swami Gnanananda who gave him discourses in Hindu scriptures and philosophy. Swami Gnanananda was a highly educated ascetic and he worked as a professor of Nuclear Physics at the Andhra University in Visakhapatnam. Father used to visit the University to meet him whenever he had time or wanted to consult him.

He discontinued his studies as soon as he completed his matriculation so that he could use these resources to educate his younger brother Venkateshwarulu or Babayya. My father always wanted my uncle to be a doctor and set up his practice in Diwancheruvu where medical facilities were non-existent to the local farm hands and no doctor was available within an 8 mile radius. He could not motivate his brother or his son Pedda Babu to practice in the village. Of course his brother did not study medicine but that was not the case with my brother who became a doctor.

His uncle and mentor Rajananna warned him when he heard my father dropping off his schooling that he would be making a mistake in sacrificing his own career particularly when he himself was so good in studies. He reminded my father the popular saying in Telugu that there is no better religion than to improve one's own life. But my father believed in Ramayana and like Rama he too wanted to see that he gave support to his brother and so used all his resources to make him a doctor while sacrificing his own personal advancement. He hoped both of them would settle in Diwancheruvu one managing the agricultural lands and the other managing the medical practice. But my uncle did not graduate in medicine, he graduated in Agricultural Science. My father was once again happy that he will now get best scientific support from his brother in developing his farms and make them an envy of the locals. My father was disappointed once again as my uncle left for Bangalore to work in some government research station and later on became a Plant Quarantine Officer traveling from one port to another all over India but he did not settle in Rajahmundry and my father's dreams remained unfulfilled. Agriculture had become a passion for my father so he even went to Poona (Pune) once and participated in a short term course in food preservation technology. I do not think that he used this knowledge any time later in his life. But this only shows my father's advanced thinking even for his time.

My father was married to Kamala Devi the second daughter of Nookala Agastya Sastry. At that time my mother was 11 years old and since the British Government introduced Sarada act to prevent child marriages in Hindu society, the marriage was performed in Yanam a French Colony in southern India that did not implement these laws. In those days marriages were carried out before a daughter reached the age of maturity or puberty. My Grandfather Agastya Sastry, the father of the bride was not able to attend the wedding as their house in Maharashtra was burgled by his trusted servant Tukaram on a day when they were leaving for the wedding. My mother, aunt and her mother, my grandmother left without my grandfather so their trip was not affected. My grandfather remained behind to recover all the jewelry and expensive wedding clothes stolen by Tukaram, the servant of past 12 years. My grandfather was busy in submitting a police report and all the formalities associated with the case and he was detained behind and the marriage had to be performed in his absence. They lost all valuables including those of his older daughter Sarada.

My mother was therefore married by my grandfather's cousin Nookala Radha Krishnan garu. He performed Kanyadanam for my mother and my father never forgot the auspicious deed performed by my grandfather's cousin. He would send new clothes to Radha Krishnan garu on Telugu New Year day till he died. My father maintained that one cannot remain indebted to the couple performing Kanyadanam. Interestingly, when my son Dinkar married Kiranmai daughter of Dr. Krishnamurthy in Hyderabad Nookala Somesham garu, brother-in-law of Dr. Krishnamurthy was also there. He immediately recognized me and remembered old incidents and time he spent with my father as they were very frequent visitor in our house in Rajahmundry.

Thus even the marriage of my father did not go normally and my mother's father had to depute someone to perform the wedding on his behalf. I am not sure how my mother has taken the incident but the fact remains, she did not have many jewelry or silk clothes for her wedding. Even her sister Sarada who had left all her jewelry with her parents before moving to her in-laws place lost her expensive items. This fact was remembered by my grandmother and I remember her mentioning this many times to me and others in our house. I do not remember Ammamma mentioning the loss of my mother's jewelry and this remained a bone of contention between my father and grandmother. My mother as I remembered was always praying or very quiet and would not allow my father to comment on this issue as she would say words cannot be recalled so talk less and do not hurt others.

Our house was visited by many beggars and if father is busy he would get annoyed and shout at them and my mother would chide him and tell him if you do not like just say with movement of your hand or tell him to go away or to come later if you feel like giving him alms. Every time someone came from Diwancheruvu even after lunch hours she would get up and serve them without any complaint or annoyance on her face. She was kind to all and she would insist my father also do the same. I was a child and did not know the full significance of her words and now I know she was correct but how many of us follow her teachings today.

The practice of giving rice or other food items became a ritual with us and at no time anyone would be sent away without any alms. If my father was busy he would mildly request the beggar to come next day as there was no one to offer the alms and they would not complain as they understood. This was one house they would get alms at almost all times. My father was a lion with a powerful body but tender heart. He would not hurt anyone but will not tolerate any injustice. He had a very long memory and would remember all the events many years later and I think this is inherited by all of us. I remember most of these events and I am sure more of these are remembered by my brothers and sisters but then this is my story of events as I remember them. It would become a very good novel if we all combine our memories of those golden days.

My Father, The Landlord

I always remember a name plate on our house in Rajahmundry. U. Narasimha Murty, Land Lord and this remained on the wall even after the Government of India abolished Zamindari or Landlordism. Everyone followed the government directive and removed the title of Land Lord from their doors. But not my father as he was proud of this. Looking back, my father did not complete any basic education so he cannot add any degrees; but for owning the land and declaring to the whole world did not require any degrees. Every time I saw the name plate on our wall, I would remember his anecdote about Barrister Parvitasam written by Mokkapati Lakshmi Narasimham garu. He was not one of the Simha Trayam, namely Chilakamarthy Lakshmi Narasimham, Koochimunchi Narasimham and Panuganti Lakshmi Narasimham as corrected by Lakshmi Manikyam's daughter. Barrister Parvitasam was a lawyer who had gone over to London to complete his bar-at-law examination so that he could become a barrister and practice law in India. There he saw several prominent people prefixing their name with the title of Lord and he decided to become one. He thought for several days and he wired his home that "Sell Land. Remove word Land from my title of Land Lord. People back home were confused and wired for the reasons. He replied everyone is a lord here; I too want to become Lord Parvitasam like others in London." This may not be a very famous tale of Barrister Parvitasam, but it conveys the satire on the elite in those days. Yet my father continued to have that name plate on his door.

My father would always say well I am not a Lord in that sense, however, since I still have land so I am just a Landlord. In his life time he looked after four parcels of farm lands, two he inherited from my grandfather Abbayi Tata garu, one assigned to him by Rajananna in Bommuru and one entrusted by my grandmother Ammamma in Vakkalanka. I will try to capture all the details of each individual lands along with a little bit of the history.

1. Diwancheruvu

Diwancheruvu is located almost 6 miles away from Rajahmundry on the main highway Grand Trunk Road, the first highway connecting Calcutta on the East to Pathankot in North India and being on the highway the land was of great value. My grandfather Abbayi must have seen all these advantages before investing into the property but there was one drawback. The land did not have adequate water supply even though the village was known as Diwancheruvu or Lake (Cheruvu) of Diwan. The land was not fit for crops like Paddy or sugarcane and as a result plants that did not need large quantities of water were grown on the land. The land was good for such cash crops like mango, lemon, oranges and cashew plants and once the fruits were ready for plucking the plot would be leased to contractors for collecting the crop. The contractors would bid for the crop and the highest bidder would get the contract. Each of these crops would be ready at different times and so we would receive infrequent income from the land unlike salaried person who would receive a steady monthly income. The actual income would be calculated after deducting cost of the farmhands and maintenance. The original farm was nurtured by my grandfather Abbayi and Akka and they both planted good, sturdy and healthy plants and they followed best horticultural practices available to get a better variety of fruit. Whatever income these cash crops produced, Abbayi Tata garu could not clear his debts and these fell on the shoulders of my father.

After his father died, for a long time my father remained in Rajananna's house and managed his farms by going up and down and looking after them. True they did not need personal attention and once the flowering began, the farm or a portion of the farm would be leased to the highest bidder and it became responsibility of the contractor to collect the fruits and sell it to the market. But some one was required to look after the plants after the fruits were picked for nurturing the plants for the next season. My father moved to Diwancheruvu in early forties and during Second World War he moved to Peruru to live with Rajananna there as there were strong rumors that Japanese would attack India from Visakhapatnam in the East. Pedda Babu was born in Peruru and my father returned to Rajahmundry in 1944 after he was born. He hired very good people to manage his farms.

Suryanarayana: We lived in a rental home in Innispeta, near the river Godavari and very near to the railway station so that father could go over to Gurraja Peta by train. This rental house was my place of birth and probably I was the first child in our family born in Rajahmundry. My father shuttled between Diwancheruvu and Gurraja Peta and felt that he needed someone at the farm itself to look after the farm and maintain the accounts and payment of salary to farm hands. He hired two brothers Suryanarayana and Satyanarayana and coincidentally they had the same last name Upadhyayula as my father but they were not directly related to us.

I would ask my father that since all Upadhyayula clan are related how come he does not know the relation with them. They would talk among themselves and come to a final answer that there must have been some relationship but over the years probably they lost track of the connection. One brother Suryanarayana looked after Diwancheruvu while Satyanarayana looked after Gurraja Peta. This reduced my father's travel considerably and he could devote his time both for the family and oversee the operations everywhere.

Muttayya: Most of us know of the legendary Hanuman and his devotion to Rama. But I know that my father had a Hanuman in the form of Tellamekala Muttayya. He was a Kapu and belonged to a farming community as opposed to our caste of Brahmin but was the most trust worthy person and when I look back today, my father would not have succeeded in his venture in the farm business without Muttayya. Muttayya was a local and lived in Diwancheruvu and would come to our house when summoned and in those days he would walk the entire distance of 8 miles to be there at our door step before dawn. In fact he often opened the door for our regular servant maid Appalamma. He had to walk at least for two hours and he certainly had to leave his house before 4.00 in the morning. This was not a difficult task and he would do so whenever he was wanted by my father. He was what one called in Telugu as "Nammeena Bantu' or a trusted servant of my father. My father would entrust him with the most complex things including carrying large sums of money. Even the lender would not hesitate to give money to him. He did not know reading or writing and so there was no question of writing any promissory notes or giving any thumb impression for taking the money and this was the level of trust between Muttayya and my father. I remember him carrying up to Rs 50,000/ from our lenders without any promissory note showing the trust the local business community had in Muttayya and my father.

As long as my father was in Rajahmundry, Muttayya would come whenever he was required and no questions asked. Muttayya's only son Satyanarayana was kidnapped by a gang of child lifters when he was a child and both his wife and Muttayya were worried about their son. They vowed many Gods for his safe return but of no use. His wife would come to our house and express their worries and my father also did not leave any stone unturned in searching for the missing son. After worrying a lot about her son wife of Muttayya died and Muttayya married again. Miraculously his son Satyanarayana returned back when he was about 12 years old using his smartness and the gang was captured. Unfortunately I do not know the details but I believe Satyanarayana also had an important role in this operation. Muttayya was extremely happy. Muttayya's second wife was very tall and was an imposing person but she was loyal and obedient to him and they both decided to educate their son. They did not have any children from their marriage and so Muttayya could give complete love and affection to his son Satyanarayana. He studied English and received training as a compounder and began to assist a local doctor in Diwancheruvu and began a different line of profession. Muttayya was always present at every function in our house and both my father and he would reminisce to find out who was older since there was no record of birth details of Muttayya or his date of birth. They would relate incidents to see who remembered more events and father would say may be Muttayya was older by a year or two. History is thus passed down by people with such memories.

His son Satyanarayana took charge of our lands in Diwancheruvu after Muttayya's death and Vikram had a close contact with him for a very long time. Once father died, there was less interest in holding on to the property and so the land at Diwancheruvu was sold off and Satyanarayana was well taken care by my three brothers. Satyanarayana came with his family consisting of two daughters and one son to attend Chinna Babu's second son Sriram's wedding. Grand children of Muttayya thus came to participate in the wedding of the grandson of the Lion of Danavaya Peta.

Arakula Veeranna: Story of Tellamekala Muttayya is incomplete without mention of his deputy Arakula Veeranna who was more like Hanuman to Muttayya and he would do everything Muttayya or my father would tell him. Veeranna had an advantage over Muttayya in that he knew how to ride a bicycle. His two brothers Pullayya and Narayudu also worked before Veeranna and it is unfortunate that all three of them did not live to a ripe old age. My father would tell Muttayya if only you knew bicycling, you would have traveled all over India. Even though Muttayya did not know languages to communicate, he had the ability to reach out to the people. He was illiterate but humane and to the best of my knowledge he did not have any enemies. Muttayya showed a maturity that reflected his experience and he always managed to pacify every one including my father whenever he became angry. It is true that my father would get angry quickly and if Muttayya also supported him at this time it would probably be difficult to contain his anger. But Muttayya would never let my father down and he would not precipitate things beyond control in anger. Last we saw Muttayya was in 1981 when he came to the wedding of my niece Gouthami and by then he became weak and he died in 1983 one year before my father who died in 1984.

2. Gurraja Peta

Gurraja Peta was almost 150 miles from Rajahmundry and I still do not know why my grandfather went to buy land there, but then he was an adventurous person and a good sales man must have motivated him to buy the land there. The land was sandy and supported casuarina trees and the wood would be auctioned once every 5 years or so with a good return. Here the plants were grown in rotation so that every year trees on one plot are available for sale. This required frequent visit by my father but not much of attention was needed as these plants grew well even in these dry sandy lands with minimum maintenance. In addition to casuarina trees, there were areas where the land supported paddy and coconut trees. I have never been there and so I do not know anything about it.

My father led a very adventurous life whenever he went there and he made friendship with many of the owners of the neighboring lands. Most of the owners were Raju's and belonged to a princely community and each one owned horses and were experts in horse riding and they practiced sword fights. My father also became an expert horse rider in their company and would not let anyone beat him in the race. He did not learn sword fighting but he was an expert wielder of staff and no one would dare come near him if he had a staff in his hand. This was new to these Raju families as they only knew that Brahmins believed in practicing priestly duties and were not fighters while my father could match each one of them and earned their respect. It was customary for my father to take the last train from Rajahmundry that arrived at Narasipatnam station at 4.00 am and then would travel by cart or bus to Gurraja Peta. He would be tired after this arduous journey and since he had to attend to many duties there he had to remain alert and active when he reached the lands. He would therefore fall sleep as soon as he got into the night train and would wake up as soon as he reached his destination station and he never over shot. Even in his sleep, he would say he could identify Narasipatnam station from the way the tracks clanged during change over and would wake up at the right time to get down at the destination.

Satyanarayana: My father appointed Upadhyayula Satyanarayana brother of Suryanarayana as a manager for the entire land in Gurraja Peta and whenever he would go to Gurraja Peta he would get meals cooked by Satyanarayana as my father would not eat at Raju household as they were meat eaters. He had two options; either cook his own meals or Satyanarayana would cook for him. Satyanarayana maintained all the records and accounts of income and expenses. I have not met another group of most loyal and honest people than Muttayya and these two Upadhyayula brothers and I am sure there are many who still practice honesty but I have to meet them yet. Corruption has become a way of life in India and honesty may have become a very rare characteristic in an individual. Our fire brand Prime Minister Indira Gandhi was often asked why she could not eradicate corruption from the Indian society and she replied that corruption in India is a way of life. It is a mystery that honesty continues to survive even today.

When everything was set in Diwancheruvu, father asked Suryanarayana to join his brother in Gurraja Peta and share his work. Both brothers built their houses next to each other and brought up their children well. There was one great characteristic of these brothers that my father would not tire telling us. Their mother was addicted to opium that started as a painkiller and slowly she needed her daily dose of opium before her morning meals and these brothers saw to it that she would get her dose of this banned drug every day whatever it cost them to get the drug. Their mother knew the drug was available only in black market and hence cost was sky high and told her sons that she did not mind dying and that they should not spend money for her drug, but these two sons never let her be without her dose of opium. My father did not pay them high salaries, but they still managed to support their individual families and also provide for their mother till she died of old age. This showed the strength of character of these two brothers and I respect them for that.

Gurraja Peta went to Babayya, my uncle after partition of the property and both these brothers I believe left the job and lived an independent life as they did not want to work for anyone else after working with my father. Our association with Gurraja Peta was over with this simple line of partition. I have never been to Gurraja Peta and I do not know how it looks but I wish the partition had divided both the landed properties equally between my father and my uncle. It is this partition and other issues that have been a bone of contention between the two brothers and events that happened later only fuelled the dislike so much so that my uncle in later years did not wish to have anything to do with my father and this hurt my father more than anything.

3. **Bommuru**

Bommuru belonged to Rajananna and he had purchased the land that was rockier and less fertile and like other two properties of my father was not an agricultural land but supported fruit plants. However, both Rajananna and Akka were greatly attached to Bommuru and loved any produce coming from Bommuru. Bommuru was about 5 miles away from Rajahmundry and was considered as within walking distance. Rajananna after renouncing his practice of law led a completely retired life and shuttled between Peruru and Rajahmundry. After my father bought the house in Danavaya Peta, Rajananna became our most frequent visitor primarily because he loved my father more than he loved anyone else. Everyone was afraid of Rajananna including his own children but not my father. Every time my father disagreed with angry Rajananna, I would consider that as the most heroic act.

Rajananna had two main activities one to go and swim in Godavari and second go over to Bommuru and see the progress of plants over there. Bommuru supported cash crops like Cashew and Sapota or Chickoo and he was so happy to be in the field. Rajananna did not need any vehicle to go over to Bommuru as he could easily walk the four miles distance and be back for lunch. He also had one trusted lieutenant but that person was more a 'yes sir' type and this kept Rajananna happy. Even Akka would walk over to Bommuru sometimes when her brother was in Peruru. Bommuru was situated on a small hillock and so the land there was mostly full of stones and gravel with just less than half of the property supporting any vegetation. My father had the Power of Attorney to manage Bommuru and he would use the income from the land to pay off salaries to the temporary hands and permanent resident there and he would often say the land needed more inputs like fertilizer and water to make it yield more but none of Rajananna's son was interested in the property and no one actually invested any of their own money for the betterment of the land. Bommuru was more as a past time for Rajananna as it hardly gave any returns to any of the children, but my father would say it certainly supported Rajananna since he did not remember any one sending him money after he retired.

Both Rajananna and Ammamma would stay for long periods in our house and Akka would see to it that he received very good treatment. Rajananna had very limited needs, he would drink coffee first thing in the morning, had a very light lunch and light dinner. He loved fruits and most importantly loved banana or plantains grown particularly in Kovvuru. He always said that coffee prepared by my mother Kamala tasted so much better than prepared by anyone else. Ammamma of course did not drink anything. She was frail and her back was bent forward and she walked very slowly but always gave a helping hand to my mother.

Overseeing the lands at Bommuru was cumbersome for my father because of asthma and this reduced his activities in the field. The strong and athletic person that my father was in his early days was replaced now with a paunch and became a very large person with limited mobility. In addition, he became addicted to use of Opium to get relief from his frequent bouts of asthma and this further affected his activities. He had to rest often to collect his breath and many days he would lie on the verandah of our house suffering from severe bout of asthma and breathlessness. He never received any revenue from Bommuru to give to Rajananna or his children but the feeling remained in the minds of Rajananna's offspring's that my father must be raking a pot of money from Bommuru and they were denied their fair share of revenue. I do not know why but there was no openness about this and none would sit with my father to audit the accounts of revenue and expenses from Bommuru but the feeling of distrust remained.

I was married to Ramam Mavayya's son Chitti in 1963 and this strengthened the suspicion that my father would now devour all the profits for his son-in-law that is Chitti and one person who did not appreciate this thought was Visalakshi the youngest daughter of Rajananna. Ramam garu had moved to Bombay after giving up his job in Billimora and was doing some form of business and selling insurance policies. He used to receive dividends from shares in blue chip companies like Tata and Birla and I believe much of his expenses were met from these but then he too had to run the family that consisted mostly of all non-earning members or growing children. He used to borrow money from his brother Chinna Tammu Mavayya and this continued for a long time and neither knew when or who will repay the loan. Pappu Bhyranna and Visalakshi were concerned about this and they began nurturing the thought of selling Bommuru before Rajananna passed away and so it was done. Mavayya's share was adjusted in the repayment of his debt to his brother Chinna Tammu. My father regretted that even after so many years of close association, he was not taken into confidence by members of my father-in-law's family including Ramam Mavayya and everything including sale was done rather secretively. Once Bommuru was sold, my father was free from these responsibilities but I still feel my father was treated badly.

4. **Vakkalanka**

One more land deal where my father was drawn unnecessarily and for no reason at all was to manage his father-in-law Nookala Agastya Sastry garu's property in Vakkalanka. After death of my grandfather in 1946, my grandmother began to live with us in our new house and since her other son-in-law Abbulu Peddananna was in London for higher studies, even my aunt Sarada would stay with us and their daughter Sethu was born in our Rajahmundry house. Abbulu garu returned from London and joined a private printing ink factory in Bhandup, a suburb in Bombay and my aunt went over to her husband, but my grandmother remained with us for long periods. She inherited ten acres of land at Vakkalanka which was very fertile and supported cash crops of paddy and coconuts and would give great yields. This land was given to Ayyalasomayajula Subbanna garu, a tenant farmer for maintenance and paying the returns from the crop. Tenant farmer system works like this. The farmer tills the land and grows the crop and improves the fertility of land by investing in fertilizers, takes his share after selling the produce and gives the land owner the balance. Thus the tenant gets his sustenance from the farm he tills and so he has an interest in holding on to the contract for his livelihood.

However, over a period of time after my grandfather died, relationship between my grandmother and Subbanna garu began to deteriorate. So my grandmother decided to terminate the contract. This was the start of the problem since after independence the Government of India declared that tenant farmer becomes owner if the owner of the land does not remain in the area and based on this change of law, Subbanna garu filed a petition in the local court for possession of grandmother's land. My grandmother became very much concerned about losing her land and so she requested my father to fight the case on her behalf. My mother also requested my father to help her mother in getting the land back and so my father agreed and he was then empowered to make decisions on behalf of my grandmother. The first step he took was to submit a counter petition in the court to order the tenant farmer to deposit land lords share in the court every time he sold the crop from the land. This ensured a constant flow of revenue from the land since Subbanna garu had stopped making any payments after he filed the case. However this being a civil case, the process went on for a very long time. My father had told my grandmother that he will not step in the witness stand as he would not lie and if asked a straight forward question about the status he will tell the truth when under oath. My father thus tried to fight the case without him being asked to take to the witness stand.

My grandmother now received a regular flow of income from the land in Vakkalanka after adjusting the cost of legal process. My grandmother then invited Sarada, my aunt and gave her the amount for her expenses. This transaction irritated my father and would argue with my grandmother. He charged that though she was living with one daughter, my mother, she passed on her income to the second daughter, Doddamma. Things became more complicated and caused long heated arguments between the two of them since my grandmother was not one to walk away from an argument. Next step my father did was to remove Subbanna garu and replace him with Mantha Shankaram garu brother-in-law of Chinnamanna, Rajananna's daughter, who also lived in Vakkalanka and was known to be a strong person. Thus the possession of land was taken by my father away from Subbanna garu while the case was going on. At one time in 1962 my father was called on the witness stand and during the deposition, Subbanna garu was asked a pointed question what he thought of my father. He replied that my father was a very straight forward, honest and truthful person and this statement cost Subbanna garu his possession of the land since court considered the case frivolous. The case was settled in 1965 in favor of my grandmother. The land was then passed over to her daughter Sarada and since my mother was not living we did not get any share.

My mother did not take sides in this quarrel between the two but would tell my father to remain quiet about this since she her daughter was not complaining. She would request my father to control his tongue since though he has been doing so many things good for everyone, his harsh words deprived him the benefits of all the good deeds. But my father never told a lie and would not hear any untruths from anyone else. He had a phenomenal memory and he remembered every incident that happened since he was sixteen or before. I too hate lies and remain steadfast in my belief that if a person lies he is not trustworthy and I lose my respect for them. I was never harsh like my father in my replies but that is because I was never in a position of power. I have tried to live my life by forgiving the past still I do not find any one friendly with me including my own cousins.

Den of the Lion King

On October 29, 1984 when my father died in Hyderabad, I felt I was orphaned. My mother died when I was just 13 years old but my father never allowed us to feel her loss. He became both mother and father to all of us. My pleasant memories of the association with my parents are restricted to our house in Danavaya Peta and since my father is Simham or Lion, this house was his den and he ruled from this house like a King. He was thus the Lion King of Danavaya Peta. We moved to our new house in Danavaya Peta in early June, 1946 and Chinna Babu was born in this house on 19th June, 1946 a few days later. My grandfather Agastya Sastry garu was there during finalization of the deal but he died before we moved into the new house. We thus moved away from Godavari River and this became our home for next twenty years.

All my memories still remain as fresh as if they happened just yesterday. My father had a bullock driven cart for traveling to Diwancheruvu or anywhere else when needed. I still remember that the two bullocks were of famous Mysore breed and they could carry the cart almost with the speed of a car. Father had the cart well painted and the floor had a mattress for us to seat and of course the mattress was made of hay. Over the years the cart remained in Diwancheruvu as it became more expensive maintaining the cart in our house once the cycle rickshaws became very common. My father still traveled to Diwancheruvu to oversee the plants and supervise plantation of new saplings for the next season, Akka of course could not go as she was afflicted with paralysis in 1946. She lived in that state for almost 8 years in the room behind my father where she not only slept, she also ate and bathe there in that small place. She was not able to walk but drag on her seat for her meals and bath. I remember Akka before her paralysis and I remember her to be a very tall person and all my brothers and sisters cared for her. My mother was a city girl and so her attachment to the lands was less intense than that of my father. Going to Diwancheruvu was a thrill for us, as we too were also not attached to farm activity since the farm was very far and probably father kept us away and neither my brothers nor any of my sisters knew much about the land in Diwancheruvu at that time.

Pedda Babu was a silent child and he would never ask anyone but instruct me and it was my chore to ask on his behalf. I remember even today, he had such big eyes that he would roll them and look at me so that I would understand what he wanted me to convey. He was one year older to me but I began to speak earlier to him, distinctly and very clearly and I am told I began speaking even before I celebrated my first birthday. Pedda Babu was the pet of the family as he was the first surviving son and my father or mother would not let anything happen to him. Soon after my younger brother Chinna Babu was born in June 1946 and shared affections with Pedda Babu and my life alternated between these two brothers. Both of them were very fair and each looked like the photograph of a bonny baby on the tin of Glaxo Baby Milk powder. My mother's father always ate in a sliver plate or "Vendi Kanchamu" when he was with us. One day my father's brother Babayya came to our house and I insisted that Babayya should be served food on my grandfather's silver plate and not my grandfather. He smiled and said see how she is able to perceive difference between father's relations and mother's relations. From very childhood I had been very demanding and was always ready to fight for right but I never whined. I learned to walk and talk before I was one so I had advantage of demanding attention from my parents and get what I wanted.

Our road was a main road and always very busy. At one end of the road was a roundabout or circle with the statue of Gandhiji in the middle and at the other end was a municipal park for children to play. I would tag along with my brothers to the park and play equally with the boys. I think I was very quick in sports and loved playing and so I would not return until summons came from our home. I was always the first to go to the park and I was the last to return. Once I fell down while playing and bruised my knee and did not tell anyone about it. But Chinna Babu as usual told my mother about it and she was so furious that even today I remember anger shown in her face. She burst out saying as it is you are dark and if you break your hand or legs, who will ever marry you? From that day my tomboy activities were put on hold. It was fun playing with my brothers. I was almost equal to my brothers in both studies and sports. May be this was my way of compensating my dark color and being accepted by my brothers.

I was called 'Nalla Pilla' meaning black girl by many of my close relatives and associates. I would not have minded since I was indeed very dark in those days but I felt insulted being called by some elders in my family whom I respected so much. "Nalla Pilla" name caught on and my cousins began calling me by that name. I was very sad and felt humiliated and in these times of my sorrow only two persons stood up for me: my father and my mother. My father always called me "Amma" since I was named after his mother and my mother would always chide others and would tell me, "Look do you see that caterpillar or 'Gongali'? How ugly it looks! But when the same caterpillar becomes a butterfly do you see any ugliness in it? In the same manner when you grow up, you too will be as pretty and beautiful like the colorful butterfly." This always cheered me up and with the support from both my parents I was now ready to take on the whole world.

My entire life is divided in two parts one before my mother died, the most pleasant part and the second after my mother died. Right now I am talking about that Nalla Pilla, the caterpillar or the ugly duckling. I had a very happy time in my school as everyone was very loving towards me and my time was full with my studies and friends. But the moment school closed for summer vacation, Babayya and my cousins would come from Madras or Bangalore or wherever they lived and then I will have a very miserable time with every one of them calling me Nalla Pilla. I longed for the end of holidays and for the schools to begin.

School time was the most pleasant time of my life. I loved going to the school, I loved the way teachers taught the subjects and I loved participating in all class activities. In our class I competed with Chinna Babu and other students for a place at the top. I have a good memory and ability to recall what I learnt and so even if I was sometimes inattentive in my studies whatever was spoken by my teacher would remain embedded in my brain. I could grasp every problem very quickly and for me working problems in maths was very easy as I was greatly interested in maths and scored almost full marks in the subject. Chinna Babu was not any less and we had a good time competing with each other.

Danavaya Peta House: Our house was situated on the corner of a main road with a street running by the side. It was a large house with both front yard and back yard. Front yard was expansive and in addition to many flowering plants we also kept two cows and their calf for milk in small sheds built near the far corners on both sides of our front yard. Cow is traditionally regarded as very pious animal by Hindu families and we were fortunate to be able to maintain not one but two cows. Our family was so large that the milk from two cows was not enough and our farm hand from Diwancheruvu would bring additional milk every day. There was a front 'vasara' porch (?) that had a very large and spacious open place extending from one end of the house to the other and was raised by almost two feet from the ground. This was the place where my father would sit on a school bench or on a small bed on the floor watching everything that happened around. People who came on business were entertained in the vasara and they would generally not enter the main room. On both ends of this long vasara there were two small rooms about 8 ft. x 8 ft.; one on the left from entrance was Rajananna's room and the opposite room was Pedda Babu's where electrical fuse box was located and since the radio was also kept in this room and it was also known as the radio room. My father kept a close eye on every thing happening on the outside and also inside the house. This porch or 'vasara was fifty feet by 10 feet wide and if required more than twenty guests could sleep there comfortably. The front yard was divided in two by a stone pathway running to the front gate from our main steps. Right side of this stone pathway had flowering plants and a clothes line an additional space for drying wet clothes when needed. Every room had windows and these were protected with closely placed iron bars so that no one could break through the windows.

Vasara led into the main room where there were two almirahs and both these were locked one on the right side was my fathers and opposite to that was that of Pedda Babu's. Facing the main door of the room, was a grandfather clock which was wound once every week and this job was done by my father very religiously as he could reach the clock without a step ladder because of his height. There were two framed art pictures on either side of the wall clock one was of Lakshmi and the second one was that of Saraswati. My mother had made these very colorful art works from full length calendar photograph. Front door of the main room facing the gate was decorated with a white full length curtain showing a lady holding India's tricolor flag; the lady represented Mother India and this beautiful curtain too was made by my mother. One could detect the stamp of my mother, the artist in the main room and in other rooms too.

There were three doors leading from the main room in addition to the main door. The door on the right led to my parent's bed room nearer to the radio room. This room led to another smaller vasara and the ceiling was partly open and one could see the sky line from there. This vasara was occupied by Akka, my father's grandmother and I only remember her mostly after she suffered a paralytic stroke. My father saw to it that he met all her immediate needs till she died. My father was able to keep an eye on her requirements during night and my mother would serve her meals there during the day. A servant would come daily to bring water from our well for Akka and she took her bath in the vasara as she could not walk. She dragged herself on her rump and did her daily chores. In addition to her paralysis, she also began to lose her eye sight and became virtually blind in the later part of her life. She could not see but she knew everyone coming there merely by their footsteps. Akka always said that it gave her great confidence when my father was in the next room. She could tell if my father was not feeling well by his talk and walk and became concerned if she found any difference in his movements and my father would laugh at her and say everything is fine, but he could not deceive her. Vasara was connected to a radio room known so because it had the only radio we had and so we would always be passing by her bed and she would immediately know who was passing and call each of us by our name. She was amazing and I faintly remember her to be a very tall and commanding person before she had the stroke.

The other end of this vasara led into an ante room we used to call as 'Totte Gadi" meaning room for crib, where sundry things were kept and Mamma slept in the room. The room led to the kitchen which in fact was an extension of the main house, but before you entered the kitchen there was a smaller door on the right that led to our pickles room. Pickles were prepared on a very large scale in our house and were stored in large ceramic jars with either screw top lid or plain cover with a knob. In the latter case, the mouth of the jar would be covered with a very clean muslin cloth to prevent any bacteria and fungi spoiling the pickles. The room was kept dark and no one was allowed to enter the room though there was no board to say "entry for authorized personnel only". Only authorized persons of the house observing 'Madi' were allowed and in this manner the chances of mishandling was prevented and the pickles were protected from spoilage. But often times the pickles would show mold growth and surprisingly my grandmother and also great grandmother Akka knew their medicinal properties. Any time someone cut their finger on the sharp knife, they would put the mold on the injured part as a first aid. At that time even Alexander Fleming might not have discovered penicillin, but my forefathers and their forefathers knew the value of mold or fungus and their antibiotic properties.

The door on the left of the main hall was a bed room earmarked for sons-in-laws and that room also had an extended vasara similar to that of Akka but this was used only when a lady was going through her monthly periods or for children to play. The bed room was used for sleeping by me and my sisters. The vasara attached to this bed room led to my grandmother Ammamma's room and this was her own room and she kept many important things and other tidbits in a locked trunk. This was her office room and she and my aunt Sarada would be closeted in the room whenever my aunt visited us and father would make fun of their meetings. This would irritate my grandmother and my mother would chide my father and say "bad comments would wipe away all the good things you have done so far for my mother".

In the main room either Pedda Babu or Chinna Babu would sleep. Pedda Babu had a locked almirah in the drawing room and he was the only one to have other locked almirah. Father kept money, his stock of medicines and all his account books etc. The main room led straight to our dining hall after passing through the middle space and Ammamma's room and this hall was almost 50 feet by twenty feet wide and when we are not having lunch or dinner we played all types of indoor games. Most common games we played were with stones, seeds of aritha (soapnut), and 'gacchakaya' seeds of a medicinal plant grey in color or with sea shells. Each game had its own fun but all these games were mostly on one basic principle and it was played with five of whatever it was and one would be thrown in the air and pick up the items on the floor and catch the one returning and it should not be dropped and all the four pieces are collected. You are supposed to pick them up when the first stone is in the air. The winner would declare some punishment for the loser. I do not know if these games are still being played these days when TV is so universal.

Another game similar to above but more complex was 'Chinta pickala aata (game of tamarind seeds)' played with dried seeds of tamarind and this was played immediately after drying ripe tamarind or Chintapandu. We received ripe tamarind pods between November and February and a battery of women would sit and remove the seeds from the pods before drying them in the sun for annual storage in the house. Our household was very large and so also our need for the 'Chintapandu' used almost daily for making rasam, sambhar or pulusu. As a result we had a very large number of these seeds that would be wasted otherwise. The game is not only played by children but even older women also played. These seeds were distributed as a pile and placed on the floor in front of each player and play same as other games described earlier except that here the small seeds are spread on the floor. A player would throw a leader seed high up in the air and before it comes down the player should pick up as many seeds from the floor as possible without touching the neighboring seeds. The game required good motor skill and eye sight. Loser would be asked to give a certain number of seeds to the winner and thus either lose some of these seeds or gain some and finally the game would end and the final winner gets the entire lot of those seeds or Chinta pickalu. The game was played by many players mostly by girls. You may not believe, but Pedda Babu was an excellent player and he could beat many of us. The counting in this game was also different and intricate; Four seeds of the pile was called 'Poonji', five 'Poonji (20 seeds) make one Kacchata and 8 Kacchata (160 seeds) would be one Gurram or horse and 10 gurram will make 1 elephant or to win one elephant one would need 1600 Chinta pickalu or seeds. We played many types of games some with these seeds and others with shells and when they were not available we would substitute them with Chinta pickalu after removing the color on one side and so it would be white on one side and dark brown on the other side.

Other games we played in this play ground were 'I spy', LONDON, and 'golla stambhala aata' which is a traditional version of musical chairs except that there was no music. Pedda Babu played his soccer or football and we all would join him. Another game played by group of children was 'chaakali bana' here we all form a large circle and one player would go around the circle with a napkin and drop it behind any player and if this was not detected he would begin beating the player just like a washer man 'chaakali' beating the clothes on the stone. But if the other player detects first he would run after the first player and begin beating him with the napkin. This game was played by both boys and girls and it was real fun and every one enjoyed. In summer we had so many cousins visiting us for vacation that it engaged every one of us including those older to us. We also played carom on carom board there and so the dining hall was a vital sports ground for all of us. Pedda Babu was very good at carom or you may say he was good at all the games. One more game that we all enjoyed was snake and ladder and it was fun. Playing with cards was not allowed for us children and if we get the cards and no one was watching, we played secretly. In addition to these games we also played a game called "Tokkudu Billa" by using flat pieces of tiles and we drew lines with chalk on the dining room floor. Again this was considered as a game for girls but Pedda Babu and Chinna Babu also played with me. In short if I played boys games with my brothers, my brothers joined me in girls' sports. We three were always together and had a special relationship and bonding with each other.

Our Tulsi Kota or the castle for plant Tulsi adorned our backyard almost in front of extended kitchen facing the hot water shed and next to "Nandivardhanam tree" that would bloom white flowers. Ammamma and Mamma collected these flowers every day for morning Pooja. Below this tree is the grinding stone for making idli and dosa. There is a gap after that leading to garage that was virtually a store house for coconuts and coal and fire wood and was also known as coal shed. Our well was famous as it was very deep but we also had a municipal tap and behind the well was the ladies bathroom.

Generally municipal water was used for drinking purposes and would come only for one hour every day. Our well was a life line for all of us as well as our neighbors. Danavaya Peta is situated on high grounds as a result ground water was always very deep and not every house was fortunate to get water from the aquifer even if drilled deeper. During summer months it would also provide water to needy in the area when all other wells were dry. Those who came first time to our house would love drawing water from the well but after very first day they would complain of aching arms and would let our maid draw water for them. I used to draw water from this well with ease and it certainly was good for health and certainly an exercise to my arms. Very often Muttayya, Veeranna, Pullayya or Narayana would draw water when we had very large number of guests. I had to share drawing water from the well most of the time. I do not remember how many buckets of water I would draw in a day, but I would not tire because I loved drawing water from that well.

The shed opposite the kitchen was known as hot water shed and had a large earthen fire stove to heat the water with fire wood in addition to one coal fired hot water copper boiler. The shed was my father's place for his bath and he would spend at least one hour discussing events of the day. Muttayya or someone would draw water from well to mix with hot water and prepare the water at right temperature for my father. Father would take his bath at 10.00 am and at 11.00 am he would sit for his meals. The time of his meal was very important as this was also the time for his daily dose of medicine. As I had mentioned earlier, father was afflicted with asthma and this has been going on since his childhood. Somewhere along the line, he was introduced to a small dose of opium that helped relieve him from the acute condition and that became an addiction for him throughout his life. He had to take his dose of opium every day at the same time and this should immediately be followed up with his first meal. We never had any practice of breakfast in our house and our morning meal was always done before 12.00 noon and evening dinner before 7.00 pm.

Behind the hot water shed there was another small gully that had many plantain trees and this became a favorite place for Pedda

Babu for playing his flute since my father objected to his excessive involvement with music. This was a safe place where he practiced his music but the sound would not go to the front of our house and father will not know. Pedda Babu would cut plantain leaves and make some whistles and was always creative. His interest in anything that would produce sound was so high that he would try everything available in nature for his practice. This is the general lay out of our house. Between the garage and the extended kitchen was a door leading to the side street and my mother and other women in the house would make their purchases of vegetables etc. here. Rajananna did not like women coming out on the front gate for making these purchases and so my mother had to wait for the vendors till they come at our rear door. She would tell my father to keep an eye for a particular vendor and father would tell the vendor to knock on our rear door for my mother to make her purchases. Rajananna was our guest most of the time in a year and that made life difficult for us children. Even my mother who believed in patience became angry when we children were not allowed to play freely in the front yard.

The house on the other side of this side door was that of a retired engineer Angara Narasimha Rao garu and was a very spacious house with a very good Banganpalli mango tree that was leaning over the tall wall towards the road. Every year during season, the tree would be full of raw mangoes that were very sweet and this would attract passersby and they would try to get these by throwing stones. Every time a stone hit the house he would come out and make a big fuss. Father admonished him but to no avail. His son Angara Krishna Rao was a violinist on All India Radio and was well regarded in the music circles. Not that his being a violinist made any difference to us since at that time even Pedda Babu did not have a greater appreciation of classical music. Next to our house on this side of the street, was a hotel run by Behra and he would prepare Idli's every day in a manner that we Brahmins could buy and even father would eat them. On some weekends when we all would look for a variety, father would order Idli's from this hotel and that was our only source of hotel food. The hotel was then famous for besan chutney which even today when we remember would bring memory of that unique taste. Chinna Babu maintained that he has yet to eat besan chutney as tasty as that of Behra and all his efforts to duplicate the taste did not succeed. I do not know if that hotel run by Behra is still there or for that matter if our house is still therein Rajahmundry.

In front of our house was a large house rented by three families. The family on the left to us was that of Paidamarri Satyanarayana, the middle portion was occupied by Saraswati garu and Janakamma who belonged to Chowdhari community. The third portion was occupied by a Peddamallu Satyanarayana garu and his grocery store who was nick named as "Yerra (fair) Komati" to differentiate him from next door Kothha Suryanarayana who was dark in texture. In fact he would remind me of the famous adage that a dark Brahmin and a fair Komati are not to be trusted. He also had a grocery store but with the big grocery store next door his shop was not well visited. Chinna Babu was a frequent visitor to Saraswati's house as a baby and he would run across the street every second minute and was pampered by the sisters. Both did not have any children and they loved Chinna Babu. Once when he was crossing the street, he was hit by a car belonging to Sankranti Venkata Ratnam Garu who lived almost two blocks from our house in front of the Engineer's house. We were all very much worried when we saw him unconscious, but the driver of the car assured us that he was not hurt and Chinna Babu soon opened his eyes. This was our first lesson in principles of safe walking on the road. He continued to visit Saraswati garu but was now more watchful.

Directly across our house was the famous grocery shop of Kothha Suryanarayana garu, famous because he was our credit card company and father would run credit till it is paid when father received money from the land. Any time any of us wanted any item my mother or father would ask us to go over to his shop and bring it. I never knew that he was paid money till I was much older. Once, when I was studying in another school, my classmate, daughter of a weaver gave me strings and yarns remaining after they spun the cotton and I gave them to Manikyam who would knit beautiful designs from these. I was six years old and was studying in first standard. One day, that girl asked me for money. I was surprised and asked her what money, I did not ask for these and you only gave me. She threatened me that she would come to our house and report to my father and I told her to go ahead and she came to our house and asked my father for money. Father called me to confirm and I told him that she was asking money for yarn that she gave me. I did not think we ever give money to anyone. Everything we need we get it from the shop across the street and they never asked for money, so why should she ask for money? Everyone laughed at my innocence and then father explained to me the basic of commerce and credit structure and explaining that he would pay Suryanarayana every time he received returns from the farms and that he has never received anything for free. I felt embarrassed that I did not know even this simple economics! By the way Kothha Suryanarayana became a Municipal Councilor in the later years and may also have become a Mayor but by that time we left Rajahmundry.

Next to our wall and opposite to Satyanarayana's shop used to be a small shop belonging to a washer man Yerakanna and he was drunk most evenings like most of his community and was a butt of jokes from Chinna Babu. But later the shop changed hands and Suryanarayana bought the place and set up a cycle repair shop and appointed Shyamala Rao, a good mechanic to look after the shop. We did not have much to do with the shop but the mechanic had a very melodious voice and that attracted our attention. He could sing in the same voice as famous Telugu singer Ghantasala of movie fame and we would listen to his rendering raptly every evening.

Further down the road on the left was the house of Kesapragada Narasimham garu and next to that were the police lines and quarters of local constabulary and this was the heart of Chinna

Babu's stories. At the end of the police lines the road would end into a sort of roundabout with the statue of Mahatma Gandhiji in the middle, road on right led to Khambala Cheruvu and further to Diwancheruvu; one on left led to Godavari railway station. Our road would continue to Government Paper mills and Central Tobacco Research Institute (CTRI). Vedula Narayana Murty garu, cousin of Pedda Bawa and maternal uncle to Chenulu worked there as a statistician in 1952 and during the famous flooding of river Godavari in 1953 he came to our house till the floods receded and he could go back.

On the other side of the road, two blocks on our left was local post office which we used to frequent for getting money order forms during Deepavali festivals to make Matabas. In those days these forms were available free, but subsequently government began charging one anna or six paise for each form to prevent them being misused. Next to the post office was the house of Yerukonda Venkanna garu who was a prominent cloth merchant and my father would always buy clothes from his shop only. They were seven brothers and all lived under one roof only and they would not think of separating. Interesting thing about this family was that they had seven twins in the family and all were similar twins. We used to wonder at these twins.

Municipal Park was situated diagonally across from Venkanna garu's house and this was my favorite place as I could enjoy plenty of freedom inside. The watchman for the park used to be the coachman to Rajananna and he knew my father very well. All my mischiefs were dutifully reported to my father by the watchman and so one day Pedda Babu warned him that this would not be good for him hoping that I would now be safe. But the watchman went to my father and reported the threat given by Pedda Babu and everyone laughed about it when we came back after play. I remember each and every one who lived on the street but this is not the place to talk about it.

Father ran our house like a small kingdom and he had a set of people who would be our vendors and they alone would visit us for all occasions and my memoirs would not be complete without mentioning about these people.

Kali Veeraswami: He was neither a vendor nor our farm hand but still I remember him very distinctly. As I had mentioned earlier, father had to visit our farms in Gurraja Peta and he would be away for at least a week or more during these visits. Father would request Kali Veeraswami to stay at our house during the nights and guard the house as well as keep an eye on the goings on. He was an elderly person, dark and not very hefty and always wore beads of Tulsi in his neck and ear rings. He was a devotee and would sing bhajans or songs praising our gods whenever he got an opportunity. I remember him coming to our house in the nights and sing bhajans or songs almost throughout the night. He would bring his tanpura, a string instrument and spend his time singing them melodiously and I would sit on the window sill and listen to these songs till I dropped asleep. He would thus guard our house in the night. He had one daughter and she died leaving her son Krishna in the care of her husband, but when he married again, Veeraswami brought his grandson Krishna to his house and not only supported him but also provided him with good education. My father chided Veeraswami for bringing a child since he was living all alone and he asked him if he was looking for support from him when he grew up or when he became old. Veeraswami replied, I am doing only what I think is right for the child and once he is grown up I would like him to go his own way and not support me.

Krishna was very intelligent and not only did he graduate from school, but he continued his studies and became an engineer. I remember Krishna coming to my father one day crying and so I asked my father if there was any problem with Veeraswami. Father explained to me that Krishna has now got a good position at a place away from Rajahmundry and he wanted his grandfather to come with him. He was telling my father that my grandfather looked after me when I needed and now when I have the opportunity of looking after him he would not come with me and this made him very unhappy. He requested my father to persuade Veeraswami since he would probably listen to my father only. My father was very touched with this request and he called Veeraswami and asked him why he would not go with Krishna since that would make him happy. He replied, I did not educate Krishna so that he would return my favor but I did so as my duty, so that he would become something better in life. My responsibility ends there and I wish him all happiness in his life. I will not go with him as I have lived here all my life and would like to die in this place only. He was the living example of that gardener of Akbar who was planting a sapling when he was almost sixty years old. The Emperor spoke lightly to the gardener that he would not live to eat the fruits and the gardener replied that he was not planting the sapling so that he would eat the fruits; but planting so that others will get the benefit of the plant. Veeraswami showed to us that he did not nurture his grandson because he wanted something in return from him but so that he became a good person. This incident has remained implanted in my mind.

State barber Adayya: Every alternate day, Adayya would stand at our gate and ask my father if would like a shave as mostly father shaved his beard alternate days and father normally nod his head. There was a protocol for the process; Adayya would pick up a chair from the vasara and bring it to the front yard and ask someone to bring hot water from inside as he is not allowed to go inside the house. He would then begin sharpening his razor on a leather strap and once water is brought he would then request father to sit down for a shave. Once every fifteen days, Pedda Babu and Chinna Babu had their hair cut. Adayya knew how to use razor and hair trimming machines but he did not know styles and so they would get a standard conventional haircut. They might have preferred going to a hair cutting saloon, but then as long as they stayed in Rajahmundry, Adayya cut their hair. Adayya not only cut Pedda Babu and Chinna Babu's hair, he was also called to cut hair for all male children who would come to our house during summer vacation. Cutting hair was a ritual and every one had to follow the same routine.

Adayya was father's source of local gossip and city news. He was what one would call the morning newspaper for my father. Most important role of Adayya was his band that we would hire for all marriages and other functions. Adayya was thus closely related to many events in our life.

Our Tailor Mahalakshmi: Mahalakshmi had a shop near Godavari Railway Station and he was invited for stitching clothes for everyone in the family. Fifteen days or even one month before any major festival, father would send for Mahalakshmi and when he came he would ask him to contact Yerukonda Venkanna Garu and request him to send new material for clothing for both boys and girls. A representative of Yerukonda Venkanna would come with large bundles of clothes all new arrivals and the selection committee comprising of Mother, Ammamma, Mamma, Manikyam if there, father and then they all would consider all the material brought and once choice is made, Mahalakshmi would give his estimate and once the material for everyone is selected he would pick up all the pieces and take them to his shop for making the dresses. I have mentioned about the selection committee and though we are allowed to make a suggestion, they had the veto power and this applied to even design for dresses. After this exercise when the dresses are received none of them would be stitched as per the measurement. Mahalakshmi always had the standard explanation that he had made them slightly larger as these clothes are likely to shrink after first wash and surprising thing was that they did not shrink but remained same size even after many washes. We would have preferred someone else to make clothes for us, but as long as we were in Rajahmundry, it was Mahalakshmi who stitched our clothes. His brother was a better tailor but he was not allowed to come as according to Mahalakshmi his brother did not know tailoring and I knew he was a better tailor but he never got opportunity of stitching our clothes. We were always unhappy about our clothes even though father selected very expensive material for us.

The only year we all wore fitting clothes was when father had purchased a sewing machine for my mother and this was enough for my mother to show her skills at stitching. She made so many different designs for each one of us and that was the last time.

Our washer man Naganna: Our clothes were always washed by our washer man Naganna who lived in Diwancheruvu. It was routine that Naganna would come to our house every Monday with his wife for collecting weekly clothes for washing. Since Rajahmundry is a city, they both would come neatly dressed and wore very clean clothes. I would tell his wife that she had the luxury of wearing new sarees every time since they received clothes from so many households and she would smile at me. Shop next to our house was earlier leased to a washer man Yerakanna who was more known to us for his drinking habit and he would sit in our front yard talking to my father. He would request my father to give him the clothes instead of giving to Naganna. Father would smile and tell him not worry about it as Naganna has been with the family for so many years and he would not change him. He would then talk about local politics, gossip and then leave. Father would tell him strongly not to misbehave with his wife when drunk but otherwise he was a good neighbor shop for emergency needs.

Our maid Appala Narasamma: Appala Narasamma stayed with us for a longest period of time. But before we hired Appala Narasamma we had Suramma and her daughter Lakshamma and they became very close to me because Lakshamma used to play with me. They were very good at drawing designs (muggu) on the floor of our house particularly during Sankranti and Deepavali times. They were real artists and they would always come together for working. After they left Pentamma joined us with her two daughters Samudram and Godavari and the three of them worked neatly and we did not have any reason to complain. My mother used to watch Appala Narasamma working at Kothha Suryanarayana's house and used to tell my father that she looked a very quiet and hardworking type and so they called her once but she did not want to work at our house at that time. Pentamma had some problems of her own and told my father that she would continue till a good maid was fixed for us and thus Appala Narasamma joined us. I must say that we were very lucky in having all good maids to do our routine cleaning and washing. Appala Narasamma was a loner unlike Suramma and Pentamma, and her daughter was very rich so she came alone to work at our place.

Thus Appala Narasamma became our maid since 1957 and continued to remain so till we left Rajahmundry. Her routine was same. She would come to our house at 4.30 in the morning and sweep the front yard, back yard and sprinkle water on the dried soil. By that time every one would be awake and she would clean all our utensils and then the first batch of coffee will be served. She would get her glass of coffee and that coffee would be as good as we would have since mother would not like separate treatment for maids or servants. I have seen many families buy poor grade rice for serving to their maid servants while I would always serve the same rice that we ate in spite of rationing of rice in Bombay. This is the training from my mother. She would in fact wait to see that our farm hands are served hot rice and curries when they come from Diwancheruvu as she felt they had as much right as we had. I too believe in this philosophy and feel proud that I have inherited the same nature from my mother.

Ramudu & Govindudu: These were two so called barbers whose job was to massage male members of our family before they have weekly oil bath. Both Pedda Babu and Chinna Babu would sit on a stool in their underwear every Sunday and one of the two would come and apply oil on their bodies and give them a very thorough body massage before they took their hot water bath. Barbers are known to have three professions namely one hair cutting, second body massage and third participate in a band to be played on special occasions like wedding, thread ceremony etc. Adayya was able to do two of the above tasks and Ramudu and Govindudu managed massaging. They lived in front of Park and probably worked at one of the house belonging to Jayanti Ganganna Garu. They would do odd jobs in the house when they came but otherwise we hardly noticed them. When I look back, my father really maintained a big entourage to look after so many jobs.

Painter Jhamparao: Every year our house was painted by two groups one who would white wash the house using lime and Painter Jhamparao would apply paint on the wood work after whitewash. He was a very jovial person and would make fun in lightness. He had a great confidence in his ability of painting and he would always boast about his work. He used very good paint material and these paints would dry very fast. Chinna Babu saw that he was so boastful he decided to teach him a lesson. One day as usual Jhamparao painted a window sill, door and even Gummam or elevated wood work for each door. He painted Gummam yellow and had red dots on this as a mark of auspicious design. Jhamparao finished painting the door and Gummam and went away. After about an hour later Chinna Babu came there and saw Jhamparao and asked him if the Gummam was painted and dry. Jhamparao as usual boasted that yes I had painted an hour back and now the paint would be dry and you could even sit on the Gummam and he sat down. Wet paint stuck to his khaki short and he felt so embarrassed. I felt sorry for him and was thinking that this batch of paint was probably bad but Chinna Babu was laughing away. I asked him what is so funny and he said, Sarvamangala now Jhamparao will never boast again. I had painted the Gummam after it had dried and just before Jhamparao came and like a fool he sat on the wet paint! My father was very upset about the incident and gave some extra money to Jhamparao.

Whitewash specialist Gajula Narasayya: It was an annual ritual in almost every house in those days to get the house whitewashed with lime as this would extend the life of the walls and other structures. Lime is rich in chlorine and so would also remove any bad air from the house. Our house was mostly whitewashed before every Sankranti. He was a tall lean person with a rich crop of dark wavy hair. His assistant was Dosalamma who helped Narasayya in mixing the lime and getting him new brushes, draw water from the well and so on. She would mix the lime and he would then whitewash the walls and however careful he was, the floor would be splattered with the lime and Dosalamma would clean the floor after the work is done. Narasayya reminded us of a movie character actor Ramana Reddy, but other than that he was a good worker. They would work without any supervision. Every time we have a wedding in our house, father would invite Narasayya to whitewash the house and Jhamparao would follow behind. In 1955 for instance, Narasayya had finished whitewashing the house in March before Bhanumati's wedding and in May when Ramam Mavayya's daughter baby was married he whitewashed the house once again. This was a tradition.

Cow herd Appanna: As I have mentioned before, we usually had two cows on both sides of the wall and Appanna would look after them and come every day in the morning to milk the cows. Both Appanna and Appala Narasamma would be the first in the morning to visit our house. He had some magic in his hands as most cows would submit meekly to his milking. Interestingly he had two sons and he educated one of his sons to become a double graduate and he completed his Masters in arts a very rare feat in their community. But he did not allow second son to study and trained him to follow his profession. My father would tell proudly to every one visiting our house about Appanna's son who did his MA. In any age, education is expensive and Appanna worked hard to educate his son and probably completed his duty towards his son. I lost touch with him once I left Rajahmundry after my marriage.

'Cow' Puli—Danayya and Dharmayya: At 10.00 in the morning two brothers Danayya and Dharmayya would come and take the cows for taking them to pasture in nearby grassland. This was the exercise much needed for the cows. Although they were brothers Danayya was very tall and looked very imposing like the Big Bacchan of today where as his brother Dharmayya was short and stout but anyone looking at them would still say they were brothers as their faces were so similar. They would don the makeup of tiger (Pedda Puli) during Dassera festivals and dance to the drum beats and my father would call them not Pedda Puli but Cow Puli as they were cow herds. Our cows recognized their footsteps so well that even if they are passing along the road and not coming to our house they would greet them. The cows came back from their outing, they looked contented and even a child could tie them without any difficulty. The cows were certainly very intelligent animals. I know this question would be on every one's mind that why do Hindu's worship cows and there is no direct answer in any text books. But I believe that Hindu civilization began once man began domesticating these animals. In all probabilities, cow may have been the first one among domesticated animals. Imagine if man did not have cows and farms in the beginning would he have got any time to contemplate about life, death and religion? In gratitude to his development, I believe he began giving the highest position one could give to any animal. If cow gave milk, the bullocks tilled the land and thus he now had milk and food grains at his disposal and all this because he could domesticate the cow and cows were more intelligent than most other animals. I wonder how my father was able to support such a large entourage of servants and other vendors. If Babayya or Pedda Babu had considered the opportunity they would have had if they had joined father, I am sure everything would be different and our families would be listed among few prosperous Brahmin families in East Godavari District. But father's dreams remained unfulfilled.

Graduate Jeweler: Jewelers in India are mostly from Marwari community who migrated to our parts from western parts of India. They believed in commerce and it is said that they are asked to go away and set up their own business when they are very young and they go out with one bed sheet and one tumbler or lota for keeping himself clean. The present icon of Marwari community Birla who are billionaires also started their career by going out to Calcutta with just one bed sheet and one tumbler or lota. Their only objective is to earn money and they would do this by setting up jewelry shops in any town or village and once he is set the next is giving loans to people and generally are considered as loan sharks. They would not waste their formative years in schools and studying and were satisfied with simple writing and reading and use their inherited knowledge of mathematics and are very good in calculating simple and compound interests on any loan. Another aspect of their business is to run pawn shops to hock gold and silver ornaments in return of money and generally the debtor would not be able to redeem their items and they would own the item.

It was therefore a surprise that our jeweler was not only educated but he was a graduate. My father would catch such nuances in a person and use that as his pet word for addressing and this definitely pleased them. He was an elderly gentleman always wore spotlessly clean white kurta and dhoti and a zari cap on his head. He would sport a red Tilak or yellow spot on his forehead. Jewelers in India are known to mix other metals mostly copper in gold instead of making ornaments of pure gold to make it pliable but more often giving substandard finished product and make a profit from some of the gold remaining after the finished product is ready. I have already mentioned my association with people of Marwari community at my birth on this world was heralded by a group of these business persons who had come to our house for borrowing silver coins to worship their goddess of Lakshmi or wealth. According to the tradition a jeweler is not supposed to charge for making Mangala Sutra at the time of a girls wedding and this item is never adulterated. At the time of my wedding, Mr. Morarji Desai was the finance minister and he declared a ban on purchase and sale of pure gold and pure gold ornaments in order to prevent black marketing and accumulation of black money or money that is not accounted. My father called this BA Jeweler and told him that he should not adulterate the gold used for making Mangala Sutra even though there is a ban and though he declared that he had used pure gold in making we all had our own doubts.

I would like to mention here that one incident affected my father very badly while dealing with this jeweler. In 1953 or so my aunt Gnanamba Attayya came with Chitti and Baby on vacation and while coming she also brought pure gold for making some ornaments. Father called this jeweler and told my aunt why don't you go ahead and tell him all the details and give him the job yourself. Accordingly she gave the jeweler the gold and he agreed to make the ornaments as per the design. But unfortunately, two days later he came and told my father that his house was burgled and he lost all valuables including my aunts gold. But somehow my father's name was involved in the deal since he had called the jeweler and he was accountable for the loss of gold and father tried to explain the situation. He told that he only arranged the introduction but all the dealings were done directly by Gnanamba only and my aunt understood the situation. But he was blamed and some in the family considered him responsible. My aunt Gnanamba died two years later and this remained etched deep in my father's mind. In 1955 when Baby was married, he presented two heavy gold chains for Mangala sutra one each for Baby and her older sister Lakshmi almost the same value as the gold that was lost earlier by my aunt. But every one forgot about this gift from my father and I had to correct the record much later when someone made a mention about this. This was the most unfortunate incident for my father and most everyone remembered only the loss of the gold, but not the chains he made for his nieces and my father never got any opportunity to clarify.

I am reminded another incident of similar nature that happened to me directly. When Chitti and we all went back to Bombay from Visakhapatnam, we were living in a apartment in Koliwada and Chinna Tammu Mavayya introduced us to one Parsi gentleman Nausher Khambata who told him that he could get refrigerator for less than half the market price and so Mavayya told Chitti to bring three thousand rupees and give it to Nausher and Chitti on his next visit gave the money to Mavayya and Mavayya gave to Nausher. Similarly, he also gave some money to him for a flat for his second daughter Rama and so also his sister Visalakshi who also gave him the money for some similar deal. Nobody knew at that time that Nausher was a scam artist and he would collect money from different people and would vanish. Every one of us remained quiet realizing Mavayya has been duped, but not Visalakshi and her husband Bhyranna Garu. It is unfortunate that good people get blamed in such mishaps.

The Empire: My father lived in Danavaya Peta like an Emperor and our house was his empire. Before my mother died, father would be in their bed room and would come out to meet visitors in Vasara, but after my mother died, father made vasara his office cum bed room. There were four pieces of furniture in this vasara, one was a school bench at the far end wall near Rajananna's room, a long bench in the middle of vasara on the left of main entrance and two straight backed chairs one adjoining the pillar and another chair on the right hand side of wall on the right of the main door. Father had his mattress spread on the edge of the vasara touching Pedda Babu's radio room and the back was supported with at least two high pillows as this propping up of his back helped him considerably. He had a 12" dry cell flash light next to his pillows that would throw powerful beam in the night and a walking stick or staff that would help him in disarming any intruder.

His bed was so critically positioned that at any time of night he could read the time from the wall clock on the center of the main drawing room. Of course this was a chiming wall clock and so he could hear the chimes every half an hour and he would be aware of time. His normal day time position would be to sit on the school bench after taking his coffee and either complete his account books or write Rama Koti or Shiva Koti. Koti means ten million and so he wrote ten million times each word or phrase and he had planned to complete these during his life time. I have mentioned earlier that father had a very nice handwriting and this remained for years to come and whether he had written when he was twenty, forty or sixty years of age his hand writing did not change. Whether completing his accounts or writing Koti books he always kept an eye on every thing happening in the house or around the house since he had two grown daughters to look after in addition to a very young child. He watched each of us like a hawk and did not allow anyone harm us.

He would stop writing when the time was nearing 10.00 am and he would ask for another cup of tea before going for his bath. Once he finished his bath he would open his almirah and take out a small pill box and take out a small weighed amount of opium and then sit for his meals in the back vasara or our dining hall. As soon as food was served, he would open his pill box and take out a small ball of opium and swallow before starting his meals. He would take this as a medicine every day during morning meals only. I do not know who would bring opium for father, but it must be in black market since use of opium was banned. He probably got his monthly stock and then mix with some other ingredient and then weigh out equal amounts using a very small weighing balance and prepare small balls for everyday use. He would use probably five grams of opium every day for his Asthma. He would not fast at any time as this would upset his regular dose except on Mondays when he would be fasting in the morning. In this case he would take his medicine with the evening meal. This small dose of opium was his life line and without that he would suffer.

But opium was not sufficient for his asthma and he had to take another smoke inhalant as an additional measure to maintain his normal activities. This was some powder made by some local herbal medicine company that had shown success in controlling asthma but it still was not a cure. This was made of many herbs one of them being seeds of datura which are known to be toxic. The powder is taken into a small base plate of a hookah and is lit using match and once it is lit the top hood is replaced and the smoke is inhaled. This was his lifeline in addition to his normal daily quota of opium. I believe I have never seen my father in good health and his asthma must have made him more helpless throughout his life.

He has always been a very neat person and he would always wear his clothes very neat and white. His shoes were always shining with a fresh coat of shoe polish. Every time he went out he would wear white dhoti, cream color lalchi or kurta and a zari embroidered khanduva or upper cloth giving an imposing picture. I have not seen him in any clothes except traditional. I know we all are used to this habit of cleanliness and this is probably running in our family. He mostly wore brown shoes and these would be so polished that one could see their face in it. His spotlessly white Dhoti was properly cared by the washer man. Ramam Mavayya once sent terry cloth dhoti's manufactured by Mafatlal and he found that this type of dhoti was easy to maintain and were long lasting.

Ramakoti: Father was a devout follower of Rama and believed in all the three principles believed by his role model Lord Rama. It is therefore no surprise that he began to write Ramakoti or writing phrase 'Sri Rama' in a Ramakoti book till he completed writing 100 lakh times or 10 million times to complete one Koti. He wrote these in books specially marketed with small fixed columns. My mother's death was a great shock to him and he was so disturbed that he decided to write Ramakoti and thus reduce the stresses on his mind. He thus began writing Ramakoti in 1957. No one knows this but my father was so upset with my mother's death that he ate only once during afternoon time and stopped eating in the night. He showed signs of weakness and so our family doctor Dr. Sambhayya advised him to eat both times and preserve his health. It was his routine to write at least two hours every day come what may. He was writing during wedding functions of Bhanumati and of his niece Baby. Once he decides, it is always final and he continued to write in Rajahmundry, then in Kakinada and finally when he went to Hyderabad he continued with his two series of books. His hand writing was so uniform that it remained same when he started and when he completed his work after about 25 years. This is amazing.

I do not know for certain, but I believe he completed writing 'Sri Rama' 100 lakh times, or written 'Sri Rama' Koti times, but then he did not go to present to Lord Rama in Bhadrachalam. Pedda Babu and Chinna Babu went to Bhadrachalam after my father died and presented the work to Lord Rama in the temple there. I was watching a movie "Andala Ramudu" that was based on an elderly woman who was traveling to Bhadrachalam to present her books after completing 100 lakh times or completing her Koti, but she died before she reached Bhadrachalam. It happened like that to my father also. My aunt Sarada was also writing Ramakoti and I know she was very serious about completing, but she too did not go to Bhadrachalam to present to Lord Rama. They all began writing seriously but their efforts were lost as they could not deliver personally because of their age and lack of support in the task.

Once Satya Saibaba came to Rajahmundry and addressed devotees at the local Foot Ball (soccer field) ground probably the only largest place in Rajahmundry and father took us there to listen to him. I was small so he took me on his shoulders and I do not remember if I could see him from that distant but then when he began to chant Ram, Ram, Ram there was pin drop silence and soon every one chanted with him. I remember even today that his voice was so melodious that one could just lose one self in the chant. Father could never forget the occasion and would remember his magnetic personality and melodious chanting of Rama my father's role model and he became Satya Saibaba's follower. Not that he went to visit him anywhere but he held him in highest respect. Father had so many responsibilities that he never went to visit any place for fun or for a pilgrimage. His only place of visit was Lord Satyanarayana's temple in Annavaram as that was just about 2 hours' drive from Rajahmundry or Kakinada. After going to Hyderabad all his movements were stopped. I still do not know what he desired and if these were fulfilled by us.

Shivakoti: Along with Ramakoti, father also began writing Shivakoti also known as Panchakshari since it consisted of 5 words in 1957 and this also involved writing 100 lakh times five words "Om Namah Shivaya" and since Lord Shiva was his favorite God he wanted to complete this also. He would write alternately Ramakoti and Shivakoti. He could not complete his Koti before he died and he was short by 15 lakh times and Pedda Babu and Chinna Babu went and presented his work to Lord Shiva at a temple in Srisailam. He would complain of back ache most nights after writing continuously for more than four hours and Muttayya would rub a soothing balm on his back.

Pied Piper: My father was always a favorite of babies and children. Everyone in my family left their babies on my father's bed and father would sing the bhajans he liked most and the baby if crying slept peacefully. I used to leave Gnanu at father's bed; Indira would leave Kavita with my father so that she could complete some chores. Most common bhajans was that of Lord Shiva "Chandrasekhar Chandrasekhar, Chandrasekhar Pahi Maam, Somasekhar Somasekhar, Somasekhar Trahi Maam" and he also had a very melodious voice. Virtually children of three generation have fallen asleep with these bhajans. He would otherwise chant "Sri Rama, Sri Rama Jai Jai Rama". I remember Durga when young would sleep when my father sang bhajans and if he changed a bhajans she would ask my father to sing Sri Rama once again and she was about 5 years old. My father's large bed was full with children of various ages and almost every one would be asleep by the time father finished his bhajans. He sang so many bhajans but I do not remember all.

Quotes of my father: My father was a very witty person and his wit was unique and he was always quick in repartee and the famous exchanges were mostly between my father and Ramam

Mavayya his brother-in-law. In fact they were so close that people would call them as Krishna and Arjun after the famous characters in Mahabharata where Krishna was Arjun's brother-in-law and I am giving a few samples of their closeness.

Vitamins and Tonic supplements: My father and Ramam Garu thus had a special relationship and they would each kid each other and if Ramam Garu was caught off guard, he would laugh very heartily and it was all fun to us children. Ramam garu accompanied with my aunt Gnanamba and their children came to our house from Bombay during one summer vacation. His doctor brother must have convinced him of the value of tonics and vitamins to him and since his past illness he had taken many allopathic medicines and believed in power of vitamins and tonics. We were all sitting in our back vasara and Ramam Garu was telling my father of the merits of tonics and how they would help build a child's growing body and how father must supplement diet of his children. Father listened to him very patiently and seriously and then asked him in all seriousness "I say Ramam, do you give these tonics to your children?" Ramam Garu was very pleased with the question and told my father yes of course and these have been recommended by my brother who is a famous doctor in Bombay. Father looked very serious and with a straight face told him, "in that case Ramam, I think, I will keep my children away from these tonics of yours." There was a pause and Ramam Garu burst out laughing since he saw that we were all very healthy whereas his children looked weak and thin. We all were expecting Ramam Garu to be angry and so were happy with this turn of things and we all joined in laughter. I do not remember any time my father and Ramam Garu having an argument and they were always very close.

Mineral nutrition: In another incident, Ramam garu was elaborating the benefits of minerals present in skins of fruits like apples and chickoo or Sapotas. My father and Ramam garu were having dinner when the discussions on the property of the skins of these fruits was going on and every one was listening raptly to the scientific information he was giving and father was also giving him good attention and so Ramam garu was happy. Once he stopped talking, father called Suryanarayana standing there and told him to give a coconut and a jack fruit to Ramam Garu without removing their outer skin as these skins contained lot of minerals for good health. No one understood what my father said first time, but when they all understood what he meant the first one to laugh was Ramam Mavayya who understood the quick wit of my father. They both understood each other very well.

Chinna Tammu: Once when my father was very young, he and Chinna Tammu and Pedda Tammu came for lunch and since they had something to eat just a few moments earlier Chinna Tammu told his mother Sitamma that he was not hungry and so he will eat only little. Accordingly Ammamma served him very small quantity while she served my father as usual. Before long Chinna Tammu finished the one served and asked for more and he ate almost as much as my father and Pedda Tammu were eating. When they finished their meals, father said "Chinna Tammu, if you could eat so much when not hungry, how much food would you eat if you were really hungry?" and every one began to laugh.

Chilaka Ramam garu: Chilaka Ramam garu visited us whenever he needed a vacation. He had nowhere to go and he felt at home in our house. Once he visited us in 1962 when things were not going well in his family and he was seething with anger about the interference by his father-in-law Pappu Bhyranna garu, but he could not talk back to him. He came to see my father and unload his troubles. Once he went out for a short errand and it began to rain. My father was standing at the gate holding an umbrella and he saw Chilaka Ramam garu walking slowly in this heavy rain with no signs of concern. Muttayya was also there holding an umbrella over my father also saw him getting wet and both began to see if he would hurry back home but he did not. Father came back to his position on the desk and saw that Chilaka Ramam was drenched wet so he asked him why did he not hurry when it began raining instead of getting drenched and he replied "Hamare Kanpur mein to aisa hi hota hai" meaning in our Kanpur it is always like this and this became a famous quote in our family.

Gouthami: As I had mentioned earlier, Pedda Bawa would come before any festival like a dutiful son-in-law but for some reason or other he would get upset and go back without participating in the festival. He was a very tall person more than 6 feet tall and one could see him coming from far off. As was his habit, father nicknamed Pedda Bawagaru. Once, Gouthami was standing near the gate looking at the far end of the road with my father to see if her father was coming. My father took this opportunity and asked her if she could see her father. She said no and father said there now you can see him like the station next to Anakapalle and Gouthami did not understand what my father meant. She asked him to tell her the meaning and he asked her do you know the name of the station next to Anakapalle and Gouthami looked at him for an answer. He laughed and said "Taadi" which in Telugu meant palm tree which stands tall in a farm and so also is your father who is walking past Narasimham garu's house walking tall among all the other short people. Everyone was silent and when he came and asked why they were all quiet, Gouthami told her father that Tata garu was calling you station next to Anakapalle and when Bawa garu laughed at this joke, every one began laughing and from that time definition for a tall person became "station after Anakapalle" and this became applicable to everyone who is tall.

Mavatata Garu: Mavatata Garu is maternal uncle to my mother and older brother to Ammanna garu. He lived most his life in Hyderabad and was a partner in an industrial establishment called Isola Industries along with his brother and his children. They would make phenyl for janitorial application and became very popular. One time he went away from his home, joined a group of sadhus and went over to Himalayas probably for meditation and after some time he returned back and this time he came to stay with us and my father never asked him why and welcomed him.

During his association with sadhus, he began practicing silence during waking hours and he would talk only in sign language or would keep a slate and chalk with him where he would write what he was saying. Thus one would not hear any words from his mouth. Things became more interesting with Appala Narasamma after Mavatata Garu came to live with us and I will briefly describe these incidents. One morning, Appala Narasamma came as usual and she opened front gate and heard Mavatata Garu shouting not in Telugu or Hindi but in English. She was so scared and stood at one corner shivering and began calling my father for help. Father came out and saw that Mavatata Garu was deep in sleep and was talking in his sleep. That became a joke and my father would say if Mavatata Garu is awake he is silent and if he speaks in English, he must be asleep.

The Blind and Brilliant:

Kesapragada Narasimham garu was the most interesting character living a few blocks away from our house. Kesapragada Narasimham garu was my father's very good friend and came frequently to our house for interesting discussions with my father. He was blind but was not blind by birth. He was an attorney and then became an insurance agent once he lost his eyes. He never carried a stick but would memorize the distance and steps needed to reach any place. He liked to give the appearance that he was a normal person walking on the road. He would come with an escort to our house but the escort had strict instructions that he will not guide him on the road. Once he is at the gate the escort would be asked to go back and return after an hour or so and he would occupy a chair in front of my father and begin his inquiry and discussion on current political situations. Moment Muttayya entered the gate he would turn towards the gate and greet him and "So Muttayya how is Diwancheruvu this year? Is the orange crop well or is cashew crop better?" and Muttayya would answer him as if he is talking to a normal person.

He knew the footsteps of each and every one in the family and if he heard new steps he would turn towards the steps and ask who is it and the moment he got reply he would recognize the person and start asking him the welfare of every one in his family and so on. He was an insurance agent and would tell every client to fill the forms as if he was watching each and every column on the form. He did not want anyone to know that he could not see and hence he would not wear glasses. During the later years, he began carrying blind persons folding stick while walking since he did not have an escort. The moment he entered the gate he would close his stick and remove his glasses and pretend he was as normal as any other person. He knew everyone in our family and they all knew that he was a regular visitor to our house and was very much respected. My father gave him full respect due to a very learned person and we too gave him the same respect. This experience gave me awareness that I should not disrespect people with deficiency just as I found myself being less respected just because I was dark in our entire family.

Why me, Father? Since my childhood, almost everything that was bad happened to me only and as per my nature I would run to my father and cry and finally ask him why me? Today Babloo, Vikram's oldest son asks his father the same question. He too suffered same sort of humiliations as I did. Even his father Vikram had the same feeling early on and he too may have asked the same question his son asked him much later. There is no answer except that one tends to remember unhappy events more than the ones that made them happy or it could be just brooding. But even today, I feel the same way when things do not go well, only I cannot go to father anymore.

Father's Legacy: What did our father leave for us? Yes of course he left to each of us proceeds of the property in Diwancheruvu, but then once the property was sold what else? He looked after us motherless children all through his long life giving us the love of mother in addition to that of his own. What is his legacy? It is certainly not money since most of it might have been lost once sale is done. I think he left us with the strength of praying God particularly Lord Shiva. All the three brothers would never miss any occasion of fasting and worshipping Lord Shiva. Indira is a firm believer in prayers and probably Bhanumati also. I have not been very fond of prayers though I believe in worshipping God in my own way.

Did he leave his jovial nature of trying to make everyone happy? I do not know, but he certainly left us all to face the world with confidence even when we all had passed through crises. May be he left a legacy of steadfastness or just to be good human being. Would we feel proud of my father; think about him and his greatness he showed under most adverse conditions? I do not know but I know that if father was not there for me I would not be living to write these memoirs. I am grateful to him at all times and I am proud to be dedicating this book to him.

CHAPTER 4

MY MOTHER KAMALA: THE LOTUS

My mother was born in 1917 and I asked my grandmother why was she named Kamala and she mentioned that my grandfather did not want his children to carry very long names of his relatives and so restricted to three syllables in Telugu. Accordingly he named the first child Sarada and the second child, my mother Kamala. My grandfather was born in Aduru near Amalapuram in the East Godavari District of Andhra Pradesh. He had five sisters and he was the only son. I do not remember the names of all the siblings but I would like to recapture some whom I personally know. He was older to everyone and the names that I remember are Upadhyayula Annapoornamma garu Grandmother of Dr. Krishnamurthy garu from father's side. Second one is known as Jagadamba and I do not know more about her. Third one was Ganti Seshamma garu mother of Ganti Narasimha Murty garu of Kakinada. Fourth one is Ammdiamma garu mother-in-law of Pappu Tammu of Peramma Agraharam. I do not know the sequence of each of his sisters. I believe the ancestral house in Aduru still exists but there are no records of succession.

My grandfather married Isola Manikyam but many knew her by her pet name Chellamma, the youngest child of the Isola family of Hyderabad. Her older two sisters are named as Subhadra and Ammanna respectively. They were followed by three sons; the oldest was Narasimha Sastry next Sriram Murty (Ramudu) and youngest brother was Brahmanadam. In short my mother had two aunts and three uncles and since we lived in Rajahmundry, I had the opportunity of meeting every one of them during my life time.

My grandfather Nookala Agastya Sastry was a very industrious civil engineer and moved from place to place on project work extending both in North India and South India and so the family also traveled to these places. He was a very pious person and he sported the traditional 'pilaka' on the back of his head and a very prominent 'Tilak' on his forehead and this would make some of his supervisors who were mostly British to either make fun of him or advise him against using these symbols of Hinduism. One word of disapproval from these bosses was enough to trigger angry reply from him by way of resigning his post. It was either he was posted to different places or his searching new opportunities after he quit the one he was holding but in either case the family would move from place to place. He was a good and sincere worker and so to find another opening was not at all difficult but very often he was between two jobs. His wife Chellamma was naturally upset with these expressions of short tempers with his bosses and they would therefore quarrel constantly and peace for this troubled engineer became elusive both at home and at his work place. He traveled from Cochin in Kerala to Kota in Rajasthan and from Bombay on the west to Madras in the south.

My grandfather Agastya Sastry Tata garu was relatively short unlike my other grandfather Abbayi Tata garu. My grandmother Chellamma on the contrary looked more imposing and appeared taller than my grandfather. She had a dominating nature and wanted my grandfather to be like every one, steady in his job and become very prosperous. Once he was laid off from his job in Bombay, but he did not dare tell the news to his wife but when she came to know all hell broke loose. Almost for one whole month he packed his lunch every morning and returned at regular time in the evening tired and giving an appearance that he still had a job. He knew what would happen if my grandmother came to know about it. Today when I saw a similar incident in a movie called 'Flavors' where an Indian software engineer in the USA lost his job but still would leave his house telling his wife he will be late as he had some meeting and return back only in the evening just like my grandfather did then. The movie ended happily with the unemployed engineer getting his job but not before his wife finds out through other sources. I only thought of my grandfather, obviously this is not unusual even today. He spent his day in the nearby municipal garden or in the library searching for another job. But at the end of a month the secret would be out and then he had to face serious consequences from his wife.

This is not uncommon even here in the USA with Americans as they too lose their jobs. The US was passing through a very serious recession in 2009 and many workers lost their jobs and it was reported by a news channel that many of these jobless persons pretended having a job. According to one report "For weeks after he was laid off, a person would rise at the usual time, shower, shave, don one of his company suits and head out from his home—to a job that no longer existed. He stayed away until 5 p.m., whiling away the hours at a local library or on a park bench. If he remained at home, he would stash his car in the garage so that neighbors did not see. When he lost his job in February, 2009 he was too ashamed to tell anyone except his wife and immediate family what had happened. It made no difference that 1,200 other workers received pink-slip at the same time, he felt as if he had done something wrong and did not want his family to be shamed. May be this is the reasoning of grandfather or was he more than a century ahead of his times!!!

His quality of work was so good that he was never short of opportunities. His name is inscribed on the list of engineers who constructed the tallest building in Madras or Chennai as known today on the Life Insurance Corporation building bearing testimony to his capabilities. My mother was born in Cochin on

July, 24, 1917 and my grandfather lived in Cochin for a very short time before he moved to other places and finally in Bombay (now Mumbai) the largest metropolitan city in India. She was educated in a convent school in English medium and was proficient in many languages. She was equally good in Marathi, Hindi, English and Tamil in addition to our mother tongue Telugu. She did not learn these languages because she was forced to learn local languages, but because she was good in learning any language, in fact she had a talent. She had a sharp memory and she would remember anything told to her just once. She was my grandfather's favorite daughter and he would call her lovingly 'Bujji Talli' and her older sister Sarada as 'Chitti Talli'. My mother was a very good artist and a good designer of clothes and would replicate any design she would see just once either in a book or in a shop. She loved bright colors and particularly liked red and violet and she loved all flowers and flowering plants. My grandfather was very particular about teaching Sanskrit Slokas to his daughters and the condition was that they can go out for play if they recite Slokas after him. My mother would always recite after hearing once even complicated Slokas and go out for playing before her sister Sarada could do. Her sister Sarada was a very tough baby and once she fell down from second floor balcony in Bombay, she was brought up by the pedestrians with only a few scratches. My grandmother did not come to the door for fear of seeing her daughter's dead body! Doctors examined her after the fall told that she was OK but will have some effect on her memory. Contrary to that diagnosis, my aunt Sarada or Doddamma lived for 95 years and had an excellent memory till her death in May, 2010. Both sisters were trained in classical music and my mother had very good voice. Grandfather loved my mother very dearly and she held a special place in his heart. I remember my grandmother reminiscing that my mother learned things much quicker and was also quick to catch the finer points of anything new. Both Doddamma and my mother were thus very well trained in arts and crafts suitable for ladies of the era. Have we stopped training our children these crafts or have we become victims of modern TV?

I have always seen my mother in total quietude and she never showed anger on her face even when all different people and relatives would either call my father names or quarrel with her children meaning us. I have not seen her raise her hands on any of us at any time. She had a remarkable patience with our tantrums and our fights and every time we went to her with a complaint she would offer us good advice and some cookies.

Her happiness as a child was very short lived as she was married when she was just eleven years old. My grandfather was living in Maharashtra somewhere near Bombay and the marriage was fixed with Narasimha Murty oldest son of Upadhyayula Abbayi garu of Rajahmundry and he was very happy with the match. Doddamma two years older to my mother was already married to Ganti Jagannatha Sastry or Abbulu garu the only son of Ganti Venkata Rao garu of Peruru. He was a graduate in printing ink technology and had gone to England for higher training. His higher education and services in cities may have made him a favorite son-in-law of my grandmother. My father on the other hand was a farmer and did not hold the same place in her heart. I do not know if my grandfather felt the same way about my father but since he loved my mother dearly, he must have liked my father equally if not more. I had more contact with Doddamma when I came to Bombay after my marriage in 1963. She inherited the same formidable personality of her mother and sharp eye sight of her father and she had a commanding voice in her family and both uncle Abbulu garu or Peddananna Garu and Doddamma lived a very long and happy married life. Peddananna garu died in February, 1980 whereas Doddamma died in 2009 after living a healthy old age life. My father would always have a long quarrel with Ammamma almost every day about many instances where he was slighted by her whereas Peddananna Garu received special treatment when they both were invited for the same occasion. My mother always felt sorry about this but could do nothing.

Doddamma was married under traditional normal Hindu rites in Vakkalanka, but the situation changed for my mother. British Government passed a law banning child marriages through Sarada Act (nothing to do with Doddamma) and was implementing the law strictly. My mother's wedding was therefore scheduled in Yanam then under French occupation where the British laws were not accepted. I would always tell my mother that for a person born in Cochin in Kerala State, brought up in Bombay, Madras and other metropolis, why was she destined to live in a far off village in Diwancheruvu or in Rajahmundry? She would smile and say that is what was in store for me and one cannot do anything to change my fate now.

I wonder what her married life was like and while talking to Ammamma after my mother's death she told me that my mother came into such an orthodox family where no one knew or drank coffee and mother required coffee first thing in the morning. She loved to drink her coffee very strong, but Akka was against drinking coffee in the house and would insist she drink milk. Father brought her coffee powder without Akka's knowledge so that she would get her first cup of coffee. Akka would sometimes inquire if the smell of coffee was coming from our house and father would summarily dismiss her question by saying that coffee is prepared in every house so you will smell coffee everywhere. My mother was used to using such English words like 'bath room, soap, towel, bed room' etc. because she was educated in convent schools. But use of English words was not appreciated and she began to reduce the usage of such words. But my mother had full support from my father and so life was easier for her. She was not allowed to wear sandals when going out and was allowed to wear only chappals or slippers. Manikyam was also married in a conservative family and had same problems about her habit of coffee but she did not get the same degree of support from Pedda Bawa as my mother received from my father. Akka objected to these things mother liked not because she was harsh on her grand daughter-in-law, but because these things were unheard of in families in the small towns. She insisted her meals were served by my mother when she became paralyzed and blind because she believed that others diluted milk with water before giving to her. This shows the trust she had in my mother. Ratnalu Mamma on the other hand loved my mother dearly and if mother was not well she would be very concerned. My mother would laughingly say I have a mother-in-law who loves me like a mother and a mother who treats me more like a step daughter.

My mother could sew well, knit well and do everything in a very professional manner. She needed to see a design only once and she could reproduce the same without the original design be it a new dress, a new pattern or anything and her magical hands would reproduce almost to the same perfection. She was very fair compared to her sister. My grandfather always regretted that he did not give away his daughter Kamala in marriage as a father of bride but that his cousin had to perform the ceremony of Kanya Daanam. He had to stay behind because of the robbery in his house before his departure to Yanam from Bombay. He therefore had one more reason for a soft spot for my father and mother.

After a string of failed pregnancies or short lived children Doddamma was very unhappy. Someone suggested that if they visit the famous temple of Lord Ramlingeshwar in Rameshwaram and bathe in the sea at Sethu, they will be blessed with a child who will live in good health. Both my aunt and uncle went over to Ramlingeshwar temple and soon after they were blessed with a daughter within a year after their visit. She was born in our house in Rajahmundry in July, 1948 and at that time her father was in London. There was active discussion about naming the new child and every one was trying to find a suitable name as per our traditions. My mother suddenly said why not name the child as Sethubai as she was born after taking bath in the sea at Sethu and this name was accepted unanimously by all. Sethubai is four years younger to me and three years older to Indira and we still have a good friendly relation with her. My aunt lived in different cities like Calcutta, Madras and Bombay wherever my uncle worked and visited us almost every year to meet her mother who lived with us after my mother's death in 1957.

My mother was commanded by Akka as the senior most matriarch of the family and Akka never let anyone relax as she herself was a tireless worker and my mother had to do the chores in the house like cooking and cleaning. We had servants but they could not enter the house especially for cooking etc. because of 'Madi' and my mother had to work hard in the kitchen. You do not employ a cook when two able and healthy women were managing the household! Work was never a problem for my mother and she always worked willingly without getting tired but then she was a frail person and at the end of the day when she slept she was lost to the world. Father would always remember those early days and feel sorry that she did not have a comfortable time most of her life.

What did my mother want most? She wanted peace and quiet when she was worshipping but that was not possible in the house full of people each having his or her own problems. She spent more than half of her waking hours in the kitchen and in those days cooking was done on fire wood or coal. Most of the times she would be in a wet saree to maintain "Madi". Even when she was not in the kitchen, she would cover herself with wet clothes as she was sensitive to the heat and her body would be covered full of prickly heat causing irritation even more difficult to bear. My mother would find more relief in covering herself with wet clothes and sleep on the bare floor. We did not have any electrical ceiling fans in our house till 1957 when my father set up two ceiling fans in both the bed rooms and my mother really enjoyed the feeling of cold air cooling her body. Father also bought a sewing machine at the same time and mother was so ecstatic that she went on a stitching spree of new clothes. Till this day I have never had so many clothes that she had stitched for me. She stitched Vikram so many baby clothes that it was a pleasure to groom Vikram with all those new clothes. All of us received so many new clothes and mother was so happy and jubilant that we all thought we lived in a paradise. This pleasure was short lived as she died three months later and every time I picked up new clothes for Vikram or myself or for Indira I could not resist tears streaming from my eyes. My father felt sorry throughout his life that he did not install fans for my mother earlier as she would have lived happy.

What do I remember most of my mother? So many things! Every Sunday, before we went to sleep, she would call each one of us and ask us to pack our school bags and believe me it would take more than one hour for each one of us to finish the chore. She would never let us sleep unless the school bags were ready and even then we would still find a couple of things that we forgot to pack. I always believed in being ready before time hence it never was a big problem but others were not so happy and they would feel mother was unnecessarily concerned about their school bags after all they were not kids any more. I did not have this problem with my children but I saw others struggling to keep up to the schedule on Mondays as so many things would not be seen just when we need them most. Both Gnanu and Dinkar were very particular about their school books and their home works etc. and I did not have to follow my mother's example. But every time I look back, I wonder at her foresight in preparing us to be more organized.

Today when I look back on my association with my mother, I feel I did not have opportunity of her blessings as she did not live long enough. In fact, when my mother Kamala Devi died on 27th July, 1957 I was just 12 years and 9 months old and so all my memories are packed in the short span of twelve years. I do not know more about her and so I would like to talk more about what I had learned from her from my perspective. I thought she was a yogi since she seemed to settle down comfortably anywhere whether in a city or in a village, with her parents or her parents in-laws or with all comforts of cities or minimum comforts in the village or our house. She was born in Cochin in Kerala State, well-traveled through much of India and lived mostly in cities like Bombay and Madras but finally spent all her life in Rajahmundry or in Diwancheruvu. All my memories of my mother are within the walls of that house in Danavaya Peta where we moved two years after I was born. Everything I remember about her is in this house. Looking back at the events I have always missed my mother and I believe my sister Indira and Vikram would not even remember any of what I write as they were too small. They missed all the good things that I have shared with my mother. Those who have mother may not realize the value of mother as much as those who are denied this simple association.

Father had a very large household filled with Babayya, Tocchhi, Mamma, Ammamma, Akka, my aunts who were still not married, farm hands, couple of servants and us seven children. Even in normal times each member would try to get my mother's attention or get some thing or demand something. It was not only children who had complaints or demands even elders had the demands like when they would want their coffee, should it be strong, moderate or weak or with milk and so on and this would be endless throughout the day and she listened patiently. I have not heard her raise her voice or hear her shout at any one. But if our farm hand comes from Diwancheruvu, my mother would be on her feet to serve them lunch keeping aside everything else. She would personally supervise or serve lunch as she felt it is the least one could do for their labors and loyalty. As I have mentioned Diwancheruvu is more than 6 miles away from our house and it would take them at least two hours walking or one hour on their bicycle. I would ask her how she could manage all this especially when she herself was city born and bred or is it that she inherited some of the characteristics from her mother or father. What is that made her so different from everyone else? She would smile and say that it could be that 'it was just my nature or maybe I have inherited from my mother but certainly not from my father as he is known for his short temper. I will devote rest of this chapter about all my interactions with her.

School preparations: My mother loved to read and was very broad minded about schooling and she would like that we all studied very well. Needless to say we all were bright in our studies and we also became well-disciplined in our daily activities. Credit for this goes to my mother. During week days, we would keep our school bags in proper places and pick up the bags and rush to our school next morning. On the last day of the week mostly Friday evenings, our school bags would be lying around the house and we would be busy with our weekend activities. We did not get time from all our activities and by the time Saturday was over we would be so tired that we would just drop in our beds fast asleep. We did not have our rooms or our own beds and so everyone would go to their selected places on the floor of the house and sleep. We did not know if it was hot or cold, if it was raining or if someone broke into our house or anything that would happen in the night and were dead to this world. Mother would not bother us till Sunday evening. Once we finished our evening meals, she would round each one of us and remind us that it was school time tomorrow: it was **Monday**. We would then search for our bags; our text books, note books etc. and keep them in our bags. My father would then sharpen our pencils and our bags would be packed ready. Next day morning, all we had to do was to pick up the bag and leave for school. We were never late and we were never warned by teacher for missing any homework or assignments. This one habit of ours has helped me in being well organized in almost everything in my life.

Spell Check: My mother had studied in English medium schools and she also knew so many other languages that she had probably understood the trick of teaching any language. She would make me sit and teach me how to spell in English. She would use a Telugu word "kooda balukkovdam' to learn English spellings. My mother would make me sit with her to learn the simple method of remembering the spellings. She would explain to me how to split the word phonetically in a language so simple that I would remember what she said and in this manner I learnt the language.

I did not get an opportunity of higher studies, but even today I memorize spellings in the manner she had taught me and every time I try to memorize any spelling, I remember her and her "kooda balukkovdam" and this has helped me all these years without any training.

Stringing of flowers: We had so many flowering plants in our front yard that the house would be full of fragrant smell of these flowers. Front yard would look colorful to any one from outside. We were all children and my sisters and I sported a good healthy long hair and so we all loved to adorn flowers in our hair. I love flowers even today. I would collect all the flowers and take them to my mother. Looking at my size and realizing that it would be difficult for me to string the flowers like grownups she taught me how to string flowers using toes of my feet. I would hold the twine around my thumb and start stringing each flower in the same manner as a professional flower vendor in Bombay would do. As I grew up she then taught me how to string flowerers with my hands and though this was not how we would do for our day to day use. I always felt confident that if required even today I should be able to make a flower 'veni' like one sold on roads of Bombay. It is not what I know about stringing of flowers but it is how my mother taught me that is important.

I do not know why, but my mother loved me probably more than other children or at least that is what I felt at that time. Our neighbor was one Janakamma who belonged to Kamma community and had no children of her own. Her sister Saraswati was a regular visitor to our house and she would play with Chinna Babu as he was very fair and a bonny boy. Chinna Babu would also go to their house and remain there most of the time. Saraswati once came to my mother and asked her jokingly if they could adopt Chinna Babu and Manikyam who was standing nearby and who was also very close to Saraswati asked her why not adopt Sarvamangala? She immediately replied Sarvamangala looks more like one of us so what is the point? We want someone to be as fair and good looking like Chinna Babu. My mother was hurt and she told her she may be a dark girl now but mark my words like a caterpillar one day she will become as beautiful as a butterfly and everyone will be just watching her beauty. I did not realize the significance at that time, but every time I think of this incident I feel proud that my mother felt like that about me. I do not know if she will be proud of me now, but I will always cherish those words of her till I live.

Power failure: We were living in our Danavaya Peta house and it was a new development at that time meaning the electric supply would be dependent on weather conditions. The fuse box was mounted on the electric pole just outside our house. This is a normal situation in all new developments and everywhere the situation remains same. A moderate breeze would disconnect the supply and the house would be plunged into darkness. Every time the supply was disconnected, mother would call from inside to go and check if the supply in the neighbor's house is also interrupted and my father sitting on the front porch would say, why do you look at the miseries of our neighbors when we have lost the supply and mother would say patiently, if the supply in other homes is also disconnected then the problem is larger and so it would be attended immediately by the department. But if it is restricted only to our house then we will have to send Muttayya or Veeranna to the substation on the corner of our road and call the technician to fix the fuse and pay him extra. Even to this day, I would remember mother calling us from inside to see if the neighbors have electricity and father telling her why should you worry about others when we have lost our supply and so on. My mother was very sharp and had the presence of mind to see when the supply would be restored. My father would always mention these incidents and tell us how intelligent your mother was and I felt proud.

I experienced the same situation both in Visakhapatnam and in Borivali in Bombay. When we were living in Isaka Thota in Visakhapatnam, once again the house was a new construction and so the supply would go off every now and then. In fact the supply to the whole development was irregular and so if the supply is disconnected, I would first go out to look if the supply to Ramayamma's house across the street was also disconnected. If she did not have the supply, I was positive current supply would be restored soon. Otherwise Chitti would go out on his scooter to report the problem to the local call office. In Borivali, Bombay the entire area was developed after 1980 and our apartment house Gee Bee Apartment was the last house on the road and every time we lost the supply, the children would run to see if the supply was also disconnected to other apartment complexes on the road and if not then we would reach out to our local electrician. Every time these incidents happened, I remembered my mother since I too am looking at neighbor for their supply like my mother used to do in Rajahmundry.

Vikram is currently living in Ibrahimpatnam and he faces the same situation as was for us in Danavaya Peta with more failures of power than supply of power. Vikram coined a new word "gaali deepalu" literally meaning breeze lamps. He explained to me that these lights blow off at the instance of a slightest breeze since in Ibrahimpatnam you do not need a storm to knock down the power supply.

Embroidery: I have mentioned earlier that my mother was an artist. She was always interested in any type of creative art and embroidery was one such art for her. She had a collection of all designs she had copied or traced from those published in Telugu weekly or monthly since in those there was no facility of copying directly and Xerox was not invented. This was a collection of designs she traced from other sources. In addition to these, she also had a very large collection of new designs that she had created herself. Each design was drawn on note books separated with tracing paper nicely covered. These books with some original designs were preserved by her mother or Ammamma for quite some time but later on I do not what had happened to these. In a very short period of her life and in still shorter association of mine with her, I was lost in amazement in looking at these intricate designs created by my mother and that too finding time in that mad house in Danavaya Peta! She could not pursue her hobby as she could not go shopping to bring the raw material like knitting yarn, needles etc. and a private place for her to keep them. All her knowledge was wasted there. But every time she had an opportunity she would make something of those designs. One such design made by my mother and I remember even today was the curtain bearing the image of Mother India holding a tricolor flag in her hand. This curtain would proudly adorn our main door in Rajahmundry and the whole concept and design was created by my mother. This was of course not embroidery but it was crochet work and for me this too was new at that time. Now of course I know more about crochet as I have also become familiar with this form of art in the USA.

Calendar Goddesses: We had a pair of photographs of two goddesses on both sides of our wall clock in the main room facing directly the front of the main entrance so that as soon as one entered they would see them first. One was of Lakshmi and the second one was of Saraswati. In those days the then famous Imperial Chemical Industries or ICI would come out with full length black and white picture calendars of gods and goddesses and people would buy them in the market to keep them in their homes. I do not know if my mother had seen this before or it was her own original idea but she took these pictures and mounted them on a card board on a cloth. She would then select very soft cloth for making saree out of the material to be either stitched or stuck with glue. The saree was of Red color for Lakshmi and white for Saraswati. She stitched gold color flowers or stars or any design on the saree with a finely designed zari border both on the pallu and at the border of the saree. Lakshmi is standing on a lotus flower and on her either side there were two elephants each holding a garland in their trunk. Saraswati on the other hand was sitting holding a Veena in her lap. Neck of both goddesses was decorated with gold colored beads and gold chain and her hands adorned with gold colored bangles and so on. Crown or 'kiritam' on their head was decorated with gold colored thread and stringed with white pearls and colored beads. Looking at the image no one would believe that this was all done on a photograph as it would look very real. Once the deity was ready, father framed them and these two occupied a special place in our house. Complete decoration and the art work were designed by my mother and she did it of her own imagination without the help from any books!

In addition to these two photographs, my mother also made one flower vase made entirely of buttons containing flowers. Background of the vase was made of cream muslin holding pink and blue flowers all looking so bright and attractive and this too was mounted on a frame. I think my father must have liked all these activities of my mother and since in those days one would not express their love for the spouse this may be his way of telling my mother he appreciated her art. One more such a creation of my mother was a small guava tree with green leaves and branches connected with wire and a green parrot appearing to be biting the guava fruit. We did not know the complexity of the entire art and so we used the wires and pearls and beads for decorating our dolls for Bommala Pelli and then when we realized we had spoiled her work. We began to redo the same and that is how I realized that how good an artist my mother was and how difficult it was for us to reproduce the same. I have no idea how many of her creations were lost like this and I may not even know many others. I know the wall clock is with Chinna Babu in Hyderabad but I do not know who has these framed art works and since father did not have any permanent house in the later years, he too may not have been able to preserve these precious collections of arts.

Stitching: One more area that identified her city roots was her interest in stitching clothes. She was very good and her art was inherited by Bhanumati who as far as I can remember is also as good as my mother. I too learned stitching after going to Bombay, but did not become very good at it though Indira became very good at stitching while at Jamshedpur and she passed on her art to her daughter Kavita. I was surprised to see Gnanu showing the same interest in the art of stitching clothes but her interest was short lived as she lost her interest once she migrated to the USA. Mother had a phenomenal memory and she could remember any design seen once. Every time she saw a new design; it would be imprinted in her mind and she would recreate a similar one after coming home. All this was done by my mother before her marriage as my grandparents had a machine at their home. After marriage she did not have any opportunity of stitching as she was either busy with the household duties or had to attend to her new born children. But whenever she got an opportunity she would stitch with hand without use of a sewing machine. My grandmother's Singer sewing machine was left with us for some time and Mother would stitch so many different types of clothes for all of us but then this too was short lived as Doddamma took the machine with her to Madras when they lived there. This did not stop her interest and so she would stitch clothes for Pedda Babu and Chinna Babu by hand without any machine and they still looked like they were machine stitched. When my mother did not get what she wanted she would do something different. She knew she will not get even if she demands and may be father may have known it but could not help. Finally when father did buy her a machine, she did not live long enough to enjoy the gift and father always felt guilty about it as he remembered this incident many years later.

Cross Stitch Art: The list of my mother's creations is endless. She knew cross stitch so well that she designed large pieces of art that have been framed. I had mentioned about crochet work she had done for our front door depicting Mother India. In Rajahmundry this was new and now mother introduced another form of art and that is cross stitch and this was again a totally new experience for me. After all her work in the kitchen is completed and after her siesta, mother would begin making art pieces using cross stitch. Only work I remember today was a pair of deer facing each other forming an arch with their neck was beautifully created on a light pink cloth stitched with light brown threads.

Comforters for Baby: Mother stitched beautiful comforters for infant babies popularly known in Telugu as "Bontalu". These are made by attaching about four or more old cotton sarees in a square shape and stitched with white threads and once the basic shape is completed she would attach a beautiful border and make them attractive for babies. I would like to mention here a short history of these comforters. Babies in those days were allowed to play on bare floor which was generally uneven and so to protect their very soft bodies they would be placed on these bonta and the infant happily move around the entire floor. If rubber cloth was available, it is placed over a bonta and over a cloth a baby is placed so that the baby does not wet the bonta. I remember using these Bontalu for Gnanu made very painfully by Manikyam. Manikyam inherited this art of making Bontalu for babies and I remember she made for all the babies. I do not know if Bhanumati had learnt this from mother but Manikyam would make these just like mother did.

Garlands of colored glass tube and beads: Mother began to concentrate a different form of art and that is making curtains of colored glass tubes and beads for our doors. If the door was three feet wide, the garland will be made in such a manner that the tubes will not hit the head of the person entering the room. In principles it is simple; the string of glass tubes will be longest near the hinges of the doors and become progressively smaller as it comes at the center. The beads were either round or in the form of tubes and were stringed on twine thread and these beads are available in any general fancy stores or stores selling art work. She made these curtains for most of our doors in Rajahmundry. I do not know if any of my sisters had learnt this art, but Kavita is planning to revive this art once again. I may be biased but I feel all the artistic nature of my mother has been inherited by Kavita. Pedda Babu has two daughters but I hardly know if they inherited any of these characteristics. Even Gnanu is not as versatile. Of course every artist requires an appreciative audience and money for nurturing these faculties. In addition to the above two you also need free time and with the advent of TV one finds there is always a shortage of time.

I always believe that my father appreciated her work of art and so whenever she needed any money, he did not hesitate to see that she got it. Muttayya, Suryanarayana and others were always ready to bring all the raw materials that she needed and she would steal time from her busy day to concentrate on these. In addition to these specialized artistic pieces, mother was expert in making long garlands of marigold flowers during major festivals like Dassera, Deepavali, Sankranti and Telugu new year. She was also adept in drawing long designs with white powder and colored powders on these occasions known as "Muggu or Rangavali" in Telugu and "Rangoli" in north India.

My mother was a super Mom for me and she was never second best. Both Bhanumati and Indira inherited the artistic temperament and they had the support from their spouses whereas for Manikyam this could not be continued in Anakapalle. I do not think I was good in any of the arts, but I used to weave baskets and hand purses of plastic beads while in Bombay. I have dabbled in tailoring, weaving woolen yarn to make sweaters, prepared jackets of crochet and Afghans of woolen yarn both for Gnanu and Kiranmai, but nothing spectacular since I only followed designs given in the book.

Wax models: I would sit with my mother and discuss so many things and many of which I have now forgotten, but what I remember distinctly is making wax idols. We would collect clay soil make it wet enough and mold any object or doll of silver or brass deity into the prepared clay. We used to buy wax candles from the market and melt them in a pot and pour this hot wax into the hole left by the object when removed. The wax would cool and solidify and once the clay is broken the wax model of the object would be recovered without any damage. Most of the times we would use any solid object like wooden toys or other metal objects to make the wax models and I remember we had quite a collection of the models. In addition we could also prepare wax models of living things like flowers and leaves and so on. Hibiscus flower is first put petal pressed on the clay and then push the stem of the flower into the mud so that the shape of the petals is aligned properly and the molten wax is poured and the mold would look like hibiscus flower, but then this was delicate art and so we used solid objects of metals or wood and mother would also add different colors to the molten wax that was also new to us. But then she was always full of so many ideas. I remember one incident about these idols. My mother made a Lakshmi idol with red wax and it was so beautiful and once she broke the mold and separated the red idol, a crow came from nowhere and took away the idol. We all felt that this was a bad omen but did not realize the significance till after mother died.

Color combinations to sarees: My mother wore nine yards sarees and she would always wear a matching blouse. Her favorite colors were red, violet and a type of green she would call as "Damayanti green" and she would wear mostly these colors. I would ask mother why this green is known as Damayanti green. Was Damayanti wearing saree of this color for her Swayamvaram? Mother would laugh. Even though I was very young, I would take liberty with her in cracking jokes. She would mostly wear short sleeved blouses with puffs and the print on the cloth would match the main color of the saree and then she would stitch a piping of same color on the sleeve. She would never wear a blouse that did not match her saree. Mamma in later years would tell me that wherever my mother would be, she would wear a clean saree and adorn flowers in her hair in the evening and looked fresh as if she did not do any work in the house at all and was sitting in an air conditioned room. She was always neat and well-dressed irrespective of the pressures in the house. But during day time when the temperatures were very high and humidity was also high she would be most uncomfortable and wear only wet clothes and lie on bare floor to get as much coolness as she could get from the environment.

Mangala Aarti: My mother had a very melodious voice and she would sing many songs to our delight. Even my father had a very melodious voice and this is seen in the later generation. One of my favorite songs was "Ghallu Ghalluna pada gazzelu andelu mroya kalahamsa nadakala kaliki ekkadike?" an Aarti for Goddess Parvati wife of Lord Shiva and so many other songs praising her.

In addition to these songs my mother would teach us Slokas from Sumati Satakam, Vemanna Satakam, and Krishna Satakam and would make us recite them every day in the evening. She would then teach us Pedda Bala Shiksha, a Telugu primary book of information for all ages and tell us stories from Panchatantram. Learning from mother was fun and I would clamor around her for more. Today I know so many proverbs and quotations for any occasion because of those teachings. Kiranmai, my daughter-in-law used to ask me and prepared a list of these proverbs and quotations. I don't know if she still has them with her.

Tacking: By the time I was ten years old, I was getting interested in handicrafts like stitching and sewing and who else could teach us better than my mother. She would show me how to do the tacking and how to sew. She told me that the first lesson of sewing is that you should never take a long thread as it would get entangled and you would be wasting the thread and the stitches would look untidy. I remember this even today. Next she would show me how to do the tacking and told me that the stitches for a tack should be very light before sewing with sewing machine and I told this secret to Gnanu who also followed this when she used to sew. After coming to the US no one is sewing any more and I know this art is probably lost in my family.

Tikhat: My mother had a specialty and that is making chutney for any occasion. My father would always remember that if he asked for Tikhat she would make chutney from just onions for Idli's and that tasted so good that any chutney made in hotel was not equal to what she made. She would prepare this in a matter of minutes! We would ask my father how it tasted but father could not express. I had no clue to what she made but I could not prepare one like her and my father's wish remained unfulfilled.

But when we would ask for something else, she would ask us if we would like to eat Tikhat and we all will say yes. I did not know for a long time that Tikhat was a Marathi word, Tikhat in Marathi means spicy and so she would prepare spicy chutney from all available resources like coriander, green chilli and finely cut onions and give it to us. Since we did not know what she meant by Tikhat and we called it as Ticket and she would just laugh and tell us that it is a Marathi word so you would not know. After marriage I went to Bombay heart of Maharashtra and since every one spoke Marathi there I understood what she meant by Tikhat. But even there I could not get the same taste then nor do any time now and I feel she prepared something magical for us all.

One more important preparation of my mother is brinjal chutney. I still do not know how she made since no one else prepared like that. Brinjal was cut into very small pieces and then mixed in a bowl with green chilli, coriander and lime juice. There must also be some secret ingredient in the chutney since it would taste just heavenly and again I neither know the recipe nor have I tasted similar chutney once again after my mother passed away.

Tiffin: My mother would make what is called as chow chow prepared of Poha, Murmura, roasted rice (vepudu biyyam) and she will then add her Tikhat to this and made it very tasty. In addition to this she would also serve us what I called as Manna or Amrutam. We were all hungry children and so when we returned home from school there would be some thing or other available as tiffin but there were many times she would not have any thing available in the house to make tiffin for us and it is at this time that she would give us what I call as Amrutam. Every house in those days would have what we called as Chaldi Annam which is rice kept in water over night for fermentation and the fermented rice was known as 'Chaldi Annam' and tasted very good and is considered healthy. It was said the farmers would eat this as their breakfast and not feel hungry till lunch time. Mother would add Menthikaya or Avakaya and mix this Annam with plenty of oil. She would then add thick curd to this composition and make large parcels of the mixture and give one to each one of us. It was so tasty that even today while writing about it my mouth waters. This tiffin of my mother has no parallel and I have not tasted anything better. It was Amrutam.

Sewing machine, her last possession: Finally just three months before she died, my father was able to buy one sewing machine for my mother. Mother was ecstatic and immediately she called our cloth merchant and asked him to send good dress material. She began designing and stitching new dresses for all and I still remember all new dresses she had stitched for us. She would stitch and leave the work midway and go attend to other work in the house and work on the dress once again where she left on her return.

My mother stitched beautiful clothes for Gouthami and Sekhar along with Vikram. I do not remember what she had made for the other two but I remember she had stitched a drawer full of dresses of white muslin cloth for Vikram. I would like to mention one incident involving Indira. After mother died, Manikyam began using the sewing machine very frequently and once while she was away either attending to Gouthami or some such chore, Indira who was about 7 or 8 years old, began playing with the machine and accidentally she put her finger below the sewing needle and operated the machine and the needle pierced her finger and she began to bleed copiously. Father was so furious with Manikyam for her neglect that he shouted at her and warned that if she did not take care of the machine, he will throw the machine out of the house. I know father would certainly have done so. My father had one great weakness and that is children. He would always regard children as gifts of God and so did not allow anyone harm a child in his house.

Mother's old machine was probably sent over to Anakapalle to Manikyam's house before father left Rajahmundry but I may be wrong. Indira purchased a new machine after her marriage in Jamshedpur and began stitching and she became as proficient a tailor as our mother was. Surprisingly Indira's daughter Kavita has also become an expert designer and tailor thus continuing my mother's art work. In fact Kavita is so good at designing that she designs even jewelry and our jeweler would translate these designs into gold ornaments. She is very gifted and maybe she inherited all from her grandmother.

Unusual Growth of Pumpkins: Just before my mother died we had a very unusual event not seen before or after. The white pumpkin or Ash Gourd (Budida Gummadi) used to grow in our backyard although the seed was not planted by any one. Father wanted to remove the plant as it was not considered to be good, but since we had not planted the seedling he thought it would be OK. Pedda Babu remembers particularly in that year, there was so much growth of this creeper that it spread all over our roof and blossomed into yellow/white flowers. Each flower became a large ash gourd (Budida Gummadi) weighing more than 5 to 10 kilograms each over our roof. There were so many of these that father would ask Muttayya or Veeranna to climb the roof and cut these and distribute to all our neighbors on the street. Pedda Babu is sure that our neighbors living in that area today would also remember this incident. Those who saw the site said this was such a unusual site that it bode ill omen and my mother died soon after. One more sign of bad omen was the growth of a hand shaped mushroom and since we did not want the mushroom in our backyard, we cut it and the surprise was that the mushroom appeared to be bleeding as red colored fluid came out of it. This too was considered as a sign of bad things to come but no one knew what it was. In the hindsight we now know that this was indication of coming death of our mother.

Last Dinner made by my mother: I remember event leading to my mother's death and particularly the dinner she had served a day before. The cook was Gopalam a young chap who was not a very good cook and we were complaining to mother about his cooking and so my mother decided to cook the meal all by herself. The day was Wednesday and the date was 25th July, 1957. She prepared 'potlakaya kobbari kura', 'tomato perugu pacchadi' and 'pappu charu' and called us all to sit together to eat our dinner. My father was there and so also all of us were there except Manikyam who was in Anakapalle. Bhanumati wanted to eat later but she too joined because of her insistence. The whole family was there; father, Bhanumati, Pedda Babu, Chinna Babu, Indira and Trivikram and we all had our dinner together and that was her last meal. Once the dinner was over, mother insisted that we all sleep in the same room and I still wonder why because this was not our practice. We all sat together and she told us stories and songs and she told us all Slokas from Bhagvad Gita and it was a good family meet. My father always maintained that while most read Gita she digested the essence of Gita and led her life in a spiritual manner and maybe she had the premonition of her impending death.

I went to wake her up next day Thursday morning and she motioned me with her hands asking me to go away and she did not even ask for her coffee so I went to Ammamma and she too was surprised but then she told me not to disturb her as she may not be feeling well. She was having high fever. We all went back to our usual routine; we went to our school and played in the evening forgetting that in the morning mother was not well. Father had taken my mother to Government hospital and when I asked father how mother was and he told us to sleep and we all fell asleep as soon as we hit the bed. In the hospital, the doctors were injecting saline drip and the fluid did not go into the veins as by that time she was dead but we did not know. Suddenly in the middle of night, our opposite neighbor Kothha Suryanarayana came knocking at our front door and telling us to make way for mother and for a moment we did not know what he meant by that and then they brought my mother's dead body into the house. Pedda Babu fainted at the sight. Father was also hurt as he hit a stone while escorting mother in dark and nail on his thumb was pulled off and he was bleeding profusely but he was not aware of it. He looked totally lost and like us he too did not understand as the events happened so fast. He was at that moment like a rudderless ship and did not know how he will cross the long voyage of this life all alone.

We were all heart broken, but father kept a brave face and decided to bring us all up on his own. Vikram was just about one year old so he did not know the meaning of life or death, but if he saw any one wearing conventional nine yards saree tears would roll down his eyes particularly when our Doddamma wore in a conventional manner as she looked very much like my mother to him. I have not had any discussions with Pedda Babu or Chinna Babu about this incident so I do not know even now how they felt after my mother's death. In just that moment I became very aged and mature person and I took full responsibilities of Vikram and Indira. I became a very responsible person probably more mature than my own age and this was the end of my childhood.

My mother lived like a lotus leaf and though she lived in murky waters with frequents quarrels and pettiness; she was not sullied by the murkiness. She was pure both in thoughts and action like a yogi.

CHAPTER 5

GOLDEN ERA OF MY LIFE

Danavaya Peta: My golden years were spent in our Danavaya Peta house though I was not born there. Danavaya Peta house has so many pleasant memories for me and also has a ton of events that I wish I could forget them but still they continue to haunt me. I remember most of my early incidents like they happened just yesterday and always wonder why did I grow up and not remain the same young person and continue to live the happy and care free life? I do not remember birth of Chinna Babu but I remember the part where I was doing the translation for Pedda Babu to our cooks and became "Patamma" for them or an old woman. My first memory of Pedda Babu is of a boy with very big and prominent eyes and a very short temper. He never spoke and he would convey his message only by rolling his eyes. I remember that Pedda Babu would demand a glass full of milk and will not drink milk if the glass was not filled to the brim. Mother or cook would then add water to make the glass full of milk while he was watching and Pedda Babu would then happily drink the glass full of milk. Even at that age I realized that he did not get more milk but got only more water and I tried to explain that to him. But he was happy and satisfied that the glass was full and that was the end of the argument. He would look at me, roll his eyes and I should interpret his look and convey the meaning to the other party and if I have not conveyed correctly what he wanted to convey, he would grunt

'Hooon?' and I had to begin again. Pedda Babu was not dumb but he would not speak. I still do not know why he would not speak. Was it because he did not like any one to say no to him? Anyway whatever the reason I was the buffer.

I was very sick for the first four years of my life. I was very active during the day time but I would be very sick in the evening and became breathless towards the end of the day and often times even my stomach would bloat making it even more difficult to breathe. I was born just one day before new moon or Deepavali festival on Naraka Chaturdasi day, a day of great joy as demon Narakasura was killed by Satyabhama, wife of Lord Krishna. Like the nights of the new moon I was dark and very skinny and so generally was not appealing to my own relations. Adding to my woes, I was also not healthy. My older brother Pedda Babu was very chubby and fair and was glowing like a Glaxo baby but not me. In fact my mother's cousins always joked with my mother that I was changed during my birth and my mother would laugh and tell them this was not possible because I was born in our own house in Innispeta in Rajahmundry and so there was no chance of any mix up. My father carried me on his shoulders throughout the night and I would not sleep till the early morning hours. Rajananna would inquire if I survived the night before wishing good morning to my father. I do not know how many days or months my father carried me on his shoulders but this I certainly do know if he had not shown so much of compassion and affection to me in those painful years, my story would have ended long before. I owe my life to the care given by my father and I have not seen another parent of his type for that matter anyone else that includes me also. I became very active only after I was cured of my Asthma.

Chinna Babu was a very charming baby and he did not cry much and any one coming to our house would love to cuddle and carry him. My sister Manikyam had a very good friend Saraswati who would come to our house to hold and play with Chinna Babu. Her sister Janaki was married but had no children yet and she would tell Manikyam that she would like to adopt a Brahmin child and wanted to adopt Chinna Babu. Manikyam told her to adopt me instead of Chinna Babu and Janakamma replied that I was as dark as children in their own Chowdhari community so she would not adopt me. I want to adopt a fair child looking like Chinna Babu. This was all in fun and they were kidding. But I became so angry that I told Janakamma I will not come to their house. My mother who was listening did not keep quiet and she told Janakamma that even if you want to adopt my daughter, I will not part with her. She made up for all the pain and hurt I felt. How can people be so cruel to children?

During my early years of life I had an ear problem and puss would ooze out of my right ear and students on my bench as well as those behind me would complain of the foul smell. I would come back crying. My father would clean my ears every day morning and put a perfumed cotton swab in my ear before I left for school. The same process would be repeated before I returned to school after lunch and so on. He was patient with me and never showed any dislike while cleaning my ears. He tried so many medicines and quack treatments but my ear would not stop oozing puss. Once a country medicine man rather another quack came to our house and told my father that if the tail of a snake was turned in my ear the flow of puss would stop. My father immediately called a snake charmer and told him to turn the tail of snake in my ear. Believe it or not, flow of puss from my ears stopped from that that day till to date and I still do not know if this was a medicine or a miracle. I cannot tell you of all the things my father did for me or for all my brothers and sisters as now after so many years I have forgotten many of the incidents. Most of the times it was mother's job to look after children but in our house father looked after all of us. My mother was always busy in the kitchen preparing food for a large family and the guests who would be coming to our house continuously. When she retired in the evening she would be so tired that she would just fall asleep on the floor without any mattress or bed. When I look at the old photographs of mine even I feel surprised how dark and skinny I was! Virtually a bag of bones!! But I was still loved by my parents.

Pedda Babu and Chinna Babu did not go to elementary school but they were tutored at home. I on the other hand went to an elementary school in Jam Peta from the age of five and this school was operated by the weaver community. My older sisters Manikyam and Bhanumati studied in a missionary school Shady Girls High School and this school was a reputed school as the teachers were from England. But when my father tried to enroll me in the same school, I was denied the admission as by that time the school became very popular and there was a stiff competition for admission. My father tried continuously for three years and I was denied every time as the school selected mostly Christians. Incidentally, after four years when I was studying in 8th class, the school opened a new section and so most of the girls in my class got their admission, but father said no this time because I had more responsibilities at home now after my mother died.

My experiences in Jam Peta High School were also different. Both my brothers were admitted directly into First Form or Sixth Grade, and so for the first six classes they did not go to school. But I insisted that I will go to school and not remain at home and my father heeded my request. The first problem was the difference in their language; we speak good Telugu at home that was nearer to the written form while they spoke in a colloquial tone different from language we spoke and I tried to maintain the purity of the language. I had come from a very well to-do family and we never had to market any item either it was delivered at our door step or we could walk over to the grocery store in front of our house. The store was owned by Kothha Suryanarayana and we had a running account with him and we could just go over there for everything we needed for the school. But other children in the school had to scrimp for everything and they would not only know the costs but also where it would be available at a lower cost. One of my classmates would bring a roll of thread remaining after weaving and give them to me. I in turn would give it to Manikyam who was happy with the threads and she would use it for some embroidery or art work and so it went on for some time. She even asked me to bring more. One day the girl asked me three rupees for those pieces of threads and I was surprised and I asked her why she should charge me for the threads she had given to me. We had an argument over the matter and she threatened to complain to my father and I said go ahead and that I was not concerned. She came to our house and told my father that I refused to pay for the threads. First thing my father did was to pay her off and then asked me why I did not pay her. I told him that I did not know that one has to pay money for items like that as I have never paid anything to Suryanarayana garu our grocer. Everyone laughed and my father explained the mechanism. I came to know for the first time that Suryanarayana garu would keep an account of every item we bought and then send the bill to my father and he would pay off. Nothing was free. This was probably my first lesson in commerce. When I think about this incident I cannot believe that I was so stupid!

I joined 6th standard at National High School after five years at Jam Peta School and this school was reputed for high standard of education. In fact I got admission based on my marks in Jam Peta School but the school was slightly farther from our house. It was located near Ashoka Movie theater and was a very good school and I was very happy with the teachers and so also were the teachers with me. I was sent to this school only because my mother supported me and father respected mother. If I continued to study in National High School for 3 continuous years I would get an opportunity of participating in a statewide public examination. After 8th grade there would be a public examination run by the State and students passing this examination would be admitted directly in 9th Standard in any school. I was thrilled and wanted to prepare well for the examination and score very high marks and seek admission in Shady Girls High School once again but this time on my merit. But again this became a failed attempt. I did not continue in the National High School as I was removed from the school by my father one year later to enroll me in the sixth standard, one grade lower than current one in order to give company to Chinna Babu. Principal of the National High School requested my father to allow me to continue as I was doing very well in my class and remarked "I receive requests from parents to push their child to the higher class and here you are coming to remove your bright child so that she is enrolled in a lower class?" I too fought with my father that I did not want to join along with Chinna Babu in a lower grade and that he should allow me to continue in the current school. But father had already decided that I should study in the same grade as Chinna Babu so there was no appeal. I still do not know why he did so. Was it because he felt Chinna Babu was not serious in his studies? But his decision was final and particularly for a girl since education was not important at all for a girl child in those days and probably even now. I had to fight for my right to complete my education at every stage but never succeeded and this really affected my output. I still remember that every time I wanted to get something I had to fight for my right and this spirit has remained with me even today. I cannot tolerate injustice and I will not allow anyone to be unfair to me or anyone else.

Chinna Babu loved to talk and so he would chat and share gossip with every one before returning from the school. As soon as the last bell of the school would ring, we all would rush back home running, keep our books properly and then run out to play in the park. I was never tired of playing in the park and climb trees along with Chinna Babu and other boys. The watchman of the municipal garden knew my father. He used to drive Rajananna to court and back when he was practicing law and once Rajananna gave up his practice the driver became a watchman in the garden. He would report to my father about my tomboyish activities and I would be scolded. My mother in particular would lament that I became even darker with my outdoor activities this would make my matrimonial prospects even more difficult she would say. I told Pedda Babu that the watch man was telling our father behind our back and so he warned the watchman not to do so again. Pedda Babu was about 10 at that time. The watchman told my father about this warning also and everyone laughed out aloud.

I was very particular about everything in the house. Every evening, I would sit down and collect all the clothes from the clothes lines and fold them in an orderly fashion and put them back in their proper places, a chore not liked by anyone else. I would pluck all the flowers from the tree and string them together for all of my sisters to place in their plaits (zada). Everyone was happy to have their hairs adorned with flower but when it came to stringing them together, only I would do it with pleasure. I was not unhappy about this and wished every one shared the task with me collectively. We had so many plants of hibiscus, roses and jasmine and I would pluck flowers from all these plants. Towards the end of the day, I was so tired that I would be dead to this world before 9.00 pm.

I was not a pet among any of my grandparents mainly because of my color. My sister Manikyam was extremely fair and so also second sister Bhanumati and as I have mentioned all my other siblings would out shine one another in their fairness. Rajananna would not like me around; not because I would quarrel or fight or was a cry baby but because I was not pretty. Every Deepavali my father would send for the clothes merchant to bring rolls of clothes for us and invite our tailor Mahalakshmi who would then stitch new clothes for all of us. This was an annual ritual. Once when I was very young, we had guests in our house and I saw that their daughter of nearly my age was wearing a torn frock with so many patches. This was strange for me and I asked my father why so and my father replied that they are poor and so cannot afford good clothes. I thought for a couple of minutes and told my father that this year I did not want any new clothes for Deepavali and that give my clothes to this girl. Rajananna was standing there in the room and he was so surprised and happy to hear me say this and he told my father "Narasimham, this is the true nature of this girl. So what if she is dark? Come here baby." And he kissed my forehead probably for the first time since I was born. I do not remember the incident but I recollect my father telling about this so often that this has remained implanted in my mind. I even do not know the name of that girl but since my father has told me I am convinced this is true. Am I that good in nature? Only others will tell.

We had a cook most of the times as not only the household was very large but we also had a floating population of people getting down from the train in the morning stopping by for their lunch before boarding a boat for going to Amalapuram in the afternoon. Everyone who entered the kitchen had to take a bath before entering and wear wet clothes as 'Madi' and should be within the kitchen premises and not mix with others in the house. But often times the cook will go on French leave without informing us and the work would come to my mother. Irrespective of the fact whether we had a cook or not my mother still had a full time kitchen job. She loved drinking strong coffee at intervals before lunch as we did not have a routine like morning breakfast, lunch and dinner in the evening like what we are doing now. Only coffee would give her strength to face the world and father would see to it that she got it.

My whole life changed when she died in July, 1957 and I resigned to my fate since now I lost my only support and advisor. My mother was a very forward thinking person and believed in equal rights for women. In early 1956, my teachers wanted to nominate me as the class leader since I was always in top five and I was very punctual and methodical. When I mentioned this at home, my father immediately opposed the thought and said my job is to study and not any leadership, but then my mother intervened and asked my father where is it written that girls should not be class leaders? Unless we support in all their activities, how will they make progress later on in life? My father agreed and I submitted my name for being appointed as the class leader. Even before things would work my way, my mother died and I did not become the class leader. I did not have any time free for school work with so many responsibilities at home.

I was between two brothers and so when I complained to my father that Pedda Babu was not giving me anything my father would say you should not fight with him because he is your older brother. When Chinna Babu did not give me something I wanted father would pacify me by saying why do you fight with him after all he is younger to you. I was upset with this injustice and so one day I asked my father Pedda Babu is older to me OK so I should not fight and Chinna Babu was younger to me so I should not fight with him but then about me? Am I not younger to Pedda Babu? So he should not fight with me. In the same way, since I am older to Chinna Babu, he should listen to me and that is fair. My father would smile and tell me no you are my mother or Amma and that means you are above all these silly fights and that would make me happy. I was so naïve!

In addition to these two brothers, my sister Bhanumati and Manikyam were also looking for my services. I was a go between Manikyam and her friend Rajeshwari for exchange of books. I would take books from Manikyam to her and back. I liked going to her place as I would receive either chocolate or a pepper mint or sometimes even small change like half an anna for my effort. I loved these tidbits as I believed that I should be rewarded for my service even at that young age. I had to do all this for Manikyam because Manikyam was married by that time so she was not allowed to go out without an escort.

Bhanumati also had friends and I had to go their houses also for giving their homework books and class work books etc. She had these two friends namely Bharati and Ratnavati and all three were very close. I used to call them three 'Rati, Vati and Mati' and each would give me their note books to be given to either of the two. These three were so close that they would plan their clothes for school the next day and they were mostly inseparable. I was always happy to go over to Ratnavati's house as it was near the municipal park at the end of the road. I thus became very close to Bhanumati's friends also. Bhanumati had one more friend Datla

Prabhavati who was very beautiful and belonged to princely caste 'Rajulu' but I loved going to their house and talk to her. I was now cured of Asthma, no one could compete with me in activities and I would never remain at home. I therefore liked these visits to my sisters' friends.

Bhanumati was an artist. She could draw portrait of any one just in one sitting. She also was a good singer and could sing movie songs so well. When Pedda Babu was young and his voice did not break it would be difficult to distinguish who was singing as they both had same melodious tone. In addition to these Bhanumati was very good in tailoring and embroidery and in short, she was very good in every art. But there are some things that I did not like about her. She would finish her meals very fast and leave for school whereas I had to wait for both Pedda Babu and Chinna Babu to complete their meal and remove their plates and clean up the area. Not that I minded very much since we all three would go to school together after our meals. But I knew that Bhanumati was doing this deliberately so that she does not have to remove the plates and clean the place before going to the school. I thought she was unjust to me but I could not pick up fight with her and so at times I began to miss my meals also. But my father will not miss the reason behind my not coming for meals. He would ask me how I could become angry with any one after all I was a symbol of peace in the family. This made me happy and I would begin coming for my lunch once again. I think everyone knew my weakness that I cared for everyone, loved them all and so they would take advantage of the same. Every evening during spring and summer months I would pick jasmine and Mogra flowers and sit under the creepers and make long veni's. I will make one very large string of flowers just for me but, either Manikyam or Bhanumati would come and take them away to put in their plaits. I would complain that if they needed flowers why could they not pick them instead of taking away my flowers? Next day I will go to school without any flowers out of anger. Father told me not to string the flowers if it hurts you so much and I would agree with him. But next day once again I will go back to my routine and the same thing will be repeated once again. They would just laugh and I would forget my anger. My mother who too loved flowers would tell me not to worry about these petty things and do it since I love to do it and enjoy.

Once we joined the same school all three of us began to go to school together. Going with Pedda Babu to the school was an experience. He believed in being a staunch Brahmin and so would sport a prominent pig tail (pilaka) on back of his head and a big Tilak on his forehead. Other children in the school would make fun of him and some would even pull his pilaka and then he would fight them over the issue. He would have a fight virtually every day. He was a very good student and was good in every subject but excelled in mathematics. But he was also a very secretive and a private person. He had the only other cupboard in the house that was locked. He kept so many things in that we never knew of the many treasures he hid in them. All of us would be given chocolates or peppermints or balloons to play with and we will eat them or play with them almost immediately after we get them but not Pedda Babu. He would store them in his cupboard and eat them leisurely; by that time we had finished what we received and we would then complain. Father would also tell him that he should share the sweets with us but he would not do so and father could not force him as we were all given a fair share. One day he forgot to lock his cupboard and we examined what was in it and we were surprised to find that it contained so may sheets of drawing in pencil of portraits from Telugu magazine covers and that was the first time we came to know he was also an artist. Both Pedda Babu and Bhanumati were very good in drawing but both did not pursue the art in later years and this is because of the emphasis on education in India and only few would get encouragement in developing their arts during formative years.

Chinna Babu was something else. He inherited the good hand writing of my father and when he wrote it looked like print. He was not only a good artist like Bhanumati and Pedda Babu but he also was a good story teller. In the evening, after the school is over, Pedda Babu and I would return home but not Chinna Babu. Our school was so near that we could hear school bell from our house and so as soon as the school time is over with the final ringing of the bell, my father would wait at the front gate and he would see both me and Pedda Babu come back but not Chinna Babu. Father would be fuming standing there and after some half an hour or more Chinna Babu would come leisurely and before my father would even ask him where he was, he was ready with a story or an explanation. One day he started telling my father that he waited at the Police lines or quarters on his return as he was watching a very strange incident. My father naturally asked what happened and he said he saw wife of police constable beating her husband. So my father asked him what was so strange about it. He replied why most of the times it was only husband beating his wife but this time it was opposite. Chinna Babu then exclaimed 'Father, this was Police constables wife and how could she beat him?' Father forgot all his anger and laughed and said he may be a police constable for us but not for his wife for whom he was just a husband and situation returned back to normal. Father knew that Chinna Babu was deliberately trying to put him off by telling a story and actually hiding reason for his late coming. He would tell Muttayya in the night that he was not upset with Chinna Babu because he was late, but because he was lying to him but how could he be harsh with a motherless boy? He hated any one lying to him and he was worried Chinna Babu would get into wrong company. I think my father had a long suspicion that Chinna Babu had a tendency of straying away from his goal and that is why he wanted me to steady him by being at his side at least during his studies. Chinna Babu was very intelligent and could grasp minute details and answer any difficult problems, but to even do so he must study first and that was his major weakness.

Come summer vacation and he would be full of fun and games. Playing with Chinna Babu was fun but he generally cheated in any game. If we are playing cards, he would hide his low value cards and win the game, if playing hide and seek he would peep through closed eyes and would catch us before the count of 100 is over, but with all this it was fun playing with him. One of his favorite games was to play ghost and for this his makeup was very simple. He covered his face with father's dhoti and put his glasses over the eyes and it would be very scary to all of us children to see a white body with only glasses and no head! He was thus popular among all my cousins coming from both Bombay and Madras. One would never realize the fast pace at which summer time was spent. House would be full with children of all ages and then there would be raw mangoes, ripe mangoes, bananas, coconuts, Sapotas or Chickoos, guava, oranges and fruits of toddy palm (Tati Munjelu) for everyone to eat. We would receive jack fruit both raw and ripe from our farms in Vakkalanka. Raw jack fruit was used for curry and the ripe one would be peeled to separate the edible bulbs after removing their very large seeds. Seeds were also used for curry particularly with brinjal. Most would be sleeping on the floor as there were only two beds one for my father and the second one for the guest. There would be fights among children and grownups alike either for dress or for flowers or food or just for no reason. After all it was a big household.

Pickle Time: Summer was also the time for making pickles for the annual requirement for all our families. If my aunt from Bombay is coming she would carry her quota of pickles back with her. My uncle Babayya and his family came every year and they would take their requirement of pickles. I know it would be hard to believe when I say that pickles were not prepared with one kilo or ten kilos of raw mangoes but more than 100 kg for one season. Pickles were prepared in quantities that are unknown today and may probably be prepared only in some very large joint families today. Father would select a tree of mangoes for the pickles and the pickles were made from mangoes of the same one tree. Sometimes two trees were selected if the crop was not good. Once the mangoes arrive at home, the first job of all us children was to wash the outer skin of raw mangoes with a wet cloth to remove the sticky exudates from the surface. All children will be asked to sit with a wet cloth for cleaning the mangoes. The mangoes were then air dried before they are cut because water is the main enemy for preservation of pickles and any moisture remaining on the skin would spoil the shelf life of the mango pickles. Then Upadhyayula brothers Suryanarayana and Satyanarayana would sit with sharp knifes mounted on wooden plate (Kattipeeta) and begin cutting the mangoes in eight or twelve pieces depending on size. We were not allowed to cut as the knife was so sharp that we would chop our fingers. All this was done in the house because of 'Madi'. Now a days one can get the cutting services for mangoes from the vendor himself and this makes making pickles easier.

Measure of ingredients is also huge for this volume of pickles. It has been estimated that for every 1000 mangoes we need following volumes of ingredients and one could suitably modify the constituents if the number is more than 1000 or less than 1000. I have given the measures in kilos for new generations to understand more easily. We always measured either from number of mangoes or number of pieces and never in weight. The measure given below is for preparation of pickles from 1200 raw mangoes. Each pile of the pickle mix would be at least 3 feet high and mixing was done by the two brothers only. This was not a job for ladies. Once the preparation of the main pickles was over, father would order 500 mangoes more for Menthi Kaya and 500 mangoes for Tokku Pacchadi. Our farm also grew two types of oranges namely 'Naradabba kaya' Dabba Kaya and Nimma kaya (lemon). Pickles made from these are used for recuperating after any sickness. Everyone would take these also as per their requirement. I asked my father I see every one taking pickles to their homes for their annual requirements, but do they keep an account? Father laughed and said no one would like to talk about accounting since till this day even your Babayya has never asked me if I am running in profit or loss. I believe all of them assumed that my father was getting a lot of revenue and they had a right.

1.	Mustard Seeds from Madugulla	120 Kg
2.	Red Chilli from Gollaprolu	60 Kg
3.	Salt	40 Kg
4.	Til Oil	120 kg
5.	Turmeric	5 Kg
6.	Hing	10 Kg
7.	Fenugreek (Menthulu)	20 Kg

Every year Paramma (short for Parvati) and her family would come to our house virtually on a contract for pounding these ingredients into powder in a wooden receptacle with long wooden staff with iron base (Rolu and Rokali). Paramma sold vegetables in market rest of the year but pounding of pickle mixture during summer time was more lucrative. It used to surprise me to see one or the other member of her family pregnant and almost near to the delivery time and my grandmother would ask her how do you do this task of pounding and she would smile and say this is our way of keeping healthy and have normal deliveries. They looked very slim and sturdy with shining skin even though they were all dark and they would cover their mouth and nose before pounding the ingredients. All of us would be sneezing if we venture out during the pounding these items but because we were children we would not keep away from our back yard also. Every ingredient is strained through strainers to remove seeds and rough particles and there would be quite an amount of waste collected that Paramma would take home.

Once these are pounded each of the item would be placed on the cement floor behind the main house serving as our dining hall and Upadhyayula brothers would now be busy mixing these ingredients. Each of the ingredients is put up in the form of a pile on the floor and each ingredient is added as per the standard measure passed from generation to generation. It is a rigorous operation and has to be done in 'Madi' or wear clean clothes or often wet clothes after bath and we children are not allowed to touch them while they are mixing. We would watch them from distance and the protocol was like this. First measure quantities of mustard powder and mix this with powdered salt to prevent mustard powder from becoming balls. Chilli powder is now added to make a large pile of this spicy mixture. This pile would then be mixed from bottom up to achieve a homogenous mixture. Now they would make a large shallow pit in this mountain of mixture of mustard, salt and chilli and til oil or gingelly oil is poured in the center to make the pile wet with oil and then the cut pieces of mangoes that are air dried again added to this pile of the mixture. Taste of pickles depends on the primary measure of mustard or 'Avalu' and pickles is therefore known as Avakaya or cut pieces of raw mangoes in mustard powder. The pickles are then transferred into large earthen jars 'Banalu' almost 2 feet high and kept there for 3 days when the quantity is reduced to almost half. Then they are transferred in ceramic jars that are actually large acid bottles and some have threaded mouth while others have lid that is easy to remove. Til oil is added to the bottom of the jar covering more than two inches from bottom and the raw mango pieces along with the spicy powder is added and after every addition more til oil is added to the combined mixture of mango pieces and pickle powder so that oil is liberally mixed with the powder and the pieces of mangoes. Oil is the only preservative and so it must be seen as a free layer over the surface in each jar. Once the pickles are transferred to the jars they were stored in the pickles room and my count is that the room had the capacity of storing 20 to 30 jars. Mamma was the custodian and she alone will take out the pickles when needed for daily use.

Once the pickles are ready, they are packed in tin cans and sealed for my uncles and aunts to take with them to Madras, Bombay or wherever they are living. It is packed in the tin oil containers (Dabba) as oil would not leak from these Dabba but will leak from biscuit Dabba which are not air tight. Pickles from each jar are transferred along with plenty of oil and the cover is sealed by tinning to make it completely air tight. This is the signal for everyone to prepare to return to their own homes and father will send Muttayya to buy their tickets and see them off at the station. My uncle and his family will take as many as two or three of these dabbas for their annual requirement. If my aunt Gnanamba visits us she too would take one or two of these with her to Bombay and beyond. Of course they would not visit us every year as they had to change trains at three places between Billimora and Rajahmundry as there were no direct trains nor reservations available in trains. Travelling was an ordeal for them. If any of my father's other sisters are visiting, they too would take their share and Ratnalu Mamma would tell father about it so that more quantity of pickle is prepared. Finally my grandmother Ammamma will keep some separate for Doddamma who visits us once or twice every year and will keep some for her own sisters. Then whatever was left behind was for our consumption and with the floating population we normally ran short of pickles very soon. We had a special room to keep these pickles and the room was called pickle room or 'Avakaya Gadi' and only persons in 'Madi' are allowed to enter as otherwise the pickles may become moldy. The room was dark and all the windows were closed. Pickles remained without being affected by fungi for years in these conditions but in our house there was no need as we did not have large quantities for ourselves.

My father kept account of all expenses towards manufacturing pickles in his account book in his own very neat hand writing but I never heard any one asking about the cost of their share of pickles. My mother had a different role in the whole business. She neither questioned any one about the expenses nor stopped any one from taking pickles with them. She was a very large hearted person and this kept peace and tranquility in the joint family house hold where almost everyone was ready to pick up a fight with my father. She was a saint in real word. Father really led the life of a Landlord or Zamindar and we never felt any shortages at any time. How could he manage such an unwieldy household without having any steady income like others? Several years after my wedding I too was collecting my share of pickles and I never asked my father about neither the costs nor I paid for them.

Today, Indira is fulfilling my father's duties and has been sending me pickles every year when ready to the US by courier service. I can never thank her enough but remembering what I asked father I told Indira that she must maintain strict account or else I will not take the pickles. Kavita has been following my instructions very faithfully and I am happy that we are clearing our accounts when convenient.

In addition to Avakaya we also made large quantities of Menthikaya prepared of dried mango slices. We children had to sit and peel the skin of raw mangoes and in the days when we did not know of peelers, this was done using shells of fresh water mussels 'Aal Chippa'. A hole of about half an inch in diameter will be made in the center of the shell of a mussel and would be sharpened on stone and this was then used for peeling the mango skins. Today the potato peelers have replaced these low cost natural peelers of the old times. It may surprise many to know that mangoes sharpened the edge of knife or shells and hence the knife used for cutting mangoes becomes so sharp that one has to watch not to cut their fingers. Mango slices would then be prepared by cutting the mangoes length-wise, soak in salt water for preservation and later dried in hot sun for three days. In both the cases we are now declared off the limits and were not allowed to touch any of these dried slices since they are 'Madi'. Pedda Babu, I and Chinna Babu followed the instructions very obediently and would watch from outside and drooling over them from a distance. One summer Gnanamba attayya came for the vacation and the types of mischief her children showed were different from the ones we were used to play. They too wanted to eat these dried slices but we warned them that we cannot touch these since they are 'Madi' so they said all right if we do not touch them with our hands would it be affecting the 'Madi'? We said no and asked but how could you pick up without touching? They used dry ribs of coconut leaves that are strong and also sharp and used these to pick up the slices. They were right, since we did not physically touch the mango slices, technically we did not violate 'Madi' and we began to eat the slices whenever we liked. They tasted so good and why not after all they were forbidden slices!

In addition to Menthikaya we also prepared lime pickle and pickle from a different variety of orange known as 'Naradabbakaya'. Lime pickle was not liked by most so it was prepared in less quantity for export and Naradabbakaya pickle was purely medicinal and was prepared once and kept for a long time and every one would take it in small quantities and naturally it was also not prepared in large quantities. After sickness, when mouth tastes bitter and one loses appetite, recuperating patients were given rice mixed with Naradabbakaya pickle and that would make the sense of taste return to normal.

Movie times

Next big operation in our house was going for a movie. We would go in two or three batches for any movie so that we get seats in the same row. It would always be a Saturday and that too a 3.00 pm matinee show. At one O'clock, father would tell the cycle rickshaw puller to come to our house at 2.30 and then we will all be asked to be ready based on their turn in that batch and each batch would be led by a grown up and responsible person. Chinna Babu would be listed in the first batch and that was the rule. A week later the second batch would be ready to go for the movie and Chinna Babu would be part of that batch as he was permitted by my father. In third batch once again Chinna Babu would be included since he begged my father and so Chinna Babu would see three times same movie while others will see it only once. He would then entertain us with the dialogues and comedy items from that movie for days to come. But to me this was unfair and I argued with my father that since Chinna Babu would sneak with all the batches, he should always be included in the last batch and my father would just laugh. Chinna Babu loved movie world and the glamour of the tinsel world and in his later years he lost his way in these and other stage related activities. Towards the end he was associated with the

Telugu TV industries producing or directing shows etc. and fully utilizing his talent of storytelling.

Indira & Me

By the time I was 7 years old, on 8th May, 1951 Indira was born and my days began to be occupied with looking after her and also going after my other activities. Indira was a chubby child and every one in our house loved her. She was extremely fair and healthy and I do not remember her crying, but still she became my liability. I would return from my school along with Chinna Babu and Pedda Babu and they would rush off to the municipal garden for playing but I could not since I had to look after Indira. I was allowed to go to the garden only if I took Indira with me. I was a very frail person and carrying Indira was no easy task. But then I would not give up my only pleasure and so every day I would carry Indira in my arms and go over to the garden. I would leave her below a tree and then join my brothers in all the sports and games. Chinna Babu would go over to our house every time his turn was over and give us a commentary on what was going on in the house and what was cooking there. One day, he went to our house and came back to announce that hot pakodas were being prepared, let us go and so we all rushed home. Half way I remembered that I had left Indira in the garden and so I rushed back to pick her up. As soon as my father saw them coming back he asked about me. Chinna Babu blurted out that I had forgotten Indira in the park and so I went back to bring her after coming half way with them. That was enough and I received such a dressing down from my parents that day that even today I remember the incident distinctly as if it happened yesterday. One thing about my father is that he never would beat us whatever may be the cause of his anger. It always surprises me even today that Indira would remain at the same place without crying when I went off to play! She would sit under the tree without any whimper and came back with me happily. But on that day, the day itself was hot and Indira became so flushed red that my parents were worried but fortunately Indira was back to her normal shade by evening.

Father had purchased a rocking horse for Chinna Babu when he was about 4 years old because he demanded it. Father could not dodge his request and finally he bought one for him. It was a colorful piece and made from very strong wood and so as usual remained on the front verandah. When Indira was just about six months old, she was able to sit in a balanced manner without falling. One day my father just put her on the rocking horse in order to change his hand as he was carrying Indira for a long time and he was surprised to see that Indira was rocking very actively on the horse without any support. From that day onwards, the rocking horse of Chinna Babu became her rocking horse and she would not let anyone else to sit on the horse. She was healthy and looked older than her age and she was taller than normal babies her age and she would always tag behind me. One day, when I was drawing water from our well, Indira was standing near me without my knowledge and I also did not see Indira. Indira went near the well and just pulled the bucket out of the well with so much force that the bucket just flew out of the well and hit her on the head. I shouted in fear that she was hurt seriously but she did not even cry and was alright except that there was a scar on her forehead. In 2008 when I was in India, we began talking about the scar on her head and she told me the scar is visible only when she parted her hair in the middle and I joked that since she did not have brains, I just polished that part of her brain and we all laughed.

Celebration of Festivals

1. Sankranti:

Year starts with Sankranti that comes in the middle of January and every year it would be celebrated for three days namely 13th January, Bhogi, 14th January, real Sankranti and 15th January the Kanumu. Everyone who worked for us would come to our house to receive gifts of new clothes for self and their family. Our cattle would be decorated and their horns painted in bright colors. This is considered as the most important day for all the farm hands and so it would also be for their owner. We would wet the soil in front of our gate and make designs in chalk powder and you could see ladies in every house outside doing artistic designs (Muggu) with chalk powder and fill them with bright colors. On 15th January known as Kanumu, no one will travel and it is said that even crow would not fly on Kanumu for fear of becoming darker. On 13th January, children are given oil bath with 'Regi pandu' also known as 'bere' in Hindi, soaked chana and copper coins and the olders in the family bless them. This is a custom for most families but not in Ganti family. Our routine would be to wear new clothes on Bhogi and Sankranti day eat lot of sweats. It is compulsory on Sankranti day to eat pumpkin pulusu with sweet potatoes or 'Dhappalam' and curry of yam 'kanda'. On 15th January or Kanumu day, farm animals are worshipped and 'gaare' and 'aavadalu' made of black urad dal forms the main dish. Most significant event on Kanumu is the hot water bath with the following chant in Telugu; "Kaki Kaki ni rupa tesukuni na rupamu nakichheya" when translated means "Dear crow please take away your dark shade and return me my original shade." In South India, Sankranti generally follows a severe winter and every one becomes darker with exposure to sun or sunbathing. The skin became rough and dark or tanned and that is why this is chanted signifying change of season. On this day it is said the sun would enter in Makar Rashi and that is why the day is known as Makar Sankranti. The sun now enters in the northern hemisphere or 'Uttarayanam'.

2. **Shiva Ratri:**

Shiva Ratri is the day of Lord Shiva our family deity who drank the poison remaining after churning of the oceans or Samudra Manthanam and digested the same. His throat became blue because of drinking of the poison and he is also named as Neelkantha Swami. Father would fast on the day and will not eat any food.

Many of the devotees stay awake the whole night praying and chanting Bhajans of Shiva, but my father did not believe in this so he would only fast. Interestingly on this day movie theaters are permitted to exhibit mythological movies throughout the night till next day noon. It is believed that one should observe at least one Shiva Ratri in their life time and I do not think I will ever be able to do even once.

3. Telugu New Year (Samvatsaradi):

Telugu New Year falls on New Moon day of Chaitra or Chaitra Suddha Paadyami or the first day of Telugu calendar month Chaitra. Like other festivals the house is decorated with strings of marigold flowers inter woven with mango leaves to herald the beginning of a New Year and everyone is ready to take on the events of the coming New Year. The day starts with oil bath, followed with new clothes for every one and taste of bitter chutney prepared in tamarind juice containing inflorescence of neem tree, raw mango pieces, ripe banana, green chilli and jiggery thus representing six types of tastes: namely neem flowers for bitterness, raw mango for tang, tamarind juice for sourness, green chilli for spice, jaggery for sweetness and pinch of salt for saltiness together forming the Shadruchi of tastes. In the evening father would invite our Siddhanti garu to read the almanac or Panchangam and read the future of the year. First nine days of the month are known as Rama Navaratrulu starting from the New Year day and these will be celebrated with many cultural programs and listening to story of Ramayana and on the ninth day or Ramanavami day, it is celebrated as the birthday of Lord Rama and also his wedding day.

4. Sravana: A Month of Festivals

The entire month of Sravana is full of festivals particularly for women. Every Tuesday, the newly married bride performs Mangala Gouri Vratam for five years. On the Friday just before full moon, women of all the ages perform Vara Lakshmi Vratam to pray for the wealth and long life of their husbands. This is followed by Dhanjyala Purnima on Full Moon day to replace the older Yagnopavitam with a new one an important event for all male members. It is also celebrated as a Rakhi Purnima all over India where a sister ties a thread of protection 'the Rakhi' on her brother's wrist. On 8th day after Full Moon day of Sravana, Krishnashtami birth day of Lord Krishna is celebrated with fanfare with the pranks and games played on road offering tribute to child Krishna and his childhood activities. Last day of the month is celebrated as Polala Amavasya to pray for long life of children and a special type of idli known as Kotteka Butta is prepared. Jack fruit leaves are woven in a pyramid shape and are filled with the batter of idli and steam cooked. This used to be the food item for those traveling on a boat trip since they would remain for as many as 10 days without getting spoiled believed to be due to antibiotic properties of jack fruit leaves.

5. **Vinayaka Chaturthi:**

Most important festival for my father was celebration of Vinayaka Chaturthi or birthday of Lord Vinayaka on 4th day of the month Bhadrapad. Pedda Babu, Chinna Babu and everyone in the house will take oil bath and get ready for the installation of Vinayaka. According to the tradition, he will be worshipped with twenty one types of leaves, flowers and fruits collected from far and near on a small statuette of Vinayaka decorated colorfully for his birthday. The installation and worshipping would be made by our priests and most of the times it would be Subbavadhanulu garu or Ghanapathi garu who will perform the ceremony and only boys were allowed to join the worship and not girls. The statuette of Lord Vinayaka was removed on third day and since it was made of clay, it would be immersed in our well. Sometimes we would keep the idol in granary. On this day all food items are steam cooked and according to my father this was a healthy practice since the festival comes during monsoon season. New water in the rivers and lakes are likely to contain many types of disease bearing germs and steam cooked preparations help prevent any outbreaks. After completing Pooja, everyone would do the sit up for twenty one times as a penance and hence this was also known as a festival of sit ups 'Gunjila Pandaga'. In Bombay and other parts of Maharashtra, the celebrations last for 10 days and on the 14th day of Bhadrapada Masam or Anant Padmanabha Chaturdashi, the idols of Vinayaka or Ganesh is carried with fanfare to the nearest beach and is immersed there. Immersion of Ganesh is a big deal in Maharashtra and the occasion is participated by everyone irrespective of their caste, a great unifying event.

6. Dassera:

Although Dassera festival continues for ten days and we used to do that in earlier days, but as far as I remember in our house we used to observe only three days before Dassera namely, Durgashtami, Mahanavami and Vijay Dasami or Dassera. On Dassera day all of us will receive new clothes and as per the tradition we will seek blessings of elders by bowing at their feet and we would get money in addition to their blessings. Our house was corner house and many times the locals would hold public functions on Dassera on the street adjoining our house and this included street plays. Schools were closed and we had lots of fun.

7. Attla Tadiya:

The day falls on the third day after Full Moon of Aswijam (according to Indian Almanac) month soon after Dassera festivals and is primarily a ladies function and they celebrate by playing on swings and other feminine games. Women decorate their hands with mehendi. After a full day's fast the day ends with a form of Dosa known as Attulu. My father loved these Attulu with chutney made from unripe tamarind. This day precedes another similar function celebrated in North India popularly known as 'Karava Chowth' that is observed on 4th day or one day after Attla Tadiya. Married ladies look at the reflection of rising moon through a sieve and super impose the sieve on reflection of husband's image before breaking the fast. In both the regions it is customary to view moon before partaking the food and particularly for us this would be difficult. In Rajahmundry, this was start of second monsoon and very often one would not be able to see the moon because of clouds and so remain without food.

8. **Deepavali:**

Deepavali had a special significance for my father and every one in our family. It was my birthday and father would always tell me that generally a birth day is a personal matter for most but in your case it is celebrated all over India and wherever Indians live. He would do the worshipping of Goddess Lakshmi and begin distributing sweets and new clothes to everyone. He would tell me that when I was born, Marwari business men from nearby shops came to our house and collected silver coins for their Puja. The silver coin was then returned with additional 10 more coins. This practice continued as long as we lived in Innispeta which one could say had a busy market with a good Marwari population and was sort of downtown and Godavari Railway station was also very near.

In the tradition of Upadhyayula family, Kotteka Butta are prepared on the new moon day of Deepavali unlike in Ganti family. My father would religiously see that Kotteka Butta is prepared every Deepavali and he would get honey like sugary syrup made from sugarcane juice from Vakkalanka for this event. Then the fireworks would start where not only children but even older person like my father actively joined in the fireworks with a gusto matching his own children.

My father felt a special thrill of participating in the fireworks every Deepavali season. When most of the families buy their requirements of fire crackers, father would make his own every year. He would buy all the raw materials and make a variety of fire crackers sitting at home such as Matabas, flower pots (Chicchu

Buddi), 'Tara Juvva' or rockets and 'Pichika' or flying saucer (my translation). Fifteen days before Deepavali, planning for the fireworks starts and the first task after purchasing the raw fire powder material is to dry them in sunlight so that they are not moist and give best value for the efforts. Tara Juvva was prepared by stuffing the fire powder into rolls of thick paper and since normal paper is generally thin, people used money order forms available free at the post offices. My father would ask Chinna Babu or Pedda Babu to bring some from the post office every day. Empty molds of clay flower pots commercially available in the market are filled with the gun powder and the base is sealed. These chichi Buddi would last longer than commercial ones because they were made by my father with good quality mix. Most laborious and time consuming item was filling the small hole of the 'Pichika' literally meaning sparrow or the flying saucer. These are earthen balls of about an inch in size hollow from inside with a very fine opening at one end and the gun powder is very slowly introduced into this small unit. Father would not let anyone to fill up these as they could catch fire and only Pedda Babu was allowed to do the filling. Matabas or search light was filled by me only and here we used paper from a newsletter issued by all India Radio Station called 'Vani' as these papers were glossy and stiff.

Deepavali signifies beginning of winter and so the days are shorter and as soon as we finished our supper of Kotteka Butta, all of us would go out to enjoy the fireworks. I would try to be as equal to my brothers as possible, but in some arts my brothers were better. Both Pedda Babu and Chinna Babu were very good in throwing Pichika and the way they released, it looked like a real Pichika or sparrow appearing to dive to the ground for birdseed before taking off in the sky. Sparrows pick up the grain from ground before they fly back to the tree and in the same manner these Pichika also fly away after almost touching the ground. Everyone is not an expert in achieving this trajectory of the Pichika. Chinna Babu was very good in releasing Tara Juvva. He would hold the tail of Juvva before releasing in the sky and it would go straight into the sky. Since both the brothers liked two different types of crackers, there was no competition between them but then Chinna Babu would never stick to one type and he would share our stock of the crackers like Matabas, sprinklers and strip of crackers and even Vishnu Chakrams. As a routine he would finish his quota first and then take from our stock of fire crackers. Late in the evening at some areas, there will be competition in releasing Juvva in the sky between two teams and sometimes these competitions between two parties appear as if they are at war. Juvva would be released towards each party and this would continue till either of the participants has exhausted their stock or a fire reported in the hutments nearby. Such group fightings are banned, but then on Deepavali day who could dare to implement these rules strictly? Every year because of fires in the hutments loss of property if not lives is reported but the same thing continues next year.

After the completion of our fireworks we all would return back and wash our hands thoroughly and then we would burn special type of powder 'guggilam' that is believed to neutralize the magnesium and sulfur fumes in the rooms before we go for sleep. We would be so tired that once we drop on the bed we would be fast asleep instantly and not care all the noises of crackers coming from everywhere. Next day morning after Deepavali we felt very dejected as if we had lost a friend because we had been preparing for almost one month for this important event.

Father never missed making his own fire crackers and since Deepavali would fall during second monsoon season it would rain before or after Deepavali and very often the fire crackers would become soggy. Once in 1960 it was raining continuously and we had already purchased the gun powder in advance and this has to be dried before filling the material into flower pots, Matabas or Pichika. He was sitting in the boiler room where fire was burning to make hot water for the family and the firework material was kept for drying. What happened we do not know probably a spark may have ignited the gun powder and there was so much noise that we all thought my father must have suffered serious injury but things were not bad and he recovered very swiftly. Young Murthy was crying out aloud and at that time Durga was not born. Ramam Mavayya came shortly after to our house and he scolded my father that how could you do such a thing at this age and especially when the children have lost their mother! You should watch your own health. But father did not stop and continued his enthusiasm of participating and playing with fire crackers till the day he died. He died just 5 days after Deepavali on a Monday of Kartik month. I was reading a letter from him inquiring if my son-in-law had visited us on Deepavali, when I received a telegram. I did not have courage to open the telegram and asked our neighbor Nita to open the telegram and she broke the news that father was no more. The kids in the neighborhood in Hyderabad refused to believe that he was dead, since they all had come to watch him in awe the way he played with the fire crackers even at that age. He remained a colorful personality till the end.

9. Kartik Mondays:

Deepavali is followed by Kartik month. My father was a very religious person and he believed in Lord Shiva and so he would fast on every Monday of the month Kartik and will eat only in the evening. Our family priest would come on that day and after worshipping Lord Shiva in the temple and after priest was served the first meal father and everyone else will break their fast and take their meals. In fact our priest Subbavadhanulu garu or Ghanapati garu had instruction to offer Archna in Lord Shiva's temple every day throughout this month. It is believed that the God of Death 'Mrityadevata' is likely to strike if Lord Shiva was not worshipped on this month, but then my father who was devout follower of Shiva died in the month of Kartik that too Monday in the month of Kartik. Where is the truth in the belief?

Floodings of the Century

Godavari River (Flooding of Twentieth Century)

In 1953 the whole town of Rajahmundry and nearby areas in the Delta region was inundated with flood waters of the river Godavari. As much as 25 lakhs cusecs of water flooded the river Godavari on 16th August, 1953 and the height of flood waters reached 19.3ft above the crest level at the Dhavaleshwaram Anicut. Several breaches in the Anicut caused water to rise on the banks and due to the flooding there was heavy damage to the property and to the lives along the coast particularly in several towns and villages in the downstream areas. This probably was the only flood that I had seen in India. On Saturday 15th August, a day before I went with father and my grandmother to see the river when the river water was still rising. Everyone in the family had visited the river earlier and they did not take me since I was running temperature but then I insisted so father brought me to see the river. We stood on the shore and watched the water rising with a thunderous noise, like of which I have never heard before and the water was very muddy and turbulent. It was a scary sight and I developed fever again in the night and my father for a change was scolded by elders for taking me to the river. According to them the sight of flood is more terrorizing and that was the reason for my fever. A rising river seeks human sacrifice and my father was concerned that I might be the one selected from my family. But that was not so and here I am with my memoirs.

I could hear the police coming in their jeeps and asking the residents in the low lying area to vacate their homes and move with essential belongings to higher ground as the river was rising very rapidly but very few took the warning seriously. After all they have been living near river Godavari and every year they experienced same type of flooding and did not move. At 2.00 am on the night of 16th, the river waters rose so rapidly that many people even did not know as they were fast asleep and many families were washed away with no account of the exact loss of life. The flood water remained for almost three weeks and so probably there is no accurate account of many houses were washed away in the floods. I did not know the extent of damage as I was too young to worry about the details, but I remember the fact that our house in Danavaya Peta became a very important center for people displaced by flooding. Our house became a virtual refugee camp.

Danavaya Peta is situated at higher levels from the rest of the city and that was the reason that very few houses had drinking water wells and when they did have wells they were very deep. Most our relations vacated their houses in Innispeta, collected their essential items and came directly to our house. I remember the following personalities: Ganti Chinna Venkata Ramiah garu and his wife, Maruvada Chenulu garu, his three brothers and their families; Karra Ishwara Rao garu of ILTD, Isola brothers of my grandmother, Subbavadhanulu garu and his family, Ghanapathi garu and his family and so also his father Somayajula garu and his family and many of the families living in Konaseema could not go back since boat services were suspended so they too remained in our house. I do not remember now who all had come. My father had given strict instructions that whoever comes at our door should not go back without food and every one would get hot food most of the times. Kitchen was going on for almost twelve hours and food was made available to those who knocked our door. Vegetables and fruits were available at three times the costs as there was limited supply of all items. But according to my father at such times of calamity one should not worry about the costs and try to provide as much as possible without looking for profits.

I would like to mention about one family in particular who came during floods and became our close relatives later on. Vedula Narayana Murty garu of Anakapalle was working as a statistician for Indian Tobacco Research Center near Sitamma Peta that was also low lying area and he came with his wife Haimavati garu and daughter Bhanumati who was of the same age as Indira and stayed in our house till the flood waters receded. After the flood waters receded, they went back and rented a house near our house in Danavaya Peta and Narayana Murty garu became very friendly with my father and would come to our house in the evening. Bhanu would come with her doll that was so life like and Indira would want to play with it. She would refuse and Indira would cry. Next day when Narayana Murty garu wanted to come to our house, Bhanu also came with him and her father told her then do not bring your doll as you are making Indira cry. She agreed she will give it to Indira and came with her doll and again Indira asked for the doll and again she would not part with her doll. Finally father bought a doll for Indira and she named the doll as Leela after her favorite singer P. Leela. She was so fond of Leela that any time during movie music if the announcer did not say P. Leela she would cry. Even now after so many years Indira still likes songs rendered by P. Leela only. Now Bhanu is married to Peri Sastry older brother of my son-in-law Ayysola Kashipati Chenulu and so Gnanu and Bhanu are related from their husband side. Hopefully Indira and Bhanu will have no issues now.

How much did my father spent during these floods when untold number of people came and ate their meals at our place for several days. There is no account and no one even inquired later out of interest. My father was probably compared as Kubera the celestial treasurer who had access to unlimited funds. A large number of people would come to our back door and collect water from the well since their wells were contaminated with flood waters and was unsafe for drinking. I worship my father for all his good actions.

Mississippi River (Flooding of 21st Century)

In my life I had the occasion of witnessing another major flooding in 2011 in the mighty river Mississippi when Chitti and I were living in Greenville, MS. We had just set up our production facility and have been having a fairly difficult time being away from Dinkar and Gnanu. We knew we were near the river but did not expect to worry about the flooding. Flooding in the river was unlike the one I had seen earlier in Godavari river where it was probably flash flooding. Here the flooding depended on the rain in the mid-west and in the north resulting in the flooding of rivers. These rivers emptied their water in the Mississippi river and so the flooding was greatly dependent on the flow of flood water in other rivers. The strange thing is that they knew about the flooding almost one month before and the weather channel would predict flooding at any particular time. In Greenville, the prediction was that flooding would occur sometime on 17th May. We were spared the effects of inundation, but our neighboring city of Vicksburg was under water for a long time. Unfortunately this water cannot recede unless it empties in the sea in the Gulf of Mexico. These were two important milestones in my life and that is why I decided to give the current title.

Life was very pleasant after the flooding in Godavari which was followed with two weddings one my sister Bhanumati and second of my cousin Sarvamangala or Baby. Rajananna Akka was living at that time and she requested Babayya to conduct marriages of Gnanamba, his oldest daughter also in Rajahmundry before she died since she was so helpless and paralytic. But he did not agree and Gnanamba's marriage was performed in Madras and my father and mother along with Indira and Baby attended the wedding. Marriages in my house were always very grand events and there are many pleasant incidents associated with each wedding.

Trivikram was born on 20th June, 1956 and this was the height of my most memorable period. My father had purchased a ceiling fan for my mother who could not tolerate hot summer days and a sewing machine since sewing and knitting was a hobby of my mother. My mother became so young at heart with these acquisitions that she would get so many different types of clothes and make dresses for every child. I remember very distinctly the dresses she had made for me from selected cloth. My mother loved red color and so she had planted red hibiscus in the front yard and they would bloom so well that even passersby would notice these flowers. Trivikram had very curly and dense hair same like mine and so he would demand that red hibiscus flowers are put in his hair and my mother would lovingly decorate his hairs with red flowers. Trivikram did not enjoy the company of our mother as she died next year just after celebrating his first birth day.

My father did not allow us to know about his expenses and debts except telling us that he had a reputation that if he sent Muttayya to the market any one would give him up to 50,000 rupees without any promissory note! He had a very large household of family and extended family and none would contribute to the expenses and still at the end of his day he died a man with no debt or "beholden to none". He maintained a large household with heavy expenses of maintenance and supporting living and floating population in our house and no one ever asked him to show the accounts of expenses. Babayya did not ask for the expenses and believed that my father was living on his share of the property and so also his children and grandchildren. The relationship became soured and there was a clamor for partition by Babayya and father told Ramam Mavayya to divide the property as per Babayya's wish and not to consult him. Even Ramam Mavayya and Chinna Tammu Mavayya did not ask for the expenses and revenue from Bommuru but disposed of the land believing that my father swallowed revenues from Bommuru and enjoyed the benefits. Ammamma and Sarada Doddamma also did not ask for any accounts of revenues and expenses from their Vakkalanka property when managed by my father but believed that he swallowed the profits and continued to believe as long as they lived. Why? Why could not they request father for the accounts when they almost took half the share of produce? Every year they would take the produce and part of the revenues by way of borrowing money when they needed? Rajananna was right.

He left a property that was free of any mortgage and when it was disposed of by my brothers they did not pay any outstanding dues.

Before partition of the property father would have income from two properties and after partition his income was reduced by half. His expenses increased tremendously with liabilities for education of my two brothers for their professional studies added to the bulging expense portfolio. Pedda Babu became a doctor in Kakinada and Chinna Babu also studied in Kakinada and became an engineer after a marathon effort. My father also moved to Kakinada and sold our Rajahmundry house and set up a new household so that expenses could be reduced. During later part of my father's life Trivikram became a sort of confidante to my father and Muttayya would share the details of my father's liabilities with him and so he became conscious of the magnitude of difficulties my father faced all his life. Trivikram also became a graduate, did his post-graduation in Chemistry and lived with my father and reduced his expenses by contributing his own income.

July 26 1957 was also the end of my Golden Years when my mother died suddenly. I became a very responsible sister to my one year old brother Trivikram and six year old Indira. My childhood days were over suddenly and I became a mature woman.

CHAPTER 6

MANIKYAM: THE GEM

Manikyam my oldest sister was born on 13th May 1936 in Hyderabad where my grandparents were living. She was born soon after the premature death of the first daughter Sarva Lakshmi and was therefore my grandfather Agastya Sastry's favorite granddaughter. She was named after his wife or my grandmother on mother's side Manikyamba but remained known to most of us as Manikyam. Since it was customary not to address either husband by his name or wife by her first name, my grandfather would call her "Devi" or goddess. The name Manikyam means Gem in Telugu and she was gem for my grandfather and was pampered by him to a fault. Most famous instance was when Manikyam was very small she wanted to drink coffee at midnight and my grandmother refused to make coffee for her as it was already late in the night. But not my grandfather, he would not hear any one denying Manikyam and so he got up and made coffee with his own hands for his pet baby and so began a long journey of Manikyam and her love for coffee that lasted all her life. Manikyam occupied the position of importance for a long time in our family since another child Annapoorna who followed Manikyam did not survive.

She was also favorite baby to our parents and always was a Most Valued Person or MVP for them. She was a great help and support to my mother and my father also considered her his right hand

173

and sought her advice on every issue after my mother's death. She was a serious child and did not believe in any mischief usual to all children and was also a very serious student and worked hard and studied diligently. I do not know if she topped her class but she studied in a convent school. She became quite proficient in sewing and other domestic arts and activities. She would not tell us anything more about her schooling and I was too young to understand the importance. I was eight years younger to her and so there was nothing common between us and we did not share any details with each other.

She had very sharp eyes like my father and could read any small letters or identify people from far away on the road. She was conservative in her thinking and extremely curious about everything and most importantly she trusted all the information she received as she believed every piece of news. She was very fair and was very active in helping my mother in her multitudes of activities. All her intellect and activities came to a sudden halt when she was married. She was married when she was just thirteen. Initially there were two proposals one from Anakapalle and second one from Vakkalanka. My mother was very keen about Vakkalanka match and so also my aunt Gnanamba. But then my grandmother's brother Narasimha Sastry garu or our Mava Tata garu had gone to Anakapalle and met the parents and he was very much impressed by their wealth and their properties. The groom Kashipati Chenulu was studying in a school and was expected to complete his matriculation examination. Groom's father Vedula Ardha Narishwararudu (Ishwarudu) garu was a very close relation to my father from his mother's side and this also made the difference and so Manikyam became daughter-in-law of Ishwarudu garu of Anakapalle and wife of his third son Vedula Kashipati Chenulu. Marriage was performed on June 12th 1949 in our Danavaya Peta House and this was the first marriage in our house. The groom Kashipati Chenulu was tall almost 6 feet high and lanky and the ladies of the bridegroom party who accompanied him were adorned with thick necklaces of gold from head to toe.

The marriage ceremony lasted for 5 days and since Manikyam was very young, she remained with us after her marriage till her nuptials.

My brother-in-law Pedda Bawa was invited by my father for every festival as is our custom and he would come early, a few days before the beginning of the festivals and for one reason or other he would become angry on small issues and return back to his home in Anakapalle without attending the actual festival. I would always kid him that he should change the routine and he should not only come early as usual but he should stay for the festivals for a change. Every time he visited us he would take us for movies, the only pastime we had in Rajahmundry and it has been always a fun. It is unfortunate that Pedda Bawa did not complete his education. He was very intelligent but somehow got in the company of others close to him who felt education or degree was for those who wanted to work. They were rich and had properties they did not have to work then why should they study? It is like since they were blessed with Goddess Lakshmi, why should they worship Goddess Saraswati? This is the magic of that place Anakapalle and my mother hoped that he would move over to our place and completes his education and that never happened. Their place in Anakapalle was thus a place for idle rich. I am narrating incidences as they have occurred with me.

Gouthami and me

Manikyam went to Anakapalle when she was fifteen years old. She did not have any children for a couple of years and then in 1956 she was blessed with a daughter, Gouthami. My mother was also pregnant and she gave birth to my youngest brother Trivikram (Vikram). Of course coincidentally my second sister Bhanumati who was also married by that time gave birth to a son Somasekhar (Shekhar) at the same time. The house now had three mothers each with an infant and each needed close attention. I was the oldest girl in the family after Bhanumati and so almost all the responsibilities fell on my young shoulders and I was just 12 years old. Food and care given to new mothers was very special and they are not expected to work at least for a period of three months after the baby is born and so I would look after their food requirements. Of course, I did not have to cook since we always had a cook in the house and then again Ammamma was staying with us. Still this distracted me from my studies. Gouthami began to grow with Trivikram as Bhanumati went back with Shekhar to her place. One year later my mother died and so Pedda Bawa allowed Gouthami to remain with us to give company to Trivikram till she completed her matriculation examination.

My association with Gouthami thus was a very long one and she became very close to me and lived like one of us. She was the friendliest person I have known and would not take offence to our kidding her at every stage. I have already mentioned about Chinna Babu and his special nature of kidding every one even my father and he would always find something to say to Gouthami. But Gouthami would bear everything with a grin. Both Trivikram and Gouthami were of same age, but Gouthami began speaking much earlier and for a long time we were worried that Trivikram may not be able to speak at all. In his frustration to make other understand what he was conveying he would become irritable. Finally he also began speaking when he was two years old and then there was no stopping to his flow. One of the most interesting conversations between Gouthami and Vikram I overheard went like this. "Vikram," Gouthami asked "I have a mother who lives in Anakapalle but where is your mother?" Vikram was so simple that he immediately answered "Silly girl, boys do not have mother. They have only Akka. But girls have mothers" For a moment Gouthami was stumped. But after thinking she again asked "But then how come Shekhar who is also a boy has mother?" This was a difficult one but Vikram always thought ahead and so he immediately said "It is like this Gouthami, some boys have mothers and others have Akka" and I could not but feel sorry for Vikram who did not even remember his own mother.

Gouthami went to the same school as Vikram and since Vikram was a task master he would not allow a single day of leave. He would never miss any school and he would not let Gouthami miss the school too. Once when her mother Manikyam came from Anakapalle, Gouthami decided to skip her school and she began complaining that she was suffering from stomachache as soon as she woke up. Even before Manikyam could sympathize with Gouthami, Vikram told Manikyam "Your daughter is not having any ache in stomach. This is all a ruse to skip her school. After all no one can see the pain in stomach and that is why she is complaining of stomach ache. This is all a drama so don't pamper her". He then shouted to Gouthami to come along with him to the school. He was a drill master and a dictator for Gouthami and Gouthami would meekly follow him. Both studied very hard and were good in their studies. But Gouthami was more interested in many other activities particularly in movies and movie songs. Her favorite heroine was Savitri, a heart throb of millions of Andhra movie goers. She often compared her features with Savitri and would tell everyone that she looked like Savitri and then Chinna Babu would make a joke of her appearances and make her cry. But this would not deter her from what she believed. She was fun to be with and was always curious about many things and was a great help to me calling me "'Pinni' want any help?" Even today I find myself closest to Gouthami because of those old associations.

Manikyam's Illness

Manikyam was living in Anakapalle so she would come to our place every now and then since Anakapalle was just three hours by train and was well connected with many private buses plying between these two places. Since 1960 Manikyam frequently suffered bouts of heavy coughing accompanied by fever. In 1962, our family doctor an homeopath Dr, Sambhayya saw that his medicines was not helping her, he advised my father to get a chest X – Ray and sputum analysis and these tests confirmed that Manikyam was suffering from Tuberculosis of lungs. My father was very much concerned and he sent her to Madras for further consultations with experts in the field. Luckily, my uncle Abbulu Pedda Nanna garu and my father's brother Babayya were living in Madras at that time. Manikyam stayed with my mother's sister Doddamma and Peddananna garu and they took her to the consultant. After a thorough examination the consultant felt that she would require a surgical operation to remove the infected tissues. Once she knew about the nature of her infection, she was very particular that she remained in isolation and kept every item of hers away from others in the house so that the disease is not spread. Initially she was reluctant to stay with my uncle Babayya as he had so many young children and they were at an age more likely to be affected, but then one day Babayya's daughter and my first cousin Sarvamangala came to visit her in Peddananna garu's place and took her to their home telling her she will also feel equally free in their house. Manikyam always cherished her stay there with Babayya and Tocchhi and all our cousins. They treated her as if she was a normal person and did not let her feel bad that she stayed with them. The doctors prescribed her a schedule of treatment and advised her to return after two months for the surgery.

My father was concerned about Manikyam's surgical operation. Surgical operation was always looked upon with fear in those days as the medical world was not as advanced as today. My father refused to take any allopathic medicines for any illness and so news of her scheduled operation worried him considerably. My father had a trusted barber Adayya, a doctor Sambhayya, a trusted Muttayya, Pilla Ghanapathi garu, a priest who would perform Pooja on all our festivals and a trusted astrologer Bandi Siddhanti garu. He sent Muttayya with a message to Siddhanti garu to come for consultation and he came immediately when he received this request. Father requested Siddhanti garu to examine Manikyam's horoscope and explain about her health as she needed an operation. Siddhanti garu went through the horoscope once again and exclaimed this cannot be! There is no operation in her horoscope so there must be some misunderstanding in this matter. Father laughed and told him that Manikyam has already gone to Madras for her surgical operation and even the date has been fixed, but Siddhanti garu was firm that there was no surgery for Manikyam in her astrological chart and challenged my father. Imagine my father's surprise when after two days he received a telegram from my uncle that as Manikyam showed a good progress with the medicines there was no need for any surgery. Immediately my father hired a cycle rickshaw and went over to Siddhanti garu's home and told him of the news and profusely thanked him for winning the challenge.

Vikram has also become our family astrologer and I would like to describe a similar incident. Chitti's first cousin Rama's daughter was passing through a difficult phase in 2011 and she was admitted to ICU and the doctors told Rama that her survival was difficult and may not live that day. Rama conveyed this news to me in US and I immediately called Vikram and told him about this condition and asked him to study her astrological chart. Like Siddhanti garu, he also said Akka, there is no threat to her life and since she is under the influence of Saturn, this illness is manifested. According to my reading of her chart, she will become fairly normal after November, 2011, but I cannot say this now because doctors in a very famous hospital have given their verdict. I spoke to Rama end November and she told me her daughter was on the road to recovery and she was staying with her in Australia. I have developed so much confidence in astrology that I too have become like my father in this respect and consult Vikram every now and then.

Manikyam returned from Madras along with Pedda Bawa, a very happy and relieved person. I would like to record here that when Manikyam went to Madras for operation, her father-in-law Ishwarudu garu sent 20,000 rupees with his second son Chinnanna to the hospital which was never used, but that showed their concern also and that they too were prepared for an expensive treatment program. There was no need for this money since the operation was cancelled and Chinnanna returned back to Anakapalle. Manikyam and Pedda Bawa returned to Rajahmundry and thus began a long ordeal for Manikyam. She was administered streptomycin injections every day. She also had to take PAS tablets every day and eat a very nutritious food. Every day she would be given bread and butter and receive other nutritious foods from hotel as recommended by the doctors and dietician as this could not be prepared in our conservative home. All through this period, Gouthami did not trouble her mother and would sleep with me and was thus more mature for her age. I now had to look after Gouthami, Vikram and also Indira who was not even a teen.

Manikyam was given a separate room adjoining second bed room or an ante room we knew as Rajananna's room. She would not allow anyone to come beyond the ante room and I being rebellious I would always argue with her that nothing would happen to me if I came but she would hound me out if I ever crossed the boundary. I would bring her food received from the hotel and keep it in the anteroom and she would open the door only after I closed the door of the anteroom. She would clean her plates, glasses and all utensils she touched and then disinfect them with phenyl or Dettol so that germs of tuberculosis would be killed and we all will be safe. She was very methodical and particular and she would never waver from her self-imposed discipline and exile. The treatment was a very long one but she showed improvement every day and this was very promising for all of us. After one year of treatment in 1963 she was declared free from the disease but still she would keep a distance from every one to prevent any stray chance of infection particularly during my marriage in May the same year.

Manikyam the Marriage Counselor:

Manikyam occupied a place of senior advisor in our home after our mother died and father always looked at her for her advice. In 1961, when I was sixteen my education was stopped after I completed my matriculation. Fixing my marriage at the earliest became a very important objective for both Manikyam and my father. Any amount of persuasion or tantrums from me was not helpful and I had to accept their collective decision. I was dark and so many of my own close relatives would be describing me as black and this would wean away good prospects. This worried both of them. Manikyam was a strict task master and she would not allow me read romantic stories printed in popular Telugu weekly like Andhra Prabha, Andhra Patrika or Andhra Bhoomi for fear of getting corrupted. I would fight tooth and nail with her and tell her if these periodicals were good for them why not for me? Why should I only read Chandamama? But she had so much of power that her wish became a law to me. I would not lie or deceive to any one so I followed Manikyam's instructions to the letter.

My father invited his trusted Siddhanti garu once again for consultation based on astrological charts about my future and inquired if I would ever get a suitable match after all. My father developed a very high respect for his prediction after he proved correct regarding Manikyam. He looked at my chart and told my father to stop searching for a groom for this girl. In fact a bridegroom will contact us directly. My father laughed and told him I have already been rejected by a number of prospects without even seeing and here you are saying the groom would approach us directly for her hand! It sounds like a joke to me. Once again Siddhanti garu challenged my father and my father left at that. One fine morning we received a letter from Ramam Mavayya in Bombay inquiring if my father would be amenable to marry me with his second son Chitti. This was a proposal just like Siddhanti garu had predicted. Manikyam was leaning towards the match, but my brother Pedda Babu was against the match. He said Chitti and their whole family are short tempered and we should not agree for the match under any circumstances. Manikyam also agreed that this was true and that these guys are all very short tempered and this will only hurt our Sarvamangala so why not wait to see if some better proposal comes along. How can we send Sarvamangala to such a far off place like Bombay? As coincidence would have it Siddhanti garu again stopped by couple of days after we received this proposal and so father put our dilemma to him. He looked at both the horoscopes and told my father we should not hesitate in accepting the proposal and that I will be very happy and have a very bright future. This tilted the balance in favor of my marriage with Chitti and here I am.

It is not that I was not consulted but how could I say what I wanted and so I left it to Manikyam and father to decide. I had nothing against Chitti, but then I was not very keen on marriage since I wanted to devote my life to service and become a teacher or a registered nurse so that I continue to look after Vikram and also be there for my father. I know nobody would support my remaining a single person in those days. This is true even today with so many advances in culture people still believe in the same age old values. A girl should be married off and this is the responsibility of a parent and so my thoughts remained with me and no one knew them as I had not told anyone. What is the use, any way my wishes will be overruled by everyone including Pedda Babu?

Manikyam & Hindi:

Manikyam was always full of ideas and with all the time available to her, she began to examine how she could employ her time meaningfully. Just then my sister Bhanumati told her that she completed the highest course in Hindi conducted by Dakshina Bharat Hindi Prachar Sabha and thus began pursuit of Hindi by Manikyam. She requested Bhanumati to send her the books of the earlier grades and Bhanumati would send them to her. It goes to the credit of Bhanumati that she kept books in good conditions even after reading them so that Manikyam received them as good as new. Here I would like to mention that married life of Manikyam was not very pleasant. No one drank coffee except Manikyam and so it would become a chore to bring coffee powder just for Manikyam and Manikyam who was so pampered by her grandfather could not live without coffee! The family was very orthodox and religious and they were required to cook meals in 'Madi' and no one without Madi could enter the kitchen. Women would take bath and cook meals in wet clothes. They did not have a municipal water supply and all the water for cooking etc had to be drawn from the well in the backyard and this water was salty. A visitor in Anakapalle could not quench his thirst with this water. She had to depend for all her requirements on the whims of my Bawa garu who would oftentimes delay purchasing. Generally flow of money for such personal accomplishments was poor. So how could Manikyam ask money for buying books for her studies and if Bhanumati had not given her these books free, even this wish of Manikyam would have remained unfulfilled.

I became a tutor for Manikyam. In our school, Hindi was a compulsory subject and every one had to pass Hindi in their matriculation or else they would not pass the exam. I would sit with her and teach her how to write the script and she would copy and learn the alphabets and then she would read our text books. Her journey began in this manner and she would save some money from what her husband would give her during his visits and pay for the tuition and examination. She started with 'Pravesh' or entry grade and completed 'Vidwan' equaling Masters in Hindi. Then what? She could not look for a job as this was unheard of in both our families. One of her old school mate had come to visit her in Rajahmundry and she suggested that she could take lessons making baskets of plastic wires and beads that had become very popular in those days. She will not have to pay any fees since the shopkeeper would come to the house and give her the design and beads to weave the baskets and they would come and collect the finished work and pay for the job done. Manikyam wanted to save what she earned this way and become independent but this thought too was short lived. My father could have helped Manikyam financially, but he did not wish to stop her from any of these activities as he liked industrious people and then Manikyam was his pet too.

Most interesting activity of Manikyam was that after reading about Gandhiji, she began weaving yarn on Charkha and I feel proud to say that she could weave a yarn proficiently from the roll of cotton.

But then again the same dilemma, what could she do with the yarn as she cannot go out and sell the yarn and who will purchase her the replenishment of cotton roll? Like all her ventures this also failed. Did Manikyam inherit my grandfather Abbayi garu's genes of entrepreneurship and failed just like him? Is this believable today? I do not think her children would believe nor would like to know this part of their history. All the three of them are well educated and could and did earn independently. Manikyam would be very happy to see all her daughters well settled and her grandchildren doing very well. Most importantly none of her children live in Anakapalle.

In this respect Manikyam was like our mother. She was not born in city but she had all the habits of a city bred person including her schooling in a convent school. She too began her life in a highly conservative family but no one supported her.

In May, 1963, I married Chitti and Manikyam participated in the ceremony from a distance only since she did not want to mix with people though declared cured of the disease. She returned to Anakapalle and began her post treatment life in the same old conservative joint family and the same old set up. We were all very concerned and we hoped Bawa garu would find some opportunity of working away from Anakapalle, but then he was not qualified for any professional positions. My father-in-law, Ramam Mavayya garu had joined his cousin Karra Annappa Tata garu and set up a cork factory in Visakhapatnam and so he suggested to my father they would welcome Chenulu in their team and so Bawa garu went to Visakhapatnam. Since they were staying in a hotel he also joined them in Hotel Ooty and this started their differences and final breakdown of the team and he returned back to Anakapalle. His side of the story was that they were expecting him to invest in the company and he would not do so and that was the reason for the breakdown of relationship. The fact remained that Manikyam continued to stay in Anakapalle.

In October, 1964 my father shifted his residence from Rajahmundry to Kakinada by selling the Danavaya Peta house as both Pedda Babu and Chinna Babu began their professional studies there. Pedda Babu was doing his medicine in Rangaraya Medical College and Chinna Babu doing his engineering in Kakinada Engineering College. It would be cheaper to have them both stay at home than paying their hostel expenses and moreover, father wanted to keep an eye on Chinna Babu's extracurricular activities like participating in plays or fulfill his ambition of becoming a movie star. My father was afraid that he will be distracted from the course by his friends. Not that this helped as father could not keep Chinna Babu in control and he continued to stray. Indira, Trivikram and Gouthami continued their studies in Kakinada; Indira did her PUC from PR College.

Gouthami

Gouthami remained with us as a part of our family and our relations became closer. In 1965, when my father was staying in Vignana Bhavan, I came for the delivery of my second child who was still born. Chitti also came to drop me and was planning to visit Visakhapatnam by an early morning bus. He kept his shirt and pant ready for his trip on a hanger and in the night, Gouthami saw someone stealing the dress along with the hanger. But she was so scared she shut her eyes tightly out of fear. The incident was funny and every one began laughing and asked why she did not shout 'thief'. Next day Chitti went to Visakhapatnam as if nothing had happened; for him this happened a second time. A few months earlier, he lost all his formal clothes he had kept on a hanger in their house in Bombay. This happened in broad day light and Ramam Mavayya was in the house! So this was one more incident for Chitti of losing his clothes. In fact Chinna Babu made this a joke about Chitti and he would warn everyone to take care of their belongings as Chitti's friend from Bombay is transferred here.

Gouthami stayed with us in Kakinada till she completed her 10th examination in 1971 and she returned back to Anakapalle to be with her parents. Her association with us for all these years has left many pleasant memories and though Manikyam was also blessed with three more children, Gouthami remained very close to me. Gouthami went back to Anakapalle, a place where it was not considered essential for girls in the family to study. What would the girls do with their degrees? As I had observed earlier, it was not a very bright option even for boys, so how can it be different for girls? But both Manikyam and Gouthami stuck to their guns and Gouthami went to Junior college in Anakapalle and completed her Intermediate examination. That was the end of her education in Anakapalle as you had to go to Visakhapatnam for higher studies. But Gouthami was firm. She continued her studies privately and completed her Bachelors and finally her Masters in Telugu. She inherited our tradition of not accepting everything quietly.

She was married to Veerabhadra Rao or known to all as Babu Rao, oldest son of Sista Suryanarayana Rao garu of Hyderabad on August, 7, 1981. The marriage was held in Hyderabad at the request of Suryanarayana garu as they wanted to share the occasion with all their friends and relatives who lived mostly in Hyderabad. It would be difficult for these people to travel to Anakapalle and the convention of holding wedding in brides home was not followed. They were expecting more than 1000 guests for dinner and I can vouch that the function was indeed attended by not less than one thousand guests and it was done in a very grand style. This was the first time we were requested to arrange a buffet dinner, a first in our family and in a cost cutting effort we did not hire professional caterers and the job was done by each of us. It is no wonder that we do not remember seeing many of the important events during the wedding. Babu Rao became more my son-in-law than Manikyam's and he became as much a part of our family as Gouthami is.

Pedda Babu gets the credit for the entire wedding who through his contacts in Osmania Hospital not only found the address of

Suryanarayana garu, he initiated marriage talks with them and had arranged for a formal meeting to see Gouthami in their house in Hyderabad. Babu Rao liked Gouthami and declared that there will be no dowry which in itself was a giant step in those days. Even today when dowry system is abolished by the Indian Government, the system is still widely prevalent not only in our community but also throughout India.

Both Manikyam and Bawa garu approved of the match since Babu Rao was already employed in State Bank of Hyderabad in a permanent position. However, the job was transferable and so Gouthami and Babu Rao will be posted anywhere in Andhra Pradesh and they may not remain in one single location. Their only condition or demand that there should be a buffet dinner for one thousand guests became a minor issue. My father was against this as this as this was not traditional style and he compared it as 'buffalo dinner' where you let loose the animals after setting up their meal in the barn. Further there was greater chance of mixing and cross contamination of the foods. He preferred the conventional method of every one sitting either on floor or on table and food is served individually. Of course he conceded to the proposal on a condition that elders in the family are served on table separately.

I never knew that Pedda Babu was extremely cost conscious and he began the cost cutting operations by renting the dinner ware from a tent house as a first step. Since there was no cleaning staff, it became our responsibility to provide clean plates and Chitti along with his two nephews Diwakar and Prabhakar executed the marathon task. They were joined later by Indira's husband Babi who had just gotten off from the train. Marriage was a grand success, but none of us were there to watch the ceremony fully as we were behind the scenes most of the time.

Deepthi: Gouthami and Babu Rao have two children the oldest son Vamshi and the younger daughter Deepthi and both are very intelligent and smart. Deepthi studied Pharmaceutical and graduated from Osmania University. Vamshi became a software engineer and worked in Mysore in a premier software institute Infosys and has come to the USA twice on projects. Deepthi completed her Bachelors in Pharmacy and then began applying for higher studies in the US and this is where history repeated itself. Her parents did not want her to go to US unless she was married and I had to tell Gouthami that almost twenty years earlier, I had to fight her parents to allow Gouthami complete her Masters. How come she is now reluctant in sending Deepthi abroad for higher studies? Since money is not a problem why not let her come to US and finish her studies? My son Dinkar agreed to support her if needed on her Visa documents and we became her guardians in the US. She came to the US and before settling in New York stayed with us for a short period and like her mother she too became very much attached to us. She joined St. John School in Queens in New York and completed her Masters in Pharmacy. On 16th May, 2010, we all participated in the graduation ceremony of Deepthi at St. John University in New York where we met her fiancé Madhav.

Deepthi was married to Madhav on 28th August, 2010 and I did not miss the opportunity and attended her wedding in Hyderabad. We had just passed through a very traumatic experience of sudden death of Kamalakar and we were very much subdued in participating in the fun and frolic. I could not see the sad face of Durga who lost her very favorite brother. Once married, Deepthi came back to the US and after a short stint at her old place in New York, she decided to migrate to Canada and be with Madhav Kumar Sambhu and that is where she is now. Deepthi and Madhav gave us a pleasant surprise when they drove to New Jersey to attend golden jubilee of our wedding on 4th May, 2013.

Vamshi:

Vamshi joined Infosys in Mysore in 2004 after completing his B.Tech in software engineering. He came to meet me and Chitti in 2006 when we went to Bangalore before proceeding to Manipal to meet Chenulu's mother and I was surprised how tall he had grown and looked so smart and handsome. Once working at Infosys he was deputed to the US on a project and I met him again when Deepthi brought him for Christmas. In 2011, he joined another company and is now posted at Hyderabad. The best part is that even Gouthami and Baburao are moving to Hyderabad as he is posted back to Hyderabad office. Adding to the series of happy events, Vamshi was married on 5th May, 2011. I could not attend the wedding as I was in the US, but I was so glad that Gouthami and Baburao fulfilled all their duties to their children and now they can look forward to a very happy retired life. My only regret was that Pedda Bawa garu missed these events but he must be blessings them from somewhere above in the heaven.

Indira's 60th Birthday: Vamshi's wedding brought all our relations very close and almost every one attended the ceremony. Pedda Babu did not come but Sita came for the wedding but could not stay long due to excessive heat in Hyderabad. Chinna Babu and Lakshmi came and they too did not remain for the entire function. Gouthami has been very close to our family more than her other sisters and this was evidenced by the special party she arranged for 60th birthday of Indira just a short time before Vamshi's wedding reception and this was a very big surprise for me when Indira told me next day on phone. All the three sisters presented Indira with a ring. I remember Gouthami and her sisters had given me and Chitti rings on my 60th Birthday when we both were in Hyderabad. It is their tradition since they had earlier given similar rings to Bhanumati and Chinna Bawa Garu.

Both Gouthami and Baburao are very forward thinking and though they are not expected to present anything to their daughter-in-law, they presented her with a gold belt or 'Vaddanam' and with the price of gold sky rocketing this could not have been cheap.

Tradition:

Gouthami had decided at the time of Deepthi's wedding that every one of the sisters and near relations would wear traditional white printed saree on "Nagavalli" day like they used to wear in the olden days. Lately, either due to time constraints or non-availability of white sarees, women began to avoid following this tradition. She decided to follow the same tradition for Vamshi's wedding. She purchased white printed sarees for all her sisters and her first cousins and presented them before wedding so that they could get matching blouses etc. and be ready for Nagavalli. Every one wore the traditional white printed sarees on Nagavalli and thus making it a memorable event. Hope others also follow the traditions where possible. I am not very conservative especially after my marriage since none in Bombay believed in old traditions. So when I saw these photographs I was very thrilled and I complimented Gouthami.

Lakshmi Prasanna:

On 22nd December, 1968 Manikyam gave birth to a baby girl in Kakinada now that we moved to Kakinada and she was named after her mother-in-law as Lakshmi Prasanna or Lakshmi in short and she was a very fair child with very attractive features. She was not much of a crier. Lakshmi was a fun for all and Indira, Gouthami and Vikram flocked around her. Manikyam was thankfully better now and she was not showing any signs of her old illness and this event brought her plenty of happiness. By the time she was six months old Manikyam went to Anakapalle with her. I did not have much contact with her during her childhood and there is very little that I could recollect particularly since I was living in Bombay.

In 1970 Chitti was transferred to Visakhapatnam and I came early in March to attend Indira's wedding and Chitti went back to Bombay and returned to Visakhapatnam later in May. He rented an apartment in Pedda Waltair near Andhra University and I moved to our new house. I would visit Anakapalle now and then and so would meet all of them there. In September, 1971, I came to Kakinada for delivery and on 22nd September, Dinkar was born in a Nursing home and I had to stay there for at least three days. Lakshmi was very intent that her mother Manikyam also goes to hospital and brings one brother for her too. No one took her seriously but one day she left the house to go over to the hospital to ask her mother who was with me to pick up one brother for her. Our next door neighbor's daughter Vijaya Lakshmi saw her going and asked her where she was going. Lakshmi told her without any hesitation that she was going to the Hospital and ask mother to bring one brother for her too like Pinni. Vijaya Lakshmi looked at this not even three years old child and said OK and went into her house. Manikyam returned home after my meals and when she did not see Lakshmi they began to call her out and Vijaya Lakshmi came out and told her that she had gone to hospital to bring one brother for her and everyone looked at her in surprise. Manikyam took the same cycle rickshaw and went in search for Lakshmi. Our house was on this side of Railway track and the hospital was on the other side in the down town and every one was worried as to where would she go she was so small. Luckily, there was a small pan shop and the owner saw this child going towards train station and asked her where was she going and she told him that she was going to the hospital to bring one brother for her. The owner understood the situation and he told her to rest a few minutes and gave her soda and a couple of chocolates and entertained her hoping her parents would come by. Lakshmi was a talkative kid and she went on talking to him and by that time Manikyam saw her and Lakshmi came back safely. One dreads the thought of what would have happened to Lakshmi if the shop keeper did not stop her.

I returned from Hospital and Dinkar was kept in a crib. Any time infant Dinkar would cry, Lakshmi would rush to him asking him what happened (Emaynidamma?) and every one was concerned that if she goes first what would she do? Chinna Babu immediately told her "Lakshmi, Dinkar is asking you not to come near him OK."

One more important feature of this baby Lakshmi is that she would always volunteer to bring water for anyone in the house. As soon as the person finished drinking his water she would sit down and demand that he or she should also bring water for her. It was fun to watch and after that very few people would ask her for water or anything else. We had a small flower bed of red marigold flowers "Banti Puvvu" and the flowers would bloom in very large numbers. Lakshmi collected all the flowers and break up all the petals first thing in the morning. Once I saw the petals all strewn around and I asked "Lakshmi, who has done this?" "Who else Pinni, your son Dinkar has done this." Mind you Dinkar was just a few days old infant at that time and it beats me why she did this. Lakshmi was fun and very quick witted baby even at that age.

Lakshmi was a brilliant student and she passed her matriculation by topping the district and she received commendation from the then Chief Minister of Andhra Pradesh and the super star of the Telugu movies N. T. Rama Rao. I do not know if this has been kept safely by Lakshmi. She was a very bright student and was excellent in her studies. She was keen to study engineering, but then the engineering college was in Visakhapatnam and so she graduated in Commerce instead. She was not only bright in her studies but was also very tactful in dealing with every one and even today Dinkar would maintain that she was a real IAS material and had she appeared for the examination she would have become the first District Collector in our family. In 1985 Manikyam died of brain hemorrhage and this made all her children self-reliant. Lakshmi was the oldest sibling since Gouthami was living in Hyderabad after her marriage in 1981 and so she would cook their meals first thing in the morning and would go to her college. According to Lakshmi her fathers' oldest sister Suri Attayya helped her during this difficult period.

In that large house Lakshmi, Yagneshwar and Kamala lived all by themselves and would have been an imposing experience for any one, but not for these three. They would keep the house in good order and if the servant maid did not come they would share that job also. Suddenly all the three of them became matured before their time. They probably did not enjoy their childhood like everyone else.

She completed her graduation in 1988 and in the same year she was married to Kashi Vishwanath of Hyderabad. His family lived in Narasipatnam but he went to Hyderabad for studies and was posted as Commercial Tax Office in Hyderabad as soon as he completed his graduation. Her studies were permanently interrupted and she became a responsible housewife and became mother of two sons Sharat and Hemant and moved from one district to another district with Vishwanath till her children reached higher classes. She then decided she will stay in Hyderabad till their education is completed and will not follow her husband and this was a wise decision. Her Oldest son Sharat is now doing his engineering in Birla Institute of Technology (BITS) opened recently in Hyderabad. The second son Hemant is doing his graduation in Commerce at Hyderabad. Now that both her sons are well set she appeared in public competitive examination for government service and was successful and was given her first posting in Anakapalle. She now works for the State Government in Hyderabad. Dinkar was right she was a material for a District Collector and even after discontinuing her studies for so many years she successfully competed and was selected for the Government service!

Yagneshwar:

One year after Dinkar was born, like Lakshmi said, she did bring a brother back from the same Hospital in Kakinada where Dinkar was born. Manikyam gave birth to her son Yagneshwar on 9th October, 1972. I do not remember much about him as in 1974 Chitti was transferred back to Bombay and I went back there so once again I miss his childhood activities. We would visit Anakapalle once in a while but there was not much connection during these short visits. He was also a very brilliant and hardworking boy and was very good in mathematics and he joined an engineering college in Vijayawada but he did not stay there even one full year and left the studies. It is possible that he could not tolerate the ragging over there though this part of his life he has not shared with anyone. In the meantime he received an opportunity of internship with the Post and Telegraph department and so he was living all alone in Kovvuru. He had passed through a stage of depression immediately after Manikyam died and he hoped that the work would help him overcome his feeling of loneliness, but then he suffered a massive sun stroke and died during night from dehydration. His landlord contacted Bawa garu and they all came there for the final rites. Yagneshwar was Manikyam's pet child and she would not let anyone hurt him and she would pamper him all she could but she could not have foreseen this event in his life. It was a big shock for Pedda Bawa and he told me that it was their obsession with the anniversaries, that he now does not have an heir to observe his own anniversary after his death.

Kamala

Four years after Yagneshwar was born, Manikyam gave birth to one more daughter on 19th January, 1976 in Kakinada as usual. Manikyam was becoming weak every year and the frequent child births did not help her any. Kamala was her father's pet and for a change Bawa would take Kamala to drop her at the school. He always wore Dhoti and an under shirt and Kamala would not let him come to her school. She would ask him to return back when the school was near because he looked more like a grandfather to her than a father. He would laugh and would not accompany to the school but drop her away from the school. Kamala thus was always demanding and she got what she wanted.

Bawa would tell me all this about Kamala as he was more free with me. Bawa would call her Kamala Rao as he was so fond of her. She was his right hand at all times and she would go willingly to neighboring shops for medicines for him or anyone in the family.

She was a fighter and there were frequent fights between Kamala and Yagneshwar and she would even argue with elders. I remember when I asked my Bawa for money before Gnanu's wedding in Anakapalle. She objected and argued with me that why should her father give money to me. "After all you have only one daughter and she is getting married whereas my father has to think of two daughters to marry, me and my sister." She was mature even at that age and was very proud. However, as we were in Bombay and it was generally difficult to visit Anakapalle and I became more distant to the children. I became closer to them during Gnanu's wedding and during my short stay in Anakapalle when I was there helping Manikyam for Gouthami's delivery.

In 1988 after Lakshmi was married, we decided to bring Kamala with me and bring her up in Bombay. The house in Anakapalle was very large and no one would know from outside if someone had attacked her in the backyard and was not secure. As long as the house was full with people it was OK but for only two people to live in that house was like living in a haunted house. In Bombay, Kamala found herself in a totally different environment and was afraid to live with us and she decided to return back to Anakapalle. I feel the loss was mine as I did not get an opportunity of knowing her better. She completed her matriculation in Anakapalle living in that house fearlessly and then she continued to complete her graduation in the Women's college in Anakapalle because by that time Pedda Bawa reconciled to give higher education for the girls. Otherwise also Kamala would have fought with her father to achieve her goal. Like her other sisters she too is very brilliant and completed her degree in first division. She would have studied further, but due to untimely demise of Yagneshwar, she became lonely and everyone felt it would be better to find a suitable match for her.

Vishwanath began his efforts to this end and found a suitable match for kamala. He knew Balaparameshwara Rao, the youngest son of Upadhyayula Siddhanti garu, Deputy Commissioner of Income Tax and introduced him to Kamala and he liked her. He immediately fixed up the match by arranging a meeting with his parents and marriage of Kamala was performed on 20th August, 1997 in Vijayawada when she was just twenty one. Bala is a software engineer and has been in many important positions and was in the USA on a short project from 1998 at the time of delivery and Kamala also joined him later along with Baby Siddhu for one year and then moved back to Hyderabad. They are blessed with a son named Siddhu after his grandfather Siddhanti garu and a daughter Manipriya named after Manikyam and they are doing well there.

Siddhu: Siddhu was born on 21st May, 1998 in Vijayawada at Gouthami's place and Gouthami looked after Kamala as if Manikyam was there and Pedda Bawa was also there to help Gouthami. Both Indira and I went over to Vijayawada before Siddhu was born to meet Kamala. Mind you in the month of May it is superhot in Vijayawada. We both got onto an air conditioned luxury bus and hoped for a comfortable travel. But in that sweltering heat, the driver switched off the a/c as soon as we got in. He explained that since we were passing through the city limits he will start once he crosses the city while driving on the highway. He started the a/c as promised and we dozed off to a fairly sound sleep but again switched off the a/c for much of the route to Vijayawada. Both Indira and I began to argue with the driver. Other passengers also joined us and finally the driver reluctantly started the a/c. Other passengers explained that this was a regular practice with the buses, even though they charge more for the facility; they shut off the a/c most of the time.

Siddhu has an inquiring nature and he went through these memoirs so closely that if he had not corrected, I may have continued to use wrong name for Bala. On 20th May, 2011 just one day before his 13th birthday, Bala and Kamala performed Yagnopavitam ceremony for Siddhu at Aduru at his grandfather Siddhanti garu's place. I have received such wonderful reports of the function that I am regretting why did I come to the US. Am I to miss all these family functions? Any way grandfather Siddhanti garu celebrated this occasion in a very grand manner and every one of my family namely Indira, Kalyan and Kavita, Vikram with Durga, Chinna Babu with Lakshmi and Pedda Babu with Sita from Bangalore made it for the occasion. Representing Pedda Bawa, Babili and Bhaskar Rao and two others had come from Anakapalle for the function presenting young Siddhu with a sliver Pooja plate and clothes for Kamala and Bala from her father's side. Other than Pedda Babu and Sita all the others from Hyderabad travelled in the same train and had a wonderful time. Siddhanti garu saw to it that everyone was well received and they did not face any inconvenience. The ceremony was done in a very proper manner and Siddhu did not show any annoyance with the long function.

Kamala's sister Gouthami and Lakshmi came with their spouses and all their children. Gouthami and Baburao came with Deepthi and newly married couple Vamshi and Madhavi whereas Lakshmi came with her two sons. It must be mentioned here that Gouthami, Lakshmi and Kamala have a very close knit relationship. As usual the climate was very hot and every effort was made by Siddhanti garu to see that all those coming for the function did not feel uncomfortable. It rained immediately after the actual muhurtam of function was over and the weather cooled down appreciably giving a relief from daunting heat and was pleasant during return journey.

Kamala's daughter Manipriya was born on 3rd December, 2003 in Hyderabad. She has been named as Manipriya after her maternal grandmother and my sister Manikyam.

Manikyam and Bawagaru:

Any day and any time I think of Manikyam I feel she suffered unjustifiably and should I say only Bawa garu is responsible? Or was it due to cultural differences? Here is a lot of difference between families on our side from those living east of Rajahmundry. Gnanamba Attayya would say bring a daughter from there and she will be a great help but do not give your daughter there as she will not adjust and that precisely what happened. As mentioned before Manikyam was pampered to a fault by her grandfather. Drinking coffee became her most important morning ritual throughout her life and this also became her lasting desire. Like my mother who also was addicted to morning coffee and came to a conservative family in Rajahmundry and Manikyam also went to another conservative family but with a difference. My mother had father's support while Manikyam did not get support from Bawa garu. In Anakapalle her father-in-law Ishwarudu garu and the entire house hold was very conservative and no one would drink coffee or tea in the morning. The morning bath would be followed by morning Sandhya Vandanam that itself would run for almost till noon. In spite of all this Manikyam was able to make and drink coffee just for herself and Bawa garu would bring coffee powder and sugar and other things for her to make her own coffee. But not every time since while Manikyam needed coffee none in her in-laws house drank coffee and probably Bawa garu was bound by the code of their family. In the joint family maintained by Ishwarudu garu, Manikyam was living with Bawa garu, parents-in-law, sisters-in-law who were married but living very close by and every one was very dominant and Manikyam was cowed down. Bawagaru also did not have free money in his hands and he had to ask his father for any such purchases and he was not comfortable in asking. In short the whole climate there was so male dominated that thinking about wife's comfort was the last thing on their list. Whatever may be merit of joint family system, Manikyam did not reap the benefits. Bawa garu's brothers set up separate family homes close by and they had more freedom and for reasons known to Bawa garu he always wanted to be part of the joint family.

Making matters worse, there was a strict discipline and every one followed 'Madi' and so almost till after noon hours every one wore wet clothes and have their meals almost at 2.00 pm when all the children and men folk finished their meals that the women would sit down to eat what remained behind. Looking at my life and also those of everyone else currently I think not only Manikyam suffered, even Bawagaru did not enjoy. If they both walked together, Manikyam would be hundred feet behind Bawagaru and so they did not even talk. I do not remember them going out for movies or for any sight-seeing all by themselves. The family was wealthy but there was no money for their own personal enjoyment. In the case of Manikyam drinking coffee was a marathon effort and she could not win all the times. I have lived in Bombay most of my adult life and so I do not know if these archaic practices of Madi are still prevalent in our conservative houses in villages or even there they have stopped and people have become more liberal. I lived in Rajahmundry in very sheltered conditions. Things were vastly different in Bombay where no one believed in Madi so I have no personal knowledge of how an orthodox conservative family lived in villages then or now. I know this description of disciplined conservative system in Anakapalle may not be known to all and most of the readers of this generation may not believe to be real unless they have someone in their own family who endured them.

When Manikyam was living with us during her illness, Gouthami also stayed with us till completion of her SSC. My father lived in perpetual debt and since Manikyam knew about these financial difficulties she would hesitate asking any money from him. This changed her nature and she became very frugal and she would spend money only when unavoidable. She would buy a frock or a gown that was at least two sizes larger for Gouthami so that whichever way she would grow meaning either in height or in weight, the frock would still fit her for a number of years. Only Gouthami probably would wear those without any complaint as she knew and understood her mother's situation. I was just five years old when Manikyam was married but from that time on I would argue with Bawagaru on every issue whether it was for his visits to us on festivals or his examinations that he did not succeed or his not trying to seek a job. He would always smile and give me pleasant answers. When I would pester him for getting a job he once laughed and said Sarvamangala "I will certainly work as a farm hand in your farm". I do not know why but he liked me and liked to hear what I said to him. This may have encouraged me and even after death of Manikyam I often took liberty to scold him. He was never short of money but by nature he would not part with money willingly. But then he was brought up in a peculiar type of conservative family. Manikyam never got benefit of any of his wealth and neither did Bawagaru. Both of them probably loved each other but then their expression of affection was different.

Manikyam spent her happiest moments in life was when she lived in one of their houses in Gandhi Nagar in Anakapalle away from the joint family in Vedula Street. The house had a small kitchen garden where they would grow vegetables and fruits. They bought all they needed including milk from vendors at the door and Manikyam felt as if she was in Rajahmundry. Her father-in-law had a number of properties and there would be a ritual to partition these by drawing chits and every time he drew his chit, Bawagaru got the ancestral house in Vedula Street and others would object and this became a messy business. I argued with Bawagaru that the whole partition was manipulated otherwise how is it that he received the ancestral house every time? I know even Bawagaru also believed the same but he would not express them to his father. Bawagaru lived in Gandhi Nagar house till the partition was finalized. But this happiness was short lived and this house went to the oldest son Peddanna and the ancestral house was once again inherited by Bawagaru and Manikyam and this time for good. It was not a very attractive house and the front porch and room was given on rent to a merchant and the back of the house was for living and this house was very dark as there were no windows. It was like a safe deposit vault and once you enter there was only one way out. Kitchen was far away from the main house, in the extension and food was cooked there on the stoves lit with fire wood. Manikyam was finding it difficult to breathe the smoke filled kitchen once again. Bawagaru did not apply for natural gas common to every house in Anakapalle for reasons best known to him. Value of the house appreciated over the years since the town grew around the place but not in Vedula Street. The famous Vedula Street remained same as built many years before and remains so even today. If a truck is parked on the street no other vehicle could pass around it including a cycle rickshaw. The street was a commerce street and during jaggery season, gud was sold bulk in truck loads, so there would be no movement of trucks unless they are fully loaded during this season.

In 1984 I came and stayed with Manikyam in Anakapalle as she needed help. Gouthami had come for delivery of her first child in July and I had to prepare for my daughter Gnanu's marriage that was to take place later in August in Anakapalle. I became close once again with Gouthami and Lakshmi but not with Yagneshwar and Kamala. I opened an account in a bank in Anakapalle to pay for all the groceries required for the wedding and thus help in sharing the expenses. On 25th July, 1984 Vamshi was born in the local nursing home and we were all thrilled and Manikyam was most happy looking after Gouthami and the young grandson. Gnanu's wedding was fixed on 8th August in a marriage hall in Anakapalle and slowly every one began trickling to Anakapalle some to participate in the marriage and some to join some of the rituals following birth of baby and so relations from Manikyam's side and those from Babu Rao side came to this house in Anakapalle and the house was full of guests and Manikyam was very happy that so many had come over to her house. This was the first function in this house after it was inherited by Manikyam and Bawa garu and it was last for Manikyam.

One year later Gouthami came again for delivery of her daughter Deepthi born on 18th October, 1985 again in local nursing home. I went to Anakapalle as Manikyam requested me to come and help her as she was feeling weak. I argued with her that why should I come every time to help you out and she made a deal that she will come to Bombay in return for delivery of Gnanu's children. I told her that she must recover her health and be strong for helping me out during the delivery of Gnanu. I believe she would have come to our house in Bombay if she had lived. But that was not to be. She was not strong by then and in fact she fainted on the eleventh day ceremony celebrating birth of the baby Deepthi.

She consulted a doctor who gave her medicines and advised her to drink plenty of coconut water. She brought medicine and took them as prescribed but she had forgotten about taking coconut water and when she requested, Bawagaru could not get good coconuts in Anakapalle and I was furious. Bawa garu's older brother Chinnanna was passing by the house and I asked him what sort of a town this is where even coconut water is not available for Manikyam. He was surprised and shocked and called a farm hand and asked him to bring coconuts from his farm and within an hour the farmhand returned with a basket full of coconuts and we gave water from one coconut every day. Vikram also came to Anakapalle at that time as he had some work in Rajahmundry. He saw the medicines she was taking and told us that these medicines should help and continue giving her coconut water. He was not a doctor but was aware about medicines. Attla Tadiya day is celebrated by making dosa's of different type and served with a sweet dish called Timmanam quite different from regular payasam. This falls one day before famous Karava Chowth day of North India. Vikram finished his dinner of Attulu (Dosa) and Timmanam early and rushed to catch his train in the evening and he was already late for Godavari Express which normally arrived punctually so he told Manikyam he will be back in another half an hour as he most likely will miss the train. But that day the train also came late and Vikram left for Rajahmundry.

I was inside the kitchen and making more Attulu (Dosas) for every one and Bawa garu had finished his share of the evening meal when I saw Lakshmi running frantically and I rushed to see what had happened. I saw Lakshmi washing the area where Manikyam vomited coffee she had taken earlier in the evening. I was angry with Lakshmi why did she not call me and she replied that I would get worried and so she did not call me. **I told her to remember that at such times she should call, shout, cry so that every one knows some thing is wrong.** I called Bhaskar Rao who lived nearby to take Manikyam to the doctor. The doctor, a different one from the earlier one, examined her and said there was nothing to worry and we should give her some pills which will make her drowsy and she will sleep. I slept next to Manikyam and felt the signs were not good but then I had no medical knowledge. I wanted to take Manikyam in a Taxi to Visakhapatnam to the hospital where she would get good treatment but as usual Bawa garu made a joke asking me if the doctor there would remove the severe pain in her head better than the doctor in Anakapalle. Manikyam was furious and told me she will go to Visakhapatnam next day at 10.00 in the morning whether he agrees or not.

I was tired after the day's work so I slept soundly but when I woke up in the night I saw that Manikyam was frothing from the mouth and I called out Bawa garu to see and he called out by her name but she did not respond but we thought she had looked at us and we decided to let her sleep. We tried to wake up Manikyam in the morning but she would not get up and so we called a cycle rickshaw and took her to the doctor. I kept her head on my shoulders and I thought I could feel her breathing and we took her into the dispensary and doctor informed us that she had died just a few minutes earlier and coincidentally the time was 10 in the morning as she had told me previous day only her destination was different. Is this what Manikyam was thinking when she used those prophetic words? Vikram was so upset that he came back and began crying and said had he remained behind he would have been able to get better medical assistance and may have even taken her to Visakhapatnam. Yagneshwar was very young and since did not have 'Upanayanam' he was not authorized to perform the final rites to his mother and so Bawagaru performed the final rites on his behalf. Although Yagneshwar was 14 years old surprisingly no one in that conservative household even thought of performing his Upanayanam ceremony. This surprised many since a Brahmin boy must have "Upanayanam" as soon as he reaches the age of eight. Since it was delayed, it was proposed to perform the same during their daughter Gouthami's wedding. But Gouthami was married in Hyderabad when he was just 11 years old so the ceremony was not performed there too. It was decided at that time the function of Upanayanam will now be performed during Lakshmi's wedding and Manikyam was looking forward to this occasion. But she died before Lakshmi's marriage and so Yagneshwar could not perform the final rites of his mother.

Manikyam's death showed that there was a degree of lethargy or unconcern from every one including members of my own family. When she visited Hyderabad in 1983, she looked so pale and weak that everyone was asking her to get a medical checkup. But she had a great trust in Pedda Babu's ability as a doctor so she said she would go to Bangalore and get his opinion but then Pedda Babu did not get an opportunity of inviting her to Bangalore for the medical checkup. She had been complaining of constant headache and she felt as if someone was pounding inside her head and this probably was a signal for cerebral hemorrhage, but then why no one thought about it? My brother is a doctor of repute and every one in my family is so knowledgeable that we should have at least considered getting her headache investigated. This could not have been done in Anakapalle as facilities were not there at that time but why not in Hyderabad when she visited. To add to her woes my father died in October, 1984 and this was the last straw for Manikyam and she felt orphaned. We believe Manikyam began losing interest in her life soon after my father died. She felt helpless. There was no one to support her now.

I had been requesting Bawa garu to get a replacement gas cylinder as the one in the house was empty since smoke from coal affected health of Manikyam, but the refill cylinder did not come. But very next day after her cremation, Lakshmi called me to inform me that two new gas cylinders have come and I burst out in anger and shouted to return those cylinders back as we can now cook using even fire wood as we did when Manikyam was alive. "Return the gas cylinders I shouted from inside." Lakshmi stood petrified looking at me as she had not seen me angry before. We finished all the functions and prayed for the peace of her soul. But on 10th day when crows were offered Pindam, they did not come indicating that her soul demanded something from those around. Vikram realized it and declared that he will personally see that Yagneshwar completes his studies by taking him to Hyderabad away from the influence of Anakapalle and that he will personally tutor him. Only then the crows came to eat the 'Pindam'. Is it possible that crows can interpret the human language to the spirits of the dead and become the carrier of message to the departed soul? Positively yes! I am convinced and it has been noticed time and again and the promises given to souls are never broken and Vikram kept his promise he had given to Manikyam. In fact Chitti's cousin in Hyderabad Situ would tell us the stories of how she would talk to crows when she lived in Madras. On death anniversary day, she would explain to crows that she had a function in the house and the food would be delayed so to come later and she confirmed they would not come before the function was over. I found it difficult to believe but then she cannot be wrong as this was her personal experience.

I did not want to leave Anakapalle until I had made safe arrangements for both Lakshmi and Kamala since Gouthami would be going back to Hyderabad along with Deepthi and Vamshi. I insisted that the rear end of the house including the backyard should be closed so that no one could enter the house from the backyard. We made cooking arrangements in the main house and when I was satisfied that things are safe I returned back to Bombay. We came again for Lakshmi marriage in 1988 in Anakapalle and now that both the sisters would be going away Kamala who was then just 12 years old could not stay in the house all alone among unhelpful neighboring relatives.

Bawa garu: After Manikyam

Life changed for this simple person after Manikyam's death. He spent most of his life sitting on the porch of their house with other idle hands making fun of those passing by in the busy street. He never realized that what he thought as fun could hurt other persons. He disagreed with Manikyam. Manikyam only had father to support her and my father would not interfere in their married life. Bawagaru became very pensive after Manikyam's death and remained so for quite some time. He invested money and cash he received from his share of land in stock market and postal savings. He spent very little on himself and his family and more in the savings. Once, he remembered some such savings he kept in a wooden box and wanted to redeem them but when he opened the box, he found to his horror that all these were destroyed by white ants. None of his savings helped Manikyam or make her life more comfortable during her life time. He was a virtuous person and did not have any bad habits; he did not smoke, drink, eat meat or anything of that nature but he never spent money on any thing he did not consider necessary. His primary occupation in Anakapalle was to perform 'Sandhya Vandanam' three times a day, eat a joint meal late in the afternoon and sit on the porch and joke about every one passing by. In the homes of Vedula clan the most important function is to participate in lavish meal after anniversaries of dead relatives and since they were all on the same street, this was almost a daily routine for every one there. I used to taunt Bawagaru that the only festivities that the Vedula clan knew were these anniversaries. They spent less time for the living and more time for the dead. By the time men folk finished their meals it would be almost 3.00 pm and the women in the house would eat only after that and mind you there would be neither coffee nor breakfast before the meal. It was a pathetic condition for women and I would rebel but Manikyam would often stop me from arguing with him.

In 1996 ten years after Manikyam died, Yagneshwar also died due to heat stroke in Kovvuru and this brought a realization of what he had been doing or missing all these years. I had gone to Vijayawada to mourn Yagneshwar when Bawagaru broke down. He told me "Sarvamangala, remember you were making fun of our anniversaries and the rituals and see today I have no one to perform my own final rites. No one is living to perform anniversaries to me and Manikyam." I told him "Bawagaru, we all make a mistake in believing that we will get an opportunity to correct all our mistakes or injustices done to others later in life over a period of time. But we forget that life is not in our hands and we may be denied this opportunity. You should only think of today and not of a future that you do not know. You thought since Manikyam was younger to you she will die after you are dead but probably never thought that this could be reversed. Similarly, you wanted many things from Yagneshwar but never gave him any love while he lived and he always missed your love and affection. You must act in present not look forward to a distant future." He became very emotional and told me that even though I was younger to him, I told him the meaning of life. I could perceive these important changes in his nature. He began to lead his simple life and he went to live wherever he was asked to live. He tried never to be a liability to his daughters or sons-in-law.

First few years after Manikyam died, he maintained the same obstinate nature but then Yagneshwar's death really broke his heart. Both Gouthami and Lakshmi had to move from city to city with their husbands as both were on transferable positions and so he too tagged along without any complaint. Most of the time however, he stayed with Lakshmi as Vishwanath liked having him at his home as he had lost his father when he was young and he was a now father figure for him. Kamala was in and out of Hyderabad and Bala was taking positions abroad so his stay with Kamala was usually short. In addition, both Bala and Kamala loved having guests at home and Kamala's house was always full of guests and most of them came unannounced. They would just drop in and leave only after their meal which is not very common these days. Both Kamala and Lakshmi proved to be good hostess to their stream of guests and they looked after every one. If Bawa Garu is taken for any functions he would go and spend time in company otherwise he stayed at home. He became ascetic. When Bhanumati lost her husband early 2009, he felt sorry he did not get opportunity to meet Chitti Bawa when he was alive.

Bawagaru died on 6th November, 2009 in Warangal. He had earlier fallen in bathroom when living with Lakshmi in Hyderabad and since Lakshmi is a working person, she realized that her father needed a constant supervision after mishap and drove him to Warangal where Gouthami who was not working could look after him. I talked to Gouthami a day before on 5th November, she told me he is doing fine and I could hear him in the background. I requested Gouthami to let me talk to him but since his teeth were hurt after his fall she told me it was painful for him to talk and so I hoped to talk to him when he was better. But he died very next day. I had gone to Dover, PA to participate in the school day celebrations of my grandson Kartik where he would be escorting his parents proudly thus contribution of Gnanu and Chenulu was recognized and appreciated by the community. I did not know or participated for such occasions for Gnanu or Dinkar in India. Just before we were leaving for the occasion, Deepthi called us and conveyed the sad news of death of her grandfather and I consoled her and asked her to come to Dover from New York if she was free, but she had some examinations going on and so she could not get away from New York and so I asked her to bear the grief courageously. After we returned from the function I called Gouthami and I was trying to give them support at this time. Indira and Vikram, Bhanumati, Sekhar and Murty and Chinna Babu they all traveled to Warangal for mourning. Lakshmi told us of the strange request of her father that his body was to be donated to the local medical institution and not cremated and this was cause of strong discussion amongst them.

This showed a totally different side of Bawagaru and how he changed over the years. He had been telling everyone that his body should be donated to local medical institution wherever he may die and he even told his grandson Hemant, second son of Lakshmi. Should they honor this unusual request? Chitti took the phone from me and asked if he had told everyone in the family and Lakshmi said he did, in which case Chitti told them they should honor his last wish. He told them the back ground of this wish and why he insisted to tell everyone about his wish. Chitti and Bawa Garu were returning after performing 10th day ritual of Babi, husband of Indira who died of cerebral hemorrhage and they were discussing the phone call from his nephew Naresh Ayyala who lives in the US. This gentleman called Indira to inquire if they donated his eye to the eye bank as that was his wish. Indira was totally surprised by this piece of information and she asked Kavita and Kalyan if they were aware about it and they both showed blank faces. None in the family knew about this wish of Babi except his nephew in the US who did not communicate when he was hospitalized and so this wish and desire remained unfulfilled. Your father and I decided at that time that wherever they go they will tell everyone in the house that this is our wish and their bodies should be donated after death. Chitti has also told every one of us and has also written in his will but we did not know about Bawa garu and his wish. Chitti emphatically told Lakshmi and others that his body was the only real possession of their father and if he wanted to use for the benefit of humanity they should honor his wish. They all agreed and felt relieved as each one of them was passing through such a stress and this affected general peace of mind for everyone.

Next they contacted the local institution Kakatiya Medical College and inquired for the formalities for donating the body. They also contacted the eye center and requested them to come and collect the eyes donated by him and they came there immediately and saw that both the cornea and the lenses were in good order and they assured Gouthami and others that these could be transplanted to those in need and that four lives will be benefited by this act. Next day the team from Kakatiya Medical College came and was profuse in their thanks and they took his recent photograph to be enlarged and mounted in the college as a donor. The news spread so fast that a local reporter from Eenadu Newspaper interviewed Babu Rao when he was in the bank. Everyone was happy that they fulfilled their father's last wish and they were now ready to take on the world if required. Bawa garu's brother or his nephews did not come after he passed away and since the final religious rites will be performed later on 14th November they are waiting to see if any of his blood relations join the rites proposed to be performed in Rajahmundry on the banks of Godavari River. It is now immaterial whether any one from either family joins the final rites in Rajahmundry. Bawagaru at least has become a famous man by his most noble deed. I do not know if Manikyam looking down at these events from above would be very happy. In recent years he had become very charitable and he would donate his money to many events; he gave 25,000 rupees for Vikram's colleague Subrahmanyam for his operation and so on. Few knew this side of his activities in recent years.

The 10th day function was performed by Babu Rao in Rajahmundry and all the three son's-in-law participated in the function. Vishwanath was sick but still he came and so also members of his family who lived nearby. Kamala and Bala came and so also Bala's parents came from Aduru. His brother Babili came to the function and so also other close relatives of Bawa Garu, his brother and his nephews from Anakapalle. Indira, Vikram, Bhanumati, Murty participated from our side. More than 40 near relatives participated on this important event, a day when every relative tries to free the soul from any dues or debts with them in person. I called him Valmiki, a sage who had transformed from a bandit.

On his death anniversary Kamala and her sisters paid a tribute to Bawagaru as given below showing their affection and love to their father who gave them company whenever they needed.

"Those we love don't go away. They walk besides us every day"

Manikyam and Bawa garu's legacy: Once all this is over and I began to contemplate the legacy these two persons left behind to their children. First thing that came to my mind is material wealth he left for his children. Based on Bawa garu's life style I know he left his three daughters a support for their needs by way of landed property in Anakapalle. I have seen all the three daughters merging into the new environment after their marriages and how they have supported their husbands in discharging their duties and responsibilities most effectively. I know every son would like to be a Rama, but does he have Sita to follow the wishes of her in-laws? In this case I believe it is true. All three daughters have achieved greater respect from parents on the side of their spouses. This is the culture and legacy passed on by Bawagaru and Manikyam. Joint family may not work always, but respect for the elders should never be sacrificed and each one of their daughters has shown this abundantly. They are making their family a well-knit one and the three sisters are always together and participate in every function collectively.

CHAPTER 7

BHANUMATI: PEERLESS PEARL

It is said that when Bhanumati was born no one even considered selecting a name for the newborn and so they began calling her Baby. But child Baby's eyes were closed and she could not even open them and there were several red round marks on her hand. Everyone was concerned about this and thought maybe she is blind and suddenly my grandmother remembered that someone in our family had vowed to Lord Suryanarayana or Sun God before she was borne to name the child after him and so this must be his way of reminding everyone of this vow. Baby was immediately christened as Bhanumati after Sun. After knowing about this incident I was very particular to confirm if anyone has vowed any gods before selecting a name for Chaitanya Gnanu's son. Like all my other siblings, Bhanumati was also very fair and shone like a pearl. I do not recollect anything about her childhood as I am four years younger to her and at that time I was not curious about my sister or brother. But the girl I remember had very dark eyes, long dark curly hair and was very chubby. I do not remember clearly but she may also have had dimples on both her cheeks. I could be wrong and now I cannot confirm.

Bhanumati also went to the Shady Girls High School in Rajahmundry along with Manikyam and was a very serious student. Apart from her studies, Bhanumati was a very good artist and she almost inherited all the artistic genes of my mother. She could sing, draw, paint, write and act in plays and sew with a degree of expertise I have not seen in any one else in my family. She could draw a portrait of a person while he was sitting and if she had an opportunity of joining any drawing class she would have excelled in portrait painting. She had a very melodious voice and could sing any movie song rendered by play back singers Leela or Sushila just as melodiously. I have not seen any household in recent days where all the children would share their life together under one roof. Of course nowadays the opportunities are limited because most of the families are limited to two and maximum three children. Pedda Babu and Bhanumati could sing any duet and there would be a great demand for their songs every night and even my father would join in the musical interludes after our early dinner. The life was real fun.

When we were children, Bhanumati would write plays and every one of us would play a part in these. The play was mostly dominated with the performance of Bhanumati and Pedda Babu with smaller role for Chinna Babu and a sort of short entry by me at times. We all enjoyed these moments and I would feel very important every time I had a bit role in their play. Mamma would make Bhanumati and Pedda Babu sing almost every night and Pedda Babu would not only sing he would also provide music to their songs. When I look at it I find that all my family members except perhaps me, were artistically inclined and each had an art to cherish and I miss the pleasure I had during all my childhood years. Mamma loved these evening interludes and she had her own request songs and they would sing these for Mamma without getting tired. I remember these songs even now. Mamma would request them to sing the following classical songs: 1 'Tulsi dalamunache' a classical song composed by Tyagaraja; 2. 'Kanakambara Dhara Dhira Kaustabha Mani' a Mangala Aarti 3. 'Shambha Shiva Anave' Swarajiti and 'Oka Mata Oka Banamu Oka Patni Vratude' by Tyagaraja and they would both sing in concert. Of course we would request popular movie songs and our requests were also met. All this was possible because we all had our dinner by 6.30 pm and we had plenty of evening time at our disposal since father would not come for early dinner. He never minded our activities and he also joined.

Bhanumati's school friends were staying nearby and I became a courier for exchanging their homework and class work books. She was very close with two friends namely Bharati and Ratnavati and I used to call them three as trio of 'tis' Rati, Mati and Vati as their names ended with 'ti' and each would give me their note books to be given to either of the two. All three of them would plan their clothes for the next day like uniform and they were mostly inseparable. I did not mind going to Bharati's house which was close to our house and Bhanumati would go there herself with no one objecting but I was very happy to go over to Ratnavati's house as it was beyond the municipal park and I could stop by at the park and play. Bhanumati was also nearing puberty hence she also could not go out in the evening and the same restriction applied to her friends also but being a very young child I was free to move about. I thus became very close to Bhanumati's friends also though I do not remember what happened to them later.

One of the important event that I remember is the function of dolls weddings or 'Bommala Pelli' which I had the occasion to organize and participate in those days and I would invite my friends and we all would have a dummy or pretend wedding of dolls. Let me explain the function of Bommala Pelli as this was performed in almost every region in the country and the famous one is the one narrated by Sharat Chandra Chaterji in his novel Parinita. In Telugu literature this function is described in Kanyashulakam which was made into a very popular movie in those days. The dolls were normally made out of the fronds of palm leaves and there was an art in making them and it was Bhanumati who would make these dolls with beautiful dresses for them from pieces of cloth collected from tailors and make them attractive for the function. She would make clothes, adorn the dolls and decorate them so artistically that everyone who came to the function would look at these with a pleasant surprise at the art of my sister. Of course all these activities stopped once Bhanumati was married and I had more than my share of responsibilities. But these occasions have left lasting impressions on me.

My association with Bhanumati was very short lived as she was married when she was just fifteen. I loved plucking flowers from the trees like Mogra, December flowers and red Kanakambara flowering plants that grew in abundance in our front yard and routinely make a mala out of these flowers and Bhanumati and even Manikyam would love putting them on their hairs but ironically none would help me in plucking or stringing the mala. During summer months I used to string the flower buds in the evening and then put them on the branches of Tulsi plants in our backyard so that the buds would be in full bloom in the morning. Both my sisters would pick up one or two from the Tulsi plant and go to their school. The largest mala was meant for me but I would always find that Bhanumati had put the one I kept separate for me and gone to her school before me. I would become very angry and leave for school crying and without putting any flowers in my hair. This was a daily routine and my father would ask me not to string flowers since I was not getting what I wanted, but then the saying "One cannot straighten the tail of a dog" or in Telugu "kukka toka" so again in the evening I plucked the flowers and string them into mala. Sometimes I felt I was doing something wrong otherwise why should I not get reward for my labor? I know I am repeating this story, just in case someone skips earlier account and just to make sure that they will read here.

We all had shared chores in the house. During lunch time it was my duty to put the dinner plates and take them after every one finished their meal and Bhanumati selected the chore of cleaning the area with water. But then every day it would so happen that since Pedda Babu was slow to complete his lunch as per his habit, Bhanumati would leave for school without cleaning and so even that chore was also left to me. In short I was doing everything from setting plates, taking them and putting them for washing and clean the area also and Bhanumati would not do a single chore. It took me a long time to realize that Bhanumati was very shrewd in distributing the chores and there was more work involved in setting up the plates and removing them after meals than simple cleaning the area with water and a mop. By the time I realized this and even consider changing the routine Bhanumati was married and so the chores again came to me one can say permanently. This is not to show that Bhanumati avoided work but that she was more intelligent in her ways and was worldlier whereas I was more a stupid one. But all said and done both of us were children and these were very minor incident that did not affect our relationships at any time. We remained attached to each other all these years.

Wedding: When Bhanumati was nearing fifteen, Ganti Venkata Rao garu of Peruru, my mother's first cousin brought a proposal from one Ganti Somasekhar Rao garu, a very wealthy merchant of coconut products, holding a large agricultural property and a prominent landlord in Peruru. His oldest son Umamaheshwara Rao had completed a course in electrical engineering and was employed by State Electricity Board. The proposal was brought in Magha Month or in January/February and this was followed by formal meeting of the groom in our house and he said yes and before we realized Bhanumati was married on March 30th, 1955 or in Chaitra Month as per the Telugu almanac. This was probably a shortest time between engagement and marriage or it was "Jhat Mangani and Phat Vivah" and we all got fully immersed in the preparation. I would like add here once again that my father did not seek out alliances for any of his daughters and it is a record that all the matches were proposed from the bridegroom's side including mine.

This was the first wedding in our house since I matured and so I remember many of the details. Other weddings in our family namely those of Indira, Pedda Babu and Chinna Babu I virtually attended as a guest and so I do not remember as many details. It is for this reason that I am trying to capture all the events to show the grand scale at which Bhanumati was married. Others were also married likewise but I was an active participant in all the preparation of her wedding and this is also history.

The marriage function lasted for three days and since this was a wedding from our parts of Andhra the list for the guests was also very large. My father asked Upadhyayula Satyanarayana and his brother Suryanarayana from Gurraja Peta to help him in the arrangements. My grandmother Ammamma's brother Isola Narasimha Sastry or Mavatata garu meaning mother's maternal grandfather also came from Hyderabad to help my father. He was a very interesting personality since he had returned his home from Himalaya to learn meditation and he began practicing Mouna or total silence during the day after his return. He would talk to us only in sign language or write on a slate. My aunt Gnanamba had died one year before so Ramam Mavayya along with his children and his parents Rajananna and Ammamma came to take part in the function. My uncle or Babayya and his family came from Madras and the house was full of all relatives and there was so much fun all around. I remember one incident so well that I would like to mention the same here. Babayya's daughter Kalpakam was just about one year old and as usual I took her with me to play and being the month of March it may have been very warm. But when I returned with Kalpakam, Tocchhi became very angry that I took her in hot sun. I had such a beating from her that it was the only unfortunate event that has remained imprinted in my mind. Today when I look back on this incident I am convinced that as a mother Tocchhi was justified in her reaction but not in thrashing me. With so many kids of same age around there were frequent fights and quarrels among us. All had come from different parts in India and belonged to different cultures and so it was natural that we did not understand each other.

My cousins Babu, Baby and Chitti came from Bombay and did not know any other language except Gujarati and they would talk in Gujarati and we all were angry that they would not share their jokes with us and talk to us in Telugu. When they did talk in Telugu, we all laughed at their Telugu so they would stop talking in Telugu. We made fun that their Telugu sounded like those in Muslim community and so it became quite complicated to interact with each other.

We had a radio in our house and this was something of a rarity in these parts and since everyone wanted to hear their favorite programs the fights would be even more intense. Baby and Chitti would like to hear Hindi songs and Pedda Babu who had the control of Radio would not let them do so saying they can hear these songs in Bombay and would remove the fuse so that they could not hear and there would be another fight. My first cousins from Madras had a different reasons for fighting with us; they believed that my father was doing injustice to their father in not sending them due share in the produce. The house was full and every one had their own personal reasons for being angry. There would be fight for every small issue or even for a non-issue. My mother would wake up early and start making coffee for every one and since coffee require more milk we would get milk from our farm and also from other sources. Even before the morning was over, the milk we received from our farms would be exhausted. Father would buy some more milk from a local dairy farm and this would be used for evening coffee and for curd next day. With at least three families and the large children population, I do not know how my father managed these expenses. But he never shirked away from his duties.

Wedding was on 30th March, but everyone came at least a month before and so for my father, the expenses began more than one month before the event. The grocery store in front of our house in Danavaya Peta was running our credit and since we depended on agricultural income he would not hurry my father for payments and everyone who wanted anything would cross the street and buy it from there on credit. Suryanarayana and Satyanarayana and

Mavatata garu were watching like hawks to see that there were less unexpected expenses. Without these three hawks, I do not know how my father could have managed the expenses of the marriage later in the month. Muttayya was virtually living in our house and his deputy Veeranna was looking after the farm in Diwancheruvu. But many times he too had to stay back to help Muttayya in the preparations. The first task before wedding was to perform Vinayaka Puja thereby declare the start of the wedding preparations and this was followed by setting up a semi-permanent structure in the front yard, a shamiana or Mandapam and the structure was covered with fronds of coconut leaves and was adorned with mango leaves strung on jute thread. Now we had the whole of front yard protected from the harsh summer sun and we spent all our time outdoors.

Just before wedding Bhanumati fell sick and she was reduced to half her original weight. Like my other brothers and sisters, Bhanumati also looked well-nourished and she could be called plump but not fat. She became as thin as me and became very weak. My father was very much worried and during this period of recuperation, Bhanumati was playing a game with Baby and her hand slipped and she hit the pillar in our porch. Father told Bhanumati that there would be no games till the wedding is over and she will have to become as strong as before. Bhanumati was not back to her normal health on her wedding day but she looked better under my father's strict supervision.

Preparations for the wedding were in full swing as the date neared and large quantities of pickles, papads, and vadiyalu were prepared. A battery of women would come to our house in the morning and pound the spices till evening singing sweet folk songs. It was wonderful hearing them sing and to my surprise I had not heard any of these songs before or after. Sweets were prepared in very large quantities and I do not remember ever seeing those quantities any time later in my life. I remember Minapasundi Laddos since they were more than 8 inches in diameter and still were uniform in shape. Raw jack fruits were brought from Vakkalanka and Suryanarayana brothers sat down grating these with a sharp knife. Grating jack fruit is an art and required very concentrated attention and these brothers did it splendidly. During grating a wooden stick would be embedded in the fruit and since jack fruit ooze out sticky milky juice and one had to apply oil on hands to be able hold steady to chop the fruit. My father also grated the jack fruit and he grated the fruit better than everyone else into a very fine powder. But most of grating was however done by the Upadhyayula brothers. At the time of wedding one did not count the number of guests but I am sure the number was very large and could have reached more than 1000 guests for the wedding lunch and five hundred guests attending all the three days of the ceremony. The wedding was attended by a large contingent of Brahmins well versed in the knowledge of Vedas and they would chant all the three Vedas in a most melodious voice in unison. Singing of Saama Veda was also known as Sadasyam and these Vedic scholars would recite them and this was a very memorable occasion for me and other children. My father was very generous to these Vedic scholars.

Bridegroom party: The bride groom party came from Peruru. Women were dressed in expensive silk sarees and adorned beautiful traditional gold ornaments the like of which I have yet to see. I just stood there in awe. They would collectively sing songs in a melodious tune suitable for every event. They had a collection of songs for such simple event like pasupu nalugu (grinding of turmeric for oil bath), bantulu aatalu (playing with balls made of flowers by the newly married couple), Appagintalu (handing the bride to her in-laws family), Pannitti Bindelu aata (both bride and groom searching a ring from a vessel filled with perfumed water), Mangala Aarti and Bukka Jallulu (throwing colored powder on the marriage party) this would go on and on. I have not heard such songs since that event. At the time of meals there would be fun songs and they would be sung between two parties each group finding faults with the other group. It was fun.

We were so busy in the proceedings that we did not notice that the wedding was over and Bhanumati went over to Peruru with her husband Chitti Bawa and her in-laws. Luckily for us Bhanumati and her husband Chitti Bawa were posted near Rajahmundry in Tadepallegudem and so every now and then they would visit us and that was another fun. I liked to be with Chitti Bawa as he was very free with money and he always seemed to have plenty of it. He would take us to Movies and to restaurants for eats, a luxury we never had as my father would never visit any hotel except get some Idli's from our neighboring Behra's hotel run by a Brahmin cook. I looked forward to their visits.

She has four children two sons Sekhar, Murty followed by daughter Durga and fourth son Kamalakar. All were born in our Danavaya Peta house in Rajahmundry. My closeness to Bhanumati increased only after my marriage when I moved to Bombay. Every time I went to Bombay or returned from Bombay, we had to take a compulsory break at Hyderabad as the connecting train to Bombay would leave only at night as there were no direct trains from Bombay to Rajahmundry. We would come to Hyderabad in the morning and we had almost a full day to spend with Bhanumati. Bhanumati had a long and very happy stay in Hyderabad and she looked after us during our short halts. In 1967 when I was going to Rajahmundry, I saw a beautiful frock in a shop for Gnanu who was just about three years old but I did not have enough money to buy it off the shelf. Like Manikyam, I too believed that expensive clothes were not suitable for growing children and decided not to buy. Bhanumati showed her artistic nature and not one but she stitched two frocks one exact replica of the frock I could not buy and one more of a different model kept ready and gave it to Gnanu on my return from Rajahmundry. It was amazing since I only knew my mother could sew any design after just seeing once and Bhanumati seemed to have inherited her quality.

I would like to mention that during her stay at Hyderabad Bhanumati became very close with Gnanamba, oldest daughter of Babayya who also had started her family life in Hyderabad as her husband was working in a Bank in Hyderabad. In 1965 Sarvamangala fourth daughter of Babayya popularly known as Chinna Sarvamangala since she was younger to me also lived in Hyderabad and she too became close to Bhanumati. Both Chinna Sarvamangala and I were of the same age and so when I got married in 1963, there was a tremendous pressure on Babayya to get her married too and so was married in 1965 and the newly married couple decided to set up their family in Hyderabad in a modest apartment. I had not seen Chinna Sarvamangala since my marriage in 1963 and when she came to know that I would be passing through Hyderabad that summer she was very excited of meeting me once again but that did not happen. Around the same period, Babayya performed Upanayanam ceremony of his oldest son Bulli Babu or Narasimha Murty in Tirupati but she was unable to participate in the function. She was cooking their meals on a kerosene stove and like my aunt Gnanamba, her saree too caught fire and she was admitted to Osmania General Hospital in Hyderabad with third degree burns and she died of her burns. Bhanumati remained at her bedside all through. Thus we did not meet again after my marriage but I still have very pleasant memories of her. I still remember how she had brought Manikyam to Babayya's house and made her welcome when she was in Madras for medical checkup in spite of the nature of her disease. She was my best friend and we had a very close relationship though we both used to often quarrel during their summer stay in our house. But we were kids.

Bhanumati moved to Repalle along with Chitti Bawa, a period that was not very good for the family life of Bhanumati. They were living in government quarters which are believed to have been built on a land that was earlier a funeral site and this probably affected the peace in the family and being a very small village even schooling was not good. It was a very short period, but remained an unpleasant one in their life. From Repalle they moved to Hyderabad again and the family became a well knit family once again.

Artistic qualities of Bhanumati were brought out during their stay in Pochampadu near Bhadrachalam. Her children were all grown up and each had completed their matriculation or was very near to it. She became the secretary to the officers' club and conducted many cultural programs and each would have one play written, directed and played Bhanumati herself. This was the golden period in Bhanumati's life. Her children also contributed actively in the club activities and Durga in particular showed a talent in sports and was champion in the district in Shuttle Badminton and Tennicoit or ring tennis a popular sport in south. I do not remember if she played ball badminton. Murty and Kamalakar could drive the office jeep and the life was extremely good for Bawa and Bhanumati.

They moved to Hyderabad once again and this time they purchased a small house in Vijayanagar Colony and this became a headquarters for us sisters and Vikram. Chitti Bawa and Bhanumati became disciples to a guru Subhdramma garu and they participated in all the discourses very actively. It brought peace to their troubled minds.

Sekhar:

Sekhar was born on October, 10th 1956 at our house in Rajahmundry and so Bhanumati came and stayed for her delivery and post-delivery recuperation for almost six months. My mother was also pregnant and so also Manikyam who was pregnant with her first child and so we had three pregnant ladies and one active young person that is me and I was just 12 years at that time but was more mature than Indira who was just a six years old child. Readers of modern India must be wondering how this could happen that mother and her two daughters all pregnant at the same time, but then this was quite common in those days.

Sequence of the three children was very interesting, Vikram my brother was born first and followed by Gouthami and Sekhar was last sort of keeping their seniority in the family. Now the house was full of baby voices and cries. Every mother was as excited about their child although my mother was also keeping an eye on her two daughters for whom this was the first experience and gave them help and guidance. Now when I look back on these kids, I feel as if the history had repeated itself. I compared them with Pedda Babu, me and Chinna Babu. Both the boys very fair and hefty whereas Gouthami was relatively dark like me. All three grew up together and they have same degree of attachment even today.

Sekhar graduated in commerce from Osmania University and joined Alwyn Metal Industries and remained there till the company shut their doors due to losses. His wedding was on the same day as that of Vikram which again is the most unusual coincidence. They both were married on 15th May, 1982. I believe Sekhar was married in the morning and Vikram was married in the evening and here the order seems to have reversed. Sekhar has two sons the oldest Umesh was born some time in 1986 and second son Dinesh was born in 1988. Both became engineers and have gone abroad for higher education. Umesh is in Texas USA whereas Dinesh is in Toronto, Canada, both very bright boys.

Now that both the sons are well set, Sekhar began to fulfill his long drawn out dream of becoming a lawyer. Sekhar studied law by picking up threads after so many years of break in his education, successfully completing and became a practicing lawyer in 2006 in his fifties. I was then staying in Hyderabad on a short visit and was staying with Indira as usual and Sekhar came to me for my blessings and I was thrilled. Sekhar and Bala went for a position in Karimnagar where they both were employed and with both the sons in the USA they had no problem in moving away from Hyderabad. He stayed for a very short period, but returned back to Hyderabad is now working for an attorney in Hyderabad.

Narasimha Murty:

Narasimha Murty was born on 28th January, 1959 at our house in Rajahmundry. He was a very active child and was prone to mischief and in the process he neglected his studies. But otherwise was an outdoor person. He too joined commerce group after his matriculation and spent a good deal of time as a college sportsman. He was known for his batting prowess and represented his college in tournaments. In fact, both Sekhar and Kamalakar were also good in cricket, but I remember most about Murty. Chinna Bawa used to talk in a lighter vein about his escapades in cricket and for a long time a new comer to the family would really believe, till he later realizes that he was kidding. Chinna Bawa kept everyone in good humor with his imaginary stories and was fun to both the children and us. Murty graduated and like Sekhar joined Alwyn Metal Industries and began his career there till he too was laid off along with Sekhar.

Murty was married on 5th June, 1985 to Krishna Kumari who was a working girl and that was something new in our family. Together they have a very good life and have two children. Mani Sekhar his oldest son was born in 1986 followed by a beautiful daughter Sravani. Like Sekhar's children, both Mani Sekhar and Sravani are engineers and Mani Sekhar is doing his post graduate in Boston USA. Sravani is doing for her post graduate studies in the US. Murty after short stints at different places became an administrator in Vikram's institute for the past many years.

Kamalakar:

Kamalakar was born on 4th March, 1962 less than two years after Durga was born. He was born on Monday or the day of Lord Shiva on Shivratri day and that is why he was named as Shiv Kamalakar. Both Durga and Kamalakar played together and were virtually inseparable as kids. He graduated in science and was very good in Maths and Physics. Like his older brothers he too was an outdoor loving person and was known to be good in many sports. He was known for his swimming abilities and could swim long distances in rivers. He learnt software development after completing his graduation and would have become a good software professional. But then he decided to venture to the US and try his luck in getting a decent profession but for a very long time he worked on small menial jobs. Our cousin Sethu's son Ramu migrated to the US along with his parents. Ramu was born here and so he is a Citizen. They saw his talent and so invited him to work with them and develop his aptitude in the software. He was assured he will get a regular employment and that they will sponsor him once he completes his additional qualifications in India. But that did not happen and this remained a bone of contention for Kamalakar.

He began his own tutorial classes in Hyderabad for teaching software programming and became fairly known in the area. In fact Kamalakar purchased a house with his own resources and he was planning to expand more. He became confident of his success and wanted to invite all his relations once he is well set since he had shunned the society as he regarded himself as a failure. This time Ramu came to Hyderabad and requested him to manage a software project. He trusted Ramu and so left his house, his tutorial classes and moved to a location closer to Ramu's house hoping for a long tenure. However, after Ramu returned to USA the project was terminated. Kamalakar became frustrated and realized that he was misguided through excessive trust and all his hopes and aspirations were shattered. He could neither restart his class nor software programming once again. In short Kamalakar had a very difficult time in adjusting to the circumstances and he did not get the opportunity to show his mettle. He was struggling for an opportunity of joining the mainstream of his family members since he felt he was a failure. I met Kamalakar in 2010 when we all went to Vikram's house in Nallagunta for my mother's death anniversary and this remained a very memorable day for me. All my nephews and nieces with their children were there including Baby and it became a very good family gathering.

His life came to a sudden end on 13th August, 2010 when he took his own life leaving a note for everyone to know the reasons for his action. News of Kamalakar's death was unbelievable. It was very difficult for us to control Bhanumati who was grief stricken since Kamalakar was her very favorite son and for Bhanumati this was a second calamity in two years. He left all his property and belongings to his wife Nirmala. His decision to take his life was not on the spur of the moment, but was planned for a long time. There were times when he would tell people that he may not live long. He told Deepthi that he will not be there for her marriage. He went to Sekhar's house that day and took blessings from his brother and sister-in-law Bala. He sent his wife Nirmala for attending Sravana Shukravaram (Fridays of Sravana month) function as this would be her last function in her lifetime as a married woman and he thus had the whole house to himself. He then called his mother on phone to tell her about what he has done and begged her forgiveness. Bhanu called everyone to rush and save him but it was too late. His sister Durga was completely devastated and did not become normal for many days. Although she attended Deepthi's wedding she was more like a zombie. Both Kamalakar and Durga had such great attachment that Durga could barely accept the reality. For Bhanumati the pain brought so many memories and she felt he was wronged and should have had a better deal in his life. She like a yogi reconciled to the situation. But now she could not stay alone. Sekhar, Chinna Babu and Vikram felt Kamalakar could have talked to them and in this manner they probably could have reduced stresses on his mind but all this was after the event. He was alone in the world at that time. Even Babayya's daughters Gnanamba and Sita came to mourn Kamalakar's death.

Vikram and Chinna Bawa garu:

Over a period of time, Vikram became very close to Chinna Bawa and he too loved to stay at Vikram's house so that he can keep an eye on his children. Durga and Vikram loved having them at their house in Ibrahimpatnam. Vikram had a good garden and Chinna

Bawa loved nurturing these trees. He was born in Peruru and had seen his father practicing agriculture and he too had a love for gardening. Vikram had one dog who would protect the house when only children were in the house and that dog became very friendly to Chinna Bawa and so for him both the plants and the pet animal became a life and he enjoyed every minute in that house.

Bhanumati and Bawa: Married life of Bhanumati was flawless and both Chinna Bawa and Bhanumati loved each other so dearly that I have yet to come across such a loving couple in my life. They remained inseparable till Chinna Bawa's death. He would not let Bhanumati do any chores that would affect her health. In later years, Bhanumati was afflicted with severe rheumatism and it was very difficult for her to even hold a glass of water in her hand and Chinna Bawa did all the chores for her. The house in Vijayanagar Colony was sold and Bhanumati and Bawagaru began to live in an ashram operated by their guru for some time. At that time Vikram bought a house in Ibrahimpatnam and he requested Bhanumati and Chinna Bawa to stay with them so that children would find someone at home when they returned from their school. He was very happy and he began cultivating a small kitchen garden as this has been his hobby. Vikram at a later date also purchased an apartment near to his tutorial college in Nallagunta and requested Bhanumati and Chinna Bawa to stay there so that he can come over there during short breaks in his classes as Ibrahimpatnam was more than 30 miles away. Chinna Bawa died of cancer on 26th January, 2009 on the Republic Day, a national holiday and thus he even arranged a holiday for his own anniversaries in coming years. Bhanumati and Bawa had a very long association of 54 years of their happy married life. He died in pain but not of unhappiness and like a yogi he was always happy in every situation of life.

But Bhanumati could not reconcile the loss of Chitti Bawa and she became weak and her body pains became unbearable. Her rheumatism could not be cured and she began to live a more sedentary life and Vikram and Durga gave her all the support. I spent much of my time with Bhanumati when possible during my stay and once I returned to the US. Bhanumati went to live with Sekhar and Bala for a while who returned back to Hyderabad from Karimnagar.

Bhanumati died on 30th March, 2013 at Vikram's house in Nallagunta. After Chinna Bawa's death and that of Kamalakar, Bhanumati virtually lost any interest in life, but she continued to live in pain both mental and that of body. Slowly she became less mobile and since almost 2012 she became mostly restricted to bed. She made a great effort to visit Chinna Babu when his family moved to their new house and though it was known that she came to see out of deep love and affection she had with Chinna Babu, she was not allowed to visit him and she went back. She would tell me and others that why not they take her brain out and transplant it in Chinna Babu? Chinna Babu's death must have also impacted her mind and she was bed ridden when I went to visit her in August, 2012. I came to India with Chitti to participate in Babloo's wedding held in Bhopal to Parul Malviya and after visiting Chinna Babu's family and offering my sympathies to Lakshmi, Lakshminarayana and Sriram, I went to see Bhanumati. Her life depended on the services of the servant girl who would help her feed, give her medicines and also take her to rest rooms. I was totally shocked to see Bhanumati in this state.

We began our preparations to go as a marriage party to Bhopal. Vikram made arrangements for everyone by air and of course Bhanumati could not travel. We all had a very pleasant time there and we returned back to Hyderabad along with Malviya family for the wedding reception. No one expected Bhanumati to come for the reception, but we were all surprised to see her coming in a wheel chair that could also be converted into a bed or a recliner. Bhanumati was very happy and she welcomed Parul with open arms. Parul would look after her like a daughter and gave her medications regularly and she looked as if she was getting back her health and was extremely happy with the full family. Every time

I called her from US, she would talk very happily with me. Two days before she died I had a very long chat with her and she was concerned that I was sounding depressed and she encouraged me not to worry and that everything will work out for the better.

We had selected 30th March for Namakaranam of Mahati, Dinkar's daughter born on 2nd March. On the previous night I received a call from Indira informing me that Bhanumati was serious and that she was going over to Vikram's house. I told her I will call her after the function. Papa from Bombay called me on 30th and when I told her that we were having Namakaranam function, she made small talk and inquired about the preparations are but I became suspicious. Finally after every one left and after Mythili and Mahati slept I called Indira to find out about Bhanumati and she told me she was no more. Vikram had called Pedda Babu in the morning and talked to him about her symptoms and suspecting a stroke Pedda Babu asked Vikram to admit her in the hospital immediately so that the doctors can examine her. Vikram called ambulance and the doctor who accompanied the ambulance felt her pulse and declared her dead. No one knew that she was dead and she died so peacefully that for both Vikram and Durga it came as a great shock. Vikram lost two very close relations in a span of one year namely Chinna Babu and Bhanumati.

Pedda Babu along with wife Sita, Kamala and Suresh came in a Taxi from Bangalore for the cremation and he just broke down and wept uncontrollably. All the time he was saying Chinna Babu, Bhanumati and he were so close that he would remember all the childhood instances very distinctly. He was right. We four had a wonderful time during our childhood. We played till the end of the day and after we had our meals, Pedda Babu and Bhanumati would entertain us with movie songs in their melodious songs. How can we ever forget those days? Chinna Babu's family moved away from us and we could not reconnect in the same old manner even though he may have wanted to do so.

Chitti Bawa garu and Bhanumati's legacy: Both Bhanumati and Chinna Bawa lived a life of minimum interference in others affairs and managed their own life quietly. They kept away from the many social occasions as they were both very private persons. Durga inherited her mother's artistic nature and became proficient in many arts but mostly in music and gave many public performances on Veena. All the four children inherited her sports-loving nature and became good in their sports of choice mostly Cricket and Badminton. What did Bawa garu leave behind for his children? He sold his property in Peruru when his sons wanted to explore the distant lands like US. He sold his house in Vijayanagar Colony when they needed money to meet their immediate needs. Both Bhanumati and Chinna Bawa were yogis in a true sense. When he died, Chinna Bawa garu did not leave any landed property or money to his children and they were all well settled but he certainly left behind a void in their life. He believed in simplicity and led a frugal life. His needs were meager and his demands very few. They shun the society and lived their own private life following the advice of their Guru. He was always seen in either shorts or very simple clothes and unless one knew him they would mistake him for a helping hand. Simplicity and non-interference in other's affairs was their primary objective in life. Bhanumati on the other hand did not speak ill of any one and kept a very balanced poise. She would not speak ill of any one after Kamalakar's death as she said that would not bring my Kamalakar back so why should I waste my breath? She lived the life of an ideal wife and mother and supported her children and their families all through her life without expecting any returns.

She had money earmarked for her ceremonies following her death. She always paid from her own account money for all her medicines and any treatments. She did not allow even Durga to spend any money on her. She died a very happy person. Both Chinna Babu and Bhanumati died a sudden death and in the case of Chinna Babu's case I always felt death did not allow us to hear his last wish. In Bhanumati's case, her life was contented and full and had no desires to name. Her favorite grandson Babloo was there at her bedside along with his lovely wife Parul. She probably did not have any last wish.

CHAPTER 8

PEDDA BABU: MUSIC MAESTRO

Lakshminarayana or Pedda Babu was born in Peruru on 9th March, 1943 when the World War II was at its height and there were shortages of all commodities and every one was running away from cities for fear of bombing. My grandfather also moved to Peruru from Hyderabad for fear of bombing by either Germans or Japanese forces the main players in the war. It is said that the enemy planes had flown over Visakhapatnam though I do not know if this actually happened, but generally there was a strong sense of fear among those living on the shores. But there was no damage to Indian coast line and the war was over before end of 1944. Pedda Babu was a very healthy baby, a son born after so many daughters and was precious to my parents and grandparents alike. My father saw that there was a shortage of baby's milk and milk products in the market so he began buying them in the black market. The famous baby's milk of that time was Condensed Milk sold by Nestle as Milk Maid popularly known in Telugu as "Golla Bhama', a product that has survived two centuries if not more. He found a trader who sold him full three months quota of these Milk Maid tins. It is not that I was a custodian of these tins or anything like that since I was not even born at that time, but I remember my father telling us about this. My father like everyone in India believed in survival and if that meant buying in the black market for supporting his children he found no reason to shirk away from his duty. He was a principled person and if someone had asked him on oath he would have declared that he bought these in the black market because he would not tell a lie, but he was totally clear that his principles did not prevent him in going to the black market for purchasing as the situation demanded.

As a child Pedda Babu was chubby and was very shy of people. In fact he did not talk for a long time and though he was one year older to me, I was his royal translator. If I did not convey his thoughts correctly, he would get very angry with me. But generally he was a very quiet child always watching, always thinking. As a child he had very few requirements one of which was his daily glass of milk filled to the brim. He would receive milk in a very tall tumbler and the tumbler must be full up to the brim. Most of the times he would get a full glass of milk but he would never compromise if the tumbler was not full. My mother or whoever is there would add water to make it full to the brim and Pedda Babu would drink the milk happily. I was younger to him but the whole thing appeared odd to me. I could not understand why should Pedda Babu object drinking milk when it was not full? How could he be happy when water was added to the glass to make it full? I tried to reason with him that he was not getting full glass of milk when water was added. He wants glass full of milk then he should not allow water to be added to make it full. My father would laugh and say if Sarvamangala could understand the oddity of making glass full with water why not Pedda Babu? But Pedda Babu would not change. I was also very small and the fact that I remember this incident indicates that it had left a very lasting impression on me and every time I talked about it even my mother would laugh at this.

Once Pedda Babu was sitting in our dining hall in Danavaya Peta house and was drinking his milk. As usual the glass was full and so Pedda Babu finished his milk without any questions but when he finished the milk everyone was stunned to see a dead wall lizard at the bottom of his glass and the wall lizards are believed to be poisonous. My father came running from outside in the vasara and picked him and sent Muttayya to bring the doctor immediately and tell him that there was a dead wall lizard in his milk. Accordingly Muttayya ran to the doctor and doctor came and emptied his stomach. Once the contents were emptied, Pedda Babu opened his eyes and my father and mother thanked God for that. One could see the relief in the eyes of my father.

Pedda Babu is older to me by more than one year and so one would expect he will look after me, but it was the other way round. In a way the roles of a brother and sister reversed from that of my father and Gnanamba, where my father was the conveyer of thoughts of his sister here I was the conveyer of thoughts of my brother. He would sit there rolling his big eyes and look at me and I would convey his demand to the others. In our house every child was pampered, but I believe he was pampered more because he was the first surviving son. It would hurt my father if any guest scolded their children or beat them up since he would never scold any one of us. Least of all Pedda Babu as he was special.

Pedda Babu had an extreme tolerance to pain and he would not cry from pain. When he was about six years old he contracted typhoid and though he recovered it left him weak and he developed a boil on his neck. Puss would ooze out of the boil and father would do the dressing every day morning, noon and evening. Pedda Babu would bear the pain during the dressing without a tear in his eyes and probably this also may have reduced his inclination of talking. Father would never tire of telling this story of the enormous patience Pedda Babu had showed all through the recovery period. He has another quality and that is of serving others when needed. Once Pedda Babu and I were fighting to get hold of a kerosene lantern as both of us wanted the same lantern and in this pulling and pushing, the lantern slipped from Pedda Babu's hands and it hit me straight on my chest and the hot base scalded my skin on the chest and I developed a large boil. Pedda Babu felt he was responsible for this accident and so he would bathe my wound and apply ointment on the skin every day till it healed. I would argue with him that he was not at a fault since I was also at the fault equally and if I had not been trying to snatch away from his hand, there would not be this accident and so he should not feel remorse. But no! Pedda Babu would not listen to any one and he nursed my wound till it healed and my skin became as normal as before. Very few know this compassionate nature of Pedda Babu.

Pedda Babu was pet child and my grandfather Agastya Sastry would watch over him like a hawk. His wish was like an order for every one and my farther saw to it that everyone followed the rule. He was though a pampered he was not a spoiled child. By the time he was five years old, father decided that he should be tutored privately till he was six years or joined 1st standard in the school.

Father requested Mr. Mohan Rao garu to tutor Pedda Babu. I remember Mohan Rao garu very distinctly. He was a fair person with dark wavy hair and very good features and was extremely good looking and his wife Sundaramma like her name was also very fair but was not as attractive. Mamma was always praising the beauty of his wife. It became a joke with Chinna Babu that every time Mamma praised someone calling her beautiful he would ask her if she looked like Sundaramma garu and Mamma would say yes and we would all laugh. The tutor would come on the front porch and if Pedda Babu was in mood he will sit down for study if not he would tell the tutor from inside there will not be any studies today. Mohan Rao garu would meekly say OK I will come tomorrow. This was how he was brought up by my parents. Once he joined the school he was very regular. He was admitted to the Danavaya Peta Municipal High School that was so close to our house and we could even hear the ringing of the school bell from our house. Mohan Rao Sir became a family friend and we had good relations with them. Almost 20 years after their marriage, his wife gave birth to a son who was also a very attractive child but did not live after celebrating his first birth day. She was heartbroken but not for long as she again gave birth to another son who grew up and became quite successful. I remember father mentioning that they also had a daughter but they had moved away so I lost contact.

Pedda Babu was very fussy about food and he did not like any curry unless it was fried and he would eat silently. He took more time eating his meals as he was always immersed in thoughts. His favorite curry was fry of any vegetable raw bananas, brinjal (eggplant) or potato, last one was his favorite. He would come for lunch from school, throw open the front gate and ask loudly what the curry was and if answer was a fry, he will enter the house otherwise he will return back to school without his lunch. Needless to say effort was always made to serve fry for lunch to all of us. Father would feel sorry if fry was not served to Pedda Babu any day as he always felt the cook should spend that much more time for a child. Of course it did not make any difference to me as I did not like to eat any curry, but I loved potato fry and rice mixed with chilli hot pickle. Pedda Babu was generally lost in thoughts during lunch just like any other time. He would normally bite his thumb when thinking and was lost to the world.

Pedda Babu was never in a hurry and he had plenty of time on his hand and no one could make him eat his meals faster when my father was around. He ate silently and would roll his big eyes in answer to any questions. Ours was a very large household and so we always had a cook to help my mother. I would reply to their queries to Pedda Babu, his answers to them and so they called me 'Paatamma' or an old lady. I talked incessantly and chatter away while Pedda Babu remained silent. I do not know when Pedda Babu became independent and I stopped translating or it may have happened naturally.

Pedda Babu was a very proud boy, proud of his heritage of being a Brahmin and he would therefore sport a small pilaka (pig tail) on his head and a prominent bottu or Tilak on his forehead. He would dare anyone to touch his pilaka and he would be fight the miscreant then and there. In spite of all these fights, he did not give up his pilaka for a very long time. He was fearless. My father loved Pedda Babu for these characteristics as he too believed in being fearless but my mother hoped he would be less adamant and avoid almost daily fights. Both Chinna Babu and I joined the same school and so we would all go together and rush back for lunch, finish our meals and rush back to school. Pedda Babu would sit there and think about some thing or other and will not get up for a long time. Bhanumati who had the chore of cleaning the floor after our meals would leave for her school in the meanwhile and so I had to wait and clean the floor after Pedda Babu completed his meals even though I finished my meals early and this was not my chore and I still feel upset about this even today.

He was undoubtedly my father's favorite and he too looked upon my father as his role model. In fact if father was going away on his business trips, he would be so upset that he would climb the tiled roof of our house in Danavaya Peta and wait for him and my mother would be worried sick down below. He would not come down. This changed my father's routine and he now preferred to go often to Diwancheruvu so that he could return the same day and would delay his visit to Gurraja Peta which needed at least two to three days away from home. Father had implicit trust on Pedda Babu and his fairness and so he was always selected for distributing sweets and toffees among children and he would do it most judiciously. We never had any complaints when he distributed sweets or toffees or fruits including ripe mangoes. This shows his strength of character and his sense of duty. But he would not tolerate if someone took advantage of him and he was intolerant to fun in such serious matters with the exception of Chinna Babu. Chinna Babu knew this weakness of Pedda Babu and he always kept him humored with his stories and jokes and in return he would receive more than others but Pedda Babu did not mind. We three were very close then and we remained very close though we are all separated by distance.

Pedda Babu was an artist, he could sing, play and draw and he could even compete with Bhanumati and was sometimes better. One day we all went to a movie called "Malleshwari" which is a story of a sculptor who went to the city to earn more money by working for the King and his childhood sweetheart also came independently and began working for the Queen. He was a very famous sculptor and in his enthusiasm of meeting his sweet heart he went inside the Queens palace without permission and this was a transgression from the point of view of the Kings court and he was awarded a death sentence. Of course this did not happen and the hero married his sweet heart. But the movie left a deep impression on all of us. As soon as we returned from the movie, Pedda Babu picked up a chisel and began hammering the stone floor in the dining hall and in no time he etched out a very beautiful image of a monkey just as N T Rama Rao, the hero of the movie sculpted the heroine's monkey. All this after watching one movie! He was then probably just about ten years old.

Father never interfered in Pedda Babu's activities. He trusted Pedda Babu to do everything correct and just. One of the most secretive passions of Pedda Babu was to go to a movie once every week. He would go for movies secretly, buy cheapest tickets and sit on the bench and watch the movie because he wanted to utilize one rupee he received from father to see more number of movies like seeing four movies by buying four anna bench class tickets. He was a movie buff then and he remains so even now. Pedda Babu thought his secret was safe with him and no one knew, but my father came to know about it from probably Muttayya or some of his farm hands and he too kept this as a secret for a long time. When we were fairly grown up he told us all about this passion of Pedda Babu and this was a surprise for even Pedda Babu. It is clear from this incident that though father did not interfere in Pedda Babu's affairs, he kept a watchful eye on him. In fact he never interfered with activities of anyone as long as they did not create wrong influence he feared in the case of Chinna Babu.

In our house there were two almirahs that were locked one was that of my father and the second one was that of Pedda Babu. Father had money and his account books and so kept them locked and Pedda Babu had so many different types of things he considered treasures that he had to keep them under lock and key. He once was given a pocket watch by my father or someone in the family that probably belonged to my grandfather since this watch was not working. Pedda Babu sat down and opened the watch and saw all the parts that made the watch work and then began to assemble the watch once again and to every one's surprise the watch began to show time. Father was extremely happy with the ingenuity of Pedda Babu and he was extremely proud of Pedda Babu. Pedda Babu had an engineering mind. If the fuse is blown off and the house is plunged into darkness, Pedda Babu would be called and he would take out the fuse wire from his almirah and reconnect so that the power was restored. He could work with mechanical or electrical machines and repair them as best or even better than the technician. Our radio was never sent to a shop for repairs as he would fix any problem. He purchased a low cost camera when he was in 10th standard and he went on taking photographs of each and every thing interesting including my wedding. He could do anything and repair most of electrical and mechanical articles but he did not continue these disciplines that he loved but was made to study medicine.

My father gave a mouth-organ or harmonica to Pedda Babu and he would not leave the instrument till he was able to play popular tunes on mouthorgan and this was a surprise to us all. We knew of his mechanical abilities but did not know that he could master harmonica. Pedda Babu was a good singer and before his voice broke, both Pedda Babu and Bhanumati would sing duets and that would be our evening entertainment program and we all looked forward to these evenings and even my father would join us in encouraging these two budding artists. Mamma loved these evening interludes and she would forward her own request songs to Pedda Babu and Bhanumati and they would sing these for her any time without getting tired. I remember these songs even now. Mamma would request them to sing the following classical songs: 1 Tulsi dalamunache; a Karnataka classical song composed by Tyagaraja; 2. Kanakambara Dhara Dhira Kaustabha Mani, A Mangala Aarti; 3. Shambha Shiva Anave: Swarajiti and 4. Oka Mata Oka Banam by Tyagaraja and they would sing like a concert. Of course we would also request movie songs and our requests would not be denied.

All our text books and notes were nicely covered with brown paper before the beginning of school by my father and we all tried to keep them in good conditions and most of the books were kept nicely and these books would later be donated to the school for poor students. Once Pedda Babu became more involved, he took charge of covering all our text books and note books with brown paper. Every home had one such person whose job it was to protect these from damage by daily use and in our house this job was taken over by Pedda Babu and he did this well till he joined Medical college. We used to get Chandamama, a monthly magazine for children and every one would fight for reading the issue the moment it was delivered in the mail. Chandamama usually became a reason for fights and cunningness of everyone involved but I never fought. My father was surprised and he would ask me why is it that I was not keen to read it? I replied that there was no need for that; after two days the issue will be lying around everywhere with no takers and I can read them at leisure. My father was impressed by my logic which to him looked more mature for my age. Just as I mentioned, I would read Chandamama at leisure and once I finished, Pedda Babu would keep the issue under lock and key. Once all the 12 issues are read by all, he would bind them with twine so that these are not lost. He would bind issues and keep them chronologically and during summer vacation all other children would read them. Unfortunately this entire collection of Chandamama was lost when people borrowed them without returning. Initially Pedda Babu would not give these to any one for fear of losing them, but then he became very unpopular and father too told him to let others enjoy and he began loaning his collection. He was very meticulous about his duties and never did he sacrifice any of his duties at any time.

Father approved all his activities except his special interest in music and Pedda Babu had to pursue his love for music behind his back. All this started with a flute that he purchased himself or may be someone in my family had given it to him. He would practice on this flute from morning to evening till he could play all the songs correctly and melodiously. Very often he forgot to attend to his regular class work. Father did not like this and would not allow this to happen and so Pedda Babu practiced his music in a small alley on the inside of our house when father was at home and would practice there for hours together and so that father would not hear the flute. Pedda Babu became very proficient in flute without tutoring. Now he could play both mouth organ and flute and was able to entertain us all in the evenings. Father wanted Pedda Babu to be focused on his future and not addicted to music, but music remained a passion and today he teaches music! He has retired from his medical profession and he has all the time for his passion.

Next he purchased a Bulbul Tarang a string instrument with a key board. Both flute and mouth organ were wind instruments and so this was a new experience for him. He followed the instruction given in a small booklet and began practicing a few songs. He began to tune songs very well on the instrument with the help of the key board. Next he removed the key board and began analyzing the principles behind the tunes and soon he began playing Bulbul Tarang without key board and he became a person of attraction for all the visitors in our family. He was always in demand to sing, play flute, play mouth organ or Bulbul Tarang and every one was fascinated by his knowledge of instruments. They would request him mostly to play the famous song "Kahin deep Jale Kahin Dil' from the movie "Bees Saal Baad" and he would play it on bulbul Tarang with or without key board. His interest in music continued even in college and I can proudly say that my brother is the only doctor I know who could play violin, guitar, Mandolin, flute and even drums.

His school life went away in playing games and musical entertainments and soon he completed his matriculation and he joined Rajahmundry Arts College for his Pre University Course (PUC) for selecting a professional course. Pedda Babu had always shown great interest in fixing things and all things engineering, but father decided that he will study medicine. I do not think father asked Pedda Babu even once about his choice but Pedda Babu did not mind and he came with good marks in his Biology, Physics and Chemistry, a study group required for medicine and he was now ready to go the medical school. But it was not that easy. Even though he was a topper in PUC, he could not get admission in a government medical school because he was a Brahmin.

At that time a Medical College in Kakinada was accepting merit students with competitive marks in exchange of a donation but my father did not have money for donation. My father went to one Jhandhyala Papayya Sastry garu to seek loan of six thousand rupees and came home to take Pedda Babu to Kakinada for enrollment in the medical college. But Pedda Babu refused and said he did not want to study medicine by paying a donation to the college and after all that even the cost of studying medicine was high. So my father went back to Papayya Sastry garu to return the money. He was surprised to see my father back with money and told my father to hold on to money and came to our house to talk to Pedda Babu. He convinced Pedda Babu that they were not doing anything wrong since he had a good score in PUC and the donation was just to give him that push to get the admission. He could return all this with interest once he became a doctor. My father wanted Pedda Babu to become a doctor so that he would fulfill his dream of a practice in Rajahmundry and both of them together would look after their properties and have a good practice. His dream now passed on from Babayya to Pedda Babu. He would daydream about going with Pedda Babu in his car, drop him at his dispensary and he would then proceed to Diwancheruvu to supervise our farm lands. But that did not happen this time also.

In 1961, Ramam garu sent a proposal for my marriage to Chitti and Pedda Babu was absolutely against the match saying these fellows are all short tempered and they would not look after Sarvamangala. But he agreed once every one in the house accepted the match. After my engagement, Chitti advised me to join local college and finish PUC since wedding would not take place for another two years. This time Pedda Babu put his foot down and told my father that he will not let me study in the college as the boys would misbehave with me as they do with other girls. My father tried to convince him that already there were many girls in the college so it should not be difficult for me to study, but in this matter he would not listen to any body and I did not go to the college. I still regret that I could not complete my education beyond matriculation. Pedda Babu joined Rangaraya Medical College in Kakinada in 1962 and he joined the college hostel and would come weekends or whenever he would have leave.

Once my marriage was fixed, Pedda Babu told my father that I needed to learn classical music and should learn to play violin and my father was very happy that Pedda Babu was so concerned about his sister. I began learning Violin very seriously and would practice diligently whenever I would get time from my daily chores and since my marriage was already scheduled, I was not that keen. But still I did well. But I remember very well every time my teacher came, Pedda Babu would find time to be near in the next room or so and looking back at the events then, I feel he was more interested in learning violin himself and I was just an instrument to getting a good teacher for him. He became very proficient in playing classical violin by the time I was married. When he was in medical college he attended classical violin classes. In 1962, Pedda Babu joined medical college in Kakinada, in 1963 I was married and in 1963 Chinna Babu finished his PUC and joined Kakinada College of Engineering and with me married father began to toy with the idea that he should also move to Kakinada to save hostel expenses and in late 1964 father decided to move to Kakinada and set up a home for Pedda Babu and Chinna Babu so that they could study well.

Pedda Babu finished his Medical studies in 1969 and began to do the internship in a village for one year before he could set up his practice. In March, 1970 Indira was married and since Pedda Babu had completed his internship also, Father began discussing Pedda Babu's marriage and he was now ready. There was a general discussion on the type of girl he would prefer. My father told him about an eligible girl in Rajahmundry who was working in a Bank there and told him this would give him an opportunity of seeing both son and daughter-in-law going off to work every morning. Pedda Babu firmly said no. A working girl will never be able to look after you and members of our family and he would therefore prefer a girl who was not very educated so that there would not be any motivation for her to seek a job. I realized for the second time that Pedda Babu was very conservative.

One Peri Srirama Murty garu of Bhandarlanka came to our house bringing three matches at three different times for Pedda Babu and he would carry the photograph and the horoscope of the prospective bride. He would tell my father I have with me 'Chitra patamu' meaning a photograph and 'Jataka chakram' meaning an astrological chart with me so why don't you compare. The first two horoscopes did not match. Finally he came with the proposal of his granddaughter Sita Mahalakshmi, daughter of Sikha Veerabhadra Rao garu of Hyderabad and luckily their horoscopes matched.

As the horoscope matched and the girl was known to be very fair, father agreed to go to Hyderabad with Pedda Babu for formal meeting and approval of the girl. We were all worried that if the other side knew Pedda Babu's weakness for Jalebis and if they feed him Jalebis, Pedda Babu will not even look at the girl and blindly say yes. One of the greatest weakness of Pedda Babu is his love for

Jalebis that continued for a very long time or till he was forced not to eat sweets. Believe me when Pedda Babu returned after saying OK, we asked him if they served him Jalebis and he said yes and we laughed out aloud. Sita Mahalakshmi or Sita for short met all the specifications of Pedda Babu. She was fair, not educated in college and apparently did not have any inclination for a job and so will look after our father and Vikram who was still studying. Finally, Peri Srirama Murty was happy that my father selected one of his proposals. Chinna Babu used the quote of 'Chitra patamu' meaning full length photograph and 'Jataka chakram' meaning horoscope synonymous with Peri Srirama Murty garu's name. One more joke was added to his long list of funny jokes and quotations.

Pedda Babu was married on 3rd December, 1970 at Bhandarlanka in Delta region of Godavari at the ancestral house of her grandparent Peri Srirama Murty. Pedda Babu was so happy that he personally invited all sisters. He first went to Anakapalle and invited Manikyam, came to Visakhapatnam where we were living at that time and invited us and proceeded to Jamshedpur to invite Indira. Bhanumati was in Repalle so he visited the town and invited her personally. All of us were very happy that Pedda Babu was getting married and we made elaborate plans to welcome the first lady of the house after death of my mother. We all met at Kakinada and boarded a chartered bus for Bhandarlanka. Babayya and Tocchhi did not come but his two daughters Gnanamba and Aruna our first cousins came. Ramam garu my father-in-law came from Bombay and so also Baby and Lakshmi. The wedding went off in a grand manner. Father had kept a fairly large stock of fire crackers for this occasion and sky was lit with fireworks in December.

Pedda Babu stayed in Kakinada and on 15th April, 1974 Sita gave birth to a Baby girl in Hyderabad named Kamala after our mother. Kamala was a very pretty and healthy child very fair and always smiling and no wonder was a darling to us all. Pedda Babu worked for a municipal hospital and a private nursing home before he decided to move over to Hyderabad. It is not the decision that surprised father, but the suddenness and the manner in which he went away to Hyderabad that surprised him. He was blessed with another daughter Aparna on 10th November 1975 at Hyderabad. Two years later on 26th September, 1977 Sita gave birth to a son named Shivram, a very red and healthy looking child. Hyderabad has always been my overnight destination and I would generally spend about a couple of days there on my way to Kakinada or to Anakapalle so I did not have much contact with the children. Later Pedda Babu set up his own family in Bangalore where he is settled permanently. We either meet at some marriage functions or I make a special visit to Bangalore and spend a few days with him and his family.

Kamala: Kamala grew up to be a very pretty young girl who became an electronics engineer and began her career in Bangalore. Dinkar was in the US working for a software company and when he saw all this he inquired if his company could invite her on a work permit to the USA. Things worked well and Kamala came to the USA in 1997 along with Dinkar and his newly wedded wife Kiranmai to the US and began her service in earnestness. During her stay in the US she met one Suresh Balakrishna a computer software engineer in New Jersey who was quite attracted to Kamala and with the blessings of his parents they were married in India in a very public function. Kamala had told Suresh and his parents that she would not be able to give them an heir due to some medical reasons, but his parents were so forward thinking that they told Kamala and Pedda Babu that this was no big deal for them. Their son Suresh liked Kamala which is more important so this was not a big issue. I met Kamala's in-laws when they were in the US visiting their son in New Jersey and was happy that they were very fine and open hearted people. I am glad that Kamala got a very good family and she is very happy. Kamala is now in Bangalore representing the company she was working in New Jersey and both of them are very happy and near to both their parents. But Kamala cannot remain contented and when she saw her Father-in-law struggling exporting his flowers, she decided to quit her job as a software engineer and joined him. Now she does not find time to rest as there are so many chores around this simple act of exporting flowers. Yet she found some time and began a company for sarees with modern designs called Tvaksati and she is now busy visiting the weavers and other artisans for her work.

Aparna: As I had mentioned before, I did not get much opportunity of knowing Aparna except that when she came to Bombay as an intern working for a legal company. Aparna was a brilliant student and topped the competitive examination in Karnataka for engineering studies. But she refused to join engineering as she had set her mind for a legal career. She told her mother that she only appeared the entrance examination just to show to her that she was not a dud. She stayed with us for almost a month during her internship with an attorney in Bombay and this was the period that we came to know more about her. One of the most famous movie singers of the yester era was Kundan Lal Saigal and Chitti had a collection of tapes of Saigal that he and his father Ramam garu would listen when they were in a mood. She saw the collection and that was that. Every day whenever she was at home she would only listen to songs and gazals rendered by KL Saigal unlike young people of her age and this appeared most striking to us. She is also very talented in classical music and played violin along with her father for Dinkar's wedding. During her stay in Bombay, Chinna Babu's son Sriram also visited us to drop his brother Lakshminarayana and we all went to Essel World an amusement park near Malad, a suburb in Bombay and all four of us had a very fabulous time there. It was my longest association with Aparna.

Although she had indicated that she had an inclination towards legal discipline, she appeared for a competitive examination for Indian Administrative Service Examination or IAS and she topped that examination also and she could have opted for Indian Foreign Service and visited different countries, but she chose to remain in India and became a District Collector appointed by the Government of India. She is married to Ganti Prasad a very handsome Ganti and has now two sons both very active and bright. Once again I lost touch with her after she left Bombay. Her territory for administration is Uttar Pradesh in North India and my visits have always been restricted to Hyderabad only so our meetings become far in between. She is still her grandparent's favorite baby. This December 15th Aparna, Prasad and Abhiram and Anirudh participated in Vikram's eldest son Bhanu's wedding in Bhopal and we reminisced the good old times in Bombay. She actively participated in all functions and even danced in Baraat in the evening.

Shivram: Shivram was born in Hyderabad on 26th November, 1977 and was a very mischievous child. In 1981, Pedda Babu had moved to Bangalore after successfully performing Gouthami's marriage and I lost contact with him except hearing from others that he was very intelligent. My next meeting with Shivram was when we had gone to Bangalore from Tirupati and stayed with Pedda Babu. Pedda Babu is a movie buff and since video tapes became a common feature, he would watch movies at home. He liked to absorb every event in the movie and if he missed any part of dialogue or if there was an argument on any sequence he would rewind and see the movie from beginning once again. This was fun to us all and so we would watch movies with Pedda Babu and his family. Shivram would go to the kitchen and at regular intervals bring hot tea for all of us and we knew then that Shivram was real fun. He too became an engineer and joined prestigious software company in Bangalore before setting up his own company. He is married to Vandana but I did not go to his wedding since I was in the US. I met his wife Vandana who was so friendly and invited us to stay with them for longer time on our next visit.

Now Pedda Babu has retired from his teaching assignments and is devoting all his time on his only interest, music. He has purchased an apartment in Bangalore and that location is also very interesting. The apartment is situated next to a plot that was supposed to have been reserved by Archeological Society but through some manipulations, some wise guy sold this property to a builder in Bombay and this person came to develop the plot for an apartment complex. When he started excavation work prior to laying foundation, a worker came across a wall and the contractor stopped work to investigate. This wall led to an underground temple of Lord Shiva and once they discovered the temple the entire work was stopped. News of a temple at the plot spread like wild fire and every one began visiting the temple with flowers and offerings. Archeology Department came to know of the temple and came to investigate and they were told that there was no sign that the property belonged to the Archeology Department. This was attributed to vandalism and the builder from Bombay agreed to make the temple more accessible with minimum amenities to the devotees before they moved out.

The temple was renovated and is now a very famous temple popularly known as Dakshina (South) Nandi Temple because Lord Shiva's famous vehicle Nandi is facing south and not north as is the normal position. Another novel feature of this temple is that in addition to Nandi facing southwards, Nandi is situated over the Shiva Lingam and not facing the Shiva Lingam the normal position in every Shiva temples all over India. Nandi bathes the Shiva Lingam from the top continuously for several centuries a tribute to our earlier architects particularly since Bangalore is facing water shortage in recent years.

I would like to remind that Lord Shiva is our family deity and my father wrote the Shiva Panchakshari one hundred thousand times in a series of note books and would observe fast on a Monday throughout the month of Kartik. This strong faith in Shiva is seen among all my brothers. This was a golden opportunity for Pedda Babu that Lord Shiva came next to his apartment complex. He now found the opportunity of playing violin every evening at no cost to the temple. Pedda Babu's house Sapta Nilayam is surrounded with so many temples that it took me more than one hour visiting them all. The one temple that I thought was so coincidental had an idol of Ganga and since my granddaughter Mythili's middle name is Gangotri or the place river Ganga began its journey from Himalayas I thought this visit was memorable.

He began visiting other temples nearby particularly Sai Baba temples and would play violin to his heart's content. The surprise is that even his wife participated in the classical singing. I remembered earlier incident when Pedda Babu began his practice and was staying in Saidabad Colony in Hyderabad. Pedda Babu would begin playing violin first thing in the morning. This would result in daily altercation between Sita and Pedda Babu and they would have argument over his practicing music. Pedda Babu used to be frustrated but now the situation has changed and they both are participating in music sessions together. My very creative and ingenious brother has become "Maestro" in real terms. He is only second to Mandolin maestro U. Srinivas (not Upadhyayula). He gave a concert on 19th December, 2012 at Vikram's son Bhanu's reception in Hyderabad to the delight of the guests.

One thing I remember most about Pedda Babu is that he has not yet forgotten my birthday and every year without fail he would call me wherever I may be. He would call me not on my birthday as per the date but on Naraka Chaturdasi day my birthday as per Telugu almanac.

Pedda Babu and Sita: Pedda Babu enjoyed his life as a Medical professional teaching to students in a Medical school. He did try practicing on a part time basis but nothing serious and he did not pursue private practice. I have never understood why Pedda Babu did not consider practicing. He is good in diagnosis and his patients trust his judgment and follow medicines prescribed by him. Manikyam was one such patient who had implicit faith in Pedda Babu and Pedda Babu alone but she never could go to him for advice. She may have been diagnosed correctly by Pedda Babu and she might have survived. Recently when Gouthami was not feeling well, I had suggested to her to send the reports of her medical tests to Pedda Babu and she was very happy with his suggestions for treatment. He is living at Bangalore hence it is difficult for them to make a trip just to consult him but irrespective of that he is the best doctor we know. I can say that because, his father-in-law Sikha Veerabhadra Rao garu waits for his treatment either when he visits him in Bangalore or Pedda Babu visits him in Hyderabad for giving him treatment and he is now in his nineties! He certainly would have made a very good practicing doctor, but then he could not have practiced music. When Chinna Babu was suffering from brain tumor Pedda Babu suggested a second opinion before selecting operation as an option. This year on 30th March, 2013 Vikram called Pedda Babu as he was concerned about Bhanumati's health. Over the phone he told Vikram to admit her to a hospital as he thought she suffered a stroke. Vikram called ambulance and before she could be taken in the ambulance the doctor accompanying the service declared her dead. His diagnosis is accurate and his medicines work most of the time. Of course of late the medicines he recommends may not be available in the market. I feel the world has lost a good healer doctor when Pedda Babu decided not to practice medicine.

Even after retirement he used to go for conducting some examinations in some of the medical schools in south and he has stopped that also since 2012. He is well positioned and may not be very rich but should be considered as leading a comfortable life. He believed in economy as he had shown in his childhood and does not believe in extravagance. He likes luxury items but everything within limits. He is extremely religious and finds good relaxation in singing songs in praise of God. His children are very well placed and he does not have to worry about them. His son lives in the apartment opposite to his and so he does not have to be concerned about him and his wife. He and Sita are leading a wonderful and happy retired life. I would like to mention here that since his visit to Aduru in 2010 where he was informed that Subrahmanya Swami is the deity of Upadhyayula family, he has started visiting Subrahmanya Swami temple in Bangalore and elsewhere.

Legacy of Pedda Babu: First and foremost he is not leaving behind another medical doctor as Shivram did not become one. I always felt father made a poor choice in making Pedda Babu a doctor because he would have made an excellent engineer. He can repair any electrical, mechanical or electronic items like a professional. Pedda Babu may not have hated medicine but he chose to teach medicine to students so that he can devote rest of his time to learning more about music. His engineering nature has been inherited by two of his children. Pedda Babu felt otherwise and he told me when I visited him a few days back that he would have enjoyed mastering music as this is his first love. I know father would never have accepted this choice of Pedda Babu. A case to mention is that of Kartik Ayysola, my grandson and Gnanu's second son who declared he would study music only and he is studying music but that is in the USA. Pedda Babu was in India and so for him such freedom in educational matter was just not possible then and even now.

He is leaving behind three children all devoted to God and leading a quiet life and doing what they like most. Aparna showed some talent of his musical genius and is good in playing violin along with him but now she does not get any time. Kamala who is a very good software engineer and occupied a very high position in a private company left software and joined her in-laws in expanding their export business. Their business is thriving and she has shown good business mind once again inherited from my grandfather! Shivram is again an independent contractor following the characteristics of his great grandfather Abbayi Tata garu. In summing up, Pedda Babu is leading a contented life and this contentment in life is what he is leaving as his legacy for posterity.

CHAPTER 9

CHINNA BABU—THE SUPER STAR

Agastya Sastry or Chinna Babu was born on 19th June, 1946 in Rajahmundry in our own home in Danavaya Peta. He was a very fair, chubby, healthy and active child with a crown of thick wavy dark hair. I do not know if he was born laughing, but he was always a very happy person always finding ways to make others laugh. I do not remember of his early childhood as he was less with me and more with Pedda Babu. Other members in the family would lovingly cuddle him and pamper him. Only one thing is clearly imprinted in my mind is that Chinna Babu would follow Pedda Babu like a shadow and would go wherever he went. In fact he would follow Pedda Babu to the roof top when my father left for his business trips and then that would be fun. Pedda Babu had become expert in coming down the roof, but Chinna Babu could not come down on his own and so would cry and someone had to help him come down.

Once when he was about five years old he was crossing the road from our neighbor Saraswati's house across the street to our house, he was hit by a car belonging to one Mr. Sankranti Narayana Rao garu's black car and he fell down. This was the only car on our street at that time and Mr. Narayana Rao was holding a very high position in either state or central government and had servants in the house and a driver to drive him around. The driver brought the car to a screeching halt and we all rushed to see what had happened and someone carried Chinna Babu inside. Fortunately he was not hurt and he had only a few scratches on his arm but he was too shaken with the incident. But this did not stop him from going across to her house. We three would spend our evening time playing in the municipal park at the end of our street and while Pedda Babu and I were fully engrossed in our games, Chinna Babu was not very particular. He would go back to our house periodically to see what was cooking and would come back and tell us about it all. It hardly mattered to us about what was happening back home as we had more important things happening on the ground. I was tom boyish and would climb almost all the trees in the park along with Pedda Babu. Chinna Babu was not adept and so would get angry especially if he was denied what he asked. He would watch for his chance and report to my father that I was climbing the trees or so on. I could see the fireworks waiting for me in the home on my return and my mother and other women members in our house scolding me that "It was difficult to find a match for a dark girl like you and now if you break your arms or legs who will marry you?" I could not argue with my parents and for a moment I would be angry with Chinna Babu and then before the evening wore out we were back with our games. Three of us really had great times together. We joined the same school as Pedda Babu and three of us would go together chattering away and I still vaguely remember that we had very lively discussions most of the times but now when I try to recollect these discussions my memory fails me. I now wish I had a better memory.

Among all the three, Chinna Babu was the most attractive one with his dark wavy hair and chubby cheeks and to match it he also had a witty nature. He could make every one laugh with his stories and anecdotes. He always followed Pedda Babu till he began his schooling. Like Pedda Babu, Chinna Babu was also tutored by Mohan Rao teacher and joined the school directly in 6th class just like his brother. My father decided that I should also join the same school and study in the same class to give support to Chinna Babu.

Father somehow was not confident about Chinna Babu from very beginning and so he wanted me to be there to challenge him. I do not think father doubted his intelligence, but felt he was prone to diversion. At that time I was studying in National High School near Ashoka Movie Theater and if I complete 8th Grade public examination I would be able to join high school directly. I was already getting very good marks and so when father told the teacher that he was removing me from their school they were surprised and requested father to reconsider. Father explained to them that he was enrolling me in another school one class lower so that I could give company to Chinna Babu. The principal was surprised and told my father that most parents come to our school to request us to promote their child to next class and here you are taking her out so that she joins a lower class! I fought with my father but with no success. I am not sure if father was able to change the course of destiny as Chinna Babu was still not focused.

Chinna Babu and I joined the same school and same class and we were brightest students in the class always holding top five positions in the class. There used to be a competition between the two of us in getting the higher grade and while I was studious, Chinna Babu had tremendous memory and would remember what he heard just once. He never studied but always remained the topper. We were the famous five who competed with each other to take the first position. Duvvuri Venkata Ramana Murty was pretty thin like me but Nemani Venkatesh and Godavarti Ranganath looked healthy. I remember Duvvuri Ramana Murty more because he lost his mother early and he was brought up by his grandmother and I would sympathize with him. Interestingly, after my mother died, his grandmother came to our house and sympathized with my father and Venkata Ramana also talked to me about my loss. I was very good in maths and more so in bits paper. It was a test with 90 questions in each subject which had to be answered in 30 minutes and all five of us would get full marks. I would even compete with Chinna Babu and get better marks once in a while. In later years, my father enrolled me in composite maths again to be with Chinna

Babu and this was downfall in my studies as I had no interest in composite maths. I began to drop my rank whereas Chinna Babu continued to remain at the top. I lost touch with others after I left school, but I was told Duvvuri Ramana Murty joined the prestigious Indian Institute of Science in Bangalore and became a very famous scientist.

Chinna Babu was very intelligent and attractive but most importantly his hand writing matched his good looks. Teachers in our school would ask Chinna Babu to write reports if there was a visit by the school inspector or any dignitary. Chinna Babu wrote like print and his style would not change even when he was tired. He had the same quality of writing till the last day of his healthy life. Both Pedda Babu and I cannot boast about our writing. He inherited his neat and excellent hand writing from my father. My father not only had excellent hand writing, but he could compress material in any given space. In the olden times most people used post cards to write letters as they cost less and father was able to add every bit of information on one side of the post card and he also had sufficient space at the back to add return address. He never used other stationery like Inland Letters or envelopes. The same text would probably require an Inland letters for everyone else. Pedda Babu has a hand writing that lived up to the reputation of a doctor even before he became one. Could this be one more reason why my father decided that Pedda Babu should become a doctor?

Chinna Babu never fussed about anything. It did not matter to him if the tumbler of milk was full or not. He had no complaints about food and enjoyed any type of curry and he would savor everything served to him. I hated lentils (pappu) and Pedda Babu would only eat fries, but Chinna Babu would eat anything. Everyone loved him because of this accommodative nature and would listen in rapt attention to his string of stories many of which were original and often not factual. Both Pedda Babu and I would come back home as soon as the school was closed but not Chinna Babu. Invariably father waited for him at the wooden gate and asks him reason for being late and he will weave an instant story. He once told father that he was coming by the side of police quarters and he saw that a cop was beaten by his wife. He asked my father how this can be after all he was the protector of law. Father laughed at this story and told him that he was a protector of law to the rest of the world but at home his wife was law. Everyone laughed over this joke and my father's anger would then evaporate. These types of stories were unending and he would thus humor my father and kept us all laughing. He kidded and made fun of everyone in the family. The large population of children visiting us during summer vacation would flock around him for the stories. He was most popular at these times. It was like soap opera or TV shows of today and if he had time these stories would continue forever.

Chinna Babu liked to kid Manikyam a lot because she was so simple and believed everything he said. Manikyam always knew that Chinna Babu was very much interested in movies and she wanted to wean him away from this and so would naturally get upset if he went for movies. As I had already mentioned earlier, our household was so large that we used divide into at least three batches for any movie going expedition. Chinna Babu would be the first one to go in the first batch, he would then go with the second batch that would be consisting mostly be of my grandmothers and then finally he will go with the third batch to see the same movie. He would thus see one movie not once but three times. If some relatives came to our house and would like to go for the movie Chinna Babu would go with them also. I would always argue with father that Chinna Babu should only be allowed to go only in the last batch, but father would laugh and allow him to go with all the batches. He loved us all so much that I have not met any father like my father. Chinna Babu would tell Manikyam that he was going for a movie today and as always Manikyam would be angry and shout at him. He would then explain to Manikyam that there is no fun going to a movie without telling her and see her angry and add "He had seen this movie previous day without telling her but he did not enjoy the movie at all". Manikyam became more annoyed and she would become emotional. Father would be enjoying the fun. We tried to explain to Manikyam that Chinna Babu would not watch a movie without telling anyone and he was only kidding her and there is no truth to it. Manikyam would laugh about it later but then the same thing repeated again after a week or two.

Manikyam was famous for her bargaining powers with vendors for every purchase and this interested Chinna Babu. He knew that Manikyam was so simple at heart that she would be satisfied with any bargain at all. Every time he saw some items purchased by Manikyam he would ask her if she had bargained properly. She would say she got it very cheap four for only one rupee after a long bargaining and Chinna Babu would quip he had seen the same item sold five for a rupee near Gandhi Statue and Manikyam would become distressed. One of the biggest jokes was that once a vendor offered Manikyam six lemons for just one rupee and Manikyam without thinking asked him why you can't give five for one rupee before she realized her mistake. Who should be there at that time but Chinna Babu? This became one more weapon in his armor for kidding Manikyam. I do not remember many other incidents but that was our Chinna Babu. When Chinna Babu was around one could not remember how time would fly as he was always full of fun and stories and I always cherished time we spent together. But I suddenly grew up when I was just in my teens after my mother's death and I lost all the fun with Chinna Babu.

We both completed our matriculation; I barely made a second class while Chinna Babu came in first class. He joined Government Arts College for doing his Pre University Course (PUC) just like Pedda Babu and began his study. It was during this period that father was concerned about the company Chinna Babu was keeping. He was keeping a close watch on Chinna Babu and tried to stop him from making friendship with idle people or in Telugu "porambhogu" persons. He believed that an idle mind is a devil's workshop and they would waste every one's time and Chinna Babu should watch his company. Chinna Babu needed someone to support him and booster his ego in his active chatter. In the process Chinna Babu was being distracted from his studies and my father felt that once he skipped one class he will not have the same enthusiasm to continue studying with same fervor. I believe father was correct in his belief and these associations have positively distracted Chinna Babu from his course.

Fortunately Chinna Babu passed his PUC examination with very high score and he was admitted in the Government Engineering College at Kakinada on the merit of his ranking. Father was very happy about Chinna Babu's achievement and Chinna Babu joined Engineering College in Kakinada and joined Pedda Babu who was already in the medical college in Kakinada. Both were living in hostels and when my marriage was fixed on 4th May, 1963, they both came from Kakinada. Towards the end of 1964, father decided to move to Kakinada and close the establishment in Rajahmundry so that he could save the expenses on hostel for both. Indira was still in school and Vikram was still very young and they could study in Kakinada and the city had a reputation for good schools. Kakinada was considered a cultural center and there were many activities in the city that had a special attraction for Chinna Babu. He could now participate in all these activities including his love for drama and Telugu plays. Father was concerned once again that Chinna Babu was spending beyond his means and watched with regret when he pawned his watch or bicycle and so on. He was unable to find any suitable company to keep Chinna Babu focused on his studies and this was telling on his results.

In June, 1971 father fixed up Chinna Babu's wedding even though he had not graduated and I for one did not like the thought and told my father as per my nature. I received support from an unexpected quarter and that was from Manikyam. We argued with father that once he is married he may not concentrate on his studies at all, but father said he was helpless. The proposal had come from the son of Rao Bahadur Venkata Rao garu for his daughter Lakshmi and since they were local residents of Kakinada it was not possible for my father to reject as Lakshmi was a very beautiful girl. It may sound surprising, but my father seems to have had a habit of performing three marriages in one year. He had done this in 1947 when he performed three marriages one my father's step sister Lakshmi, followed by his niece or Gnanamba's daughter Lakshmi and third of daughter of his cousin Visalakshi's daughter Pappu Lakshmi and this became a very famous event. Now following the same pattern, he performed Indira's wedding in March, 1970, Pedda Babu's wedding in December, 1970 and now Chinna Babu's wedding in June 1971. The wedding was performed in a grand manner as both the families were living locally and every one was enjoying the function. But somehow, the wedding became reason for the final breakdown of relationship between my father and his brother Babayya. It is not for me to judge who was right or wrong but the fact remains that Babayya did not come to our house again and when my father had gone to Visakhapatnam to console Babayya after he lost his wife, he did not meet him and conveyed the message that he was away. Father was upset about it since he saw Babayya in the backyard. Till his dying day, father always regretted the events that led to the breakdown. He loved him more than anything in the world.

In 1970, Chitti moved to Visakhapatnam on transfer and when Dinkar was about one year old and we moved to Isaka Thota. Chinna Babu lived with me till we were transferred back to Bombay in 1975. This was my next long association with Chinna Babu. We returned back to Bombay and Chinna Babu went back to Kakinada as he had graduated. Employment for graduate engineers was very difficult in Andhra but the high court gave a directive to the State Government to provide all engineering graduates with a job. Chinna Babu got his first appointment as Assistant Engineer in Andhra Pradesh State Electricity Board (APSEB) and was posted in Paloncha. Incidentally Chitti's sister Baby was living as her husband was also posted there. But soon after, Chinna Babu was transferred to Hyderabad and so he moved to Hyderabad. By that time our household in Kakinada had dwindled to only father and Vikram who too had gone to Visakhapatnam for completing his Masters in Chemistry at Andhra University. Vikram also found opening for teaching in Hyderabad and so father decided to move to Hyderabad where Pedda Babu, Chinna Babu and Vikram had jobs and so he closed the establishment in Kakinada permanently.

Chinna Babu always felt that he was destined to be a movie star but then father did not allow him to go to the film industry as it did not have a good reputation then. But once he was posted in Hyderabad, he began meeting people in television industry and he became evening news reader in Hyderabad Doordarshan and this helped him in realizing his potential as an artist. He found that his job in APSEB was a liability and so he quit the job and began acting in TV Shows and people began to associate him with his role as Parsuram in a Telugu detective series which I did not see as I was in Bombay.

It is not that father did not approve of Chinna Babu's progress in the entertainment industry but he had reservations about his ability to continue and get consistent remuneration from these shows. He would tell me that he was not worried about Pedda Babu because he will take care of himself as he loves those near to him. Chinna Babu on the other hand liked to maintain his expensive style at any cost and in the process he may neglect his own family. But father was wrong as this did not happen and Chinna Babu too loved his family as dearly and loved his children and led a very good family life. He is blessed with two sons the oldest one is Lakshminarayana named after our grandfather and the youngest one is Sriram Narasimha Murty. Both are software engineers and are well set. Lakshminarayana is settled in Hyderabad and is working in a well reputed Satyam Computers and is happy living single and with his mother after Chinna Babu died in 2012.

Sriram was in the US as a consultant for a Hyderabad based Software Company and is blessed with a son born on 28th January,

2009. Chinna Babu celebrated his grandson's first birthday in Hyderabad but I could not go as I was in the US. Chinna Babu was leading a very happy life producing many Telugu shows which not only he directed but he also portrayed lead characters. Thus he may not have become a movie star on his own right but he became a TV Star and became popular in this field. Chinna Babu has been an artist all his life and he believed he could reach the same heights as his role model Nageshwara Rao, the hero of yester years but this could not be achieved as father did not support him. But he did not lose sight and like following the North Star he continued in his path of excellence in arts and has achieved great success. I am very proud of his achievements though I have not seen any of his shows as I lived in Bombay where there was no transmissions of Telugu shows and now when he has more shows I am in the USA.

His ambition of playing an important role in a movie was fulfilled just one year before he died. He played a priest in a movie "Nenu, Nanna, Abaddam" meaning "Me, Father, a Lie" and thus he did not live in vain.

Chinna Babu and Lakshmi: Chinna Babu and Lakshmi have been very close from the day they were married till today. Both listened to each other and are compatible with each other. Lakshmi is always well dressed and never without a well ironed saree. If she is well dressed so also her house that is always well kept and clean. You will never see a speck of dirt in her house and everything will be polished like a mirror. Chinna Babu is an early riser and he will get his first coffee from her and as soon as he finished his bath he will pray to Gods in my father's tradition. All my brothers and sisters are very devout and so also my sister-in-laws. One of the most attractive places in her house is the place Lakshmi selects for worship. Every day she would do her Pooja before taking her lunch.

Chinna Babu is as devout as his other two brothers, he too believes in worshipping Lord Shiva. Some time in his later years, he became a devotee of Lord Ayyappa and would visit Shabarimala temple every year. It was necessary that he takes a vow for 41 days before visiting the temple and wear black clothes. It is a very rigorous penance and Chinna Babu followed the strict rules for his pilgrimage. I do not know what made him a follower of Lord Ayyappa, but I believe he got what he wanted.

Aduru visit: On 20th May, 2011, all our family members went to participate in Upanayanam function of Siddhu, son of Kamala and Bala Upadhyayula and Chinna Babu and Lakshmi joined the party to bless Siddhu. It was a great family gathering and relations from our side and those from Pedda Bawa side participated in the event. I am not destined to participate in such event as I am now in the USA.

Chinna Babu and his jokes

Prashnala Rao (Question Master): In Kakinada, one of our close relative Karra Gopalam garu was a fairly common visitor to our house and would come to inquire about father and share local news with him. He was working for a local school and every time he entered the front gate, he would see Muttayya and ask him "Muttayya how are things at Diwancheruvu?" Muttayya would look at him and before he could answer him, he has moved on to another person. If he saw Vikram he will ask him: "Hey Vikram so how is your college? Are you still doing chemistry as major?" Indira is seen at the other door he will inquire "Hello Indira, so how is Jamshedpur?" And so on to the next person without waiting for answers. The whole thing was a bit of unusual for all of us. But Chinna Babu understood him very well. He said he is the question Master or in Telugu "Prashnala Rao" he only asks questions and he does not require any answers. Next time he opened the gate and walked in Chinna Babu would tell us all, the "Prashnala Rao (question master) is here. Don't you worry about a thing he does not want your answers and as soon as came near us and asked questions we would only remember Chinna Babu and would control our laughter. Even father would laugh at his joke.

Our cook Isola Kamanna: We had a very old cook Kamanna in Rajahmundry who was not only expert in cooking but could cook for any number of guests coming to our Danavaya Peta house at a short notice and so if he is cooking I would feel great relief but very often during marriage season he would be contracted for cooking at the weddings and he would go away. He had one small bad habit and that he was addicted to play a game of chance called 'bracket' and Chinna Babu came to know about it. He began to watch his behavior every day. If Kamanna was irritated and was quarreling with our maid Appala Narasamma it indicated he lost his money. But if he was laughing and sharing jokes with every one indicated he had won. He would ask him if he had won any money by asking him "Kaya leka Panda" meaning did you lose of win today. Kamanna would gladly share secret with him. We would all laugh at this question. I do not know if this game of chance is still going in rural India or has it been replaced with Government Lottery, but there were many families living in poverty that would bet all their investment on 'bracket' with a hope of winning and very few would succeed as the game was mostly manipulated. Kamanna did not do well in later days but I am happy to know that his children looked after him well.

Painter Zampa Rao: In Rajahmundry my father had a set of vendors like Barber Adayya; tailor Mahalakshmi and painter Zampa Rao. Every year father would give contract to Zampa Rao for internal whitewash and painting of the house and he would tell my father "Sir, you don't worry, everything will be taken care by me." In 1963 as my wedding date came closer, my father called Zampa Rao and told him that he needs to use good paint so that they dry very fast since the time was very short. Zampa immediately replied "Sir you do not have to worry about it. Everything will dry by evening. Just leave it to Zampa." Chinna Babu decided to play a prank on Zampa Rao and once during their lunch break, he repainted one of the steps before Zampa came. As soon as Zampa came, he asked him innocently "Do you think this paint would dry by tomorrow?" Zampa Rao felt offended and said "why sir it is dry even now see" and sat down on this repainted surface and the entire bottom of his trouser got a coat of paint. Zampa Rao could not understand how this could happen and became very embarrassed and went away. Father asked Chinna Babu if he played any prank, he laughed and told him that he had applied a fresh coat just before Zampa Rao came. Father was very upset with Chinna Babu and told him not to play pranks with such people who honestly try to earn their living. I remember this because this happened for my wedding and the entire scene is in front of my eyes like a replay of a DVD.

Manikyam and Chinna Babu: Chinna Babu took many liberties with Manikyam because he knew how to needle her and she was always caught by him unawares. One of his most famous jokes was the pig tail of Gouthami. Manikyam would tie a very strong knot of the hair with a ribbon at the end of the pig tail and this amused Chinna Babu tremendously. He made a by-line "The pig tail may give way but not the knot (zada udina udutunnadi kani mudi maatram udadu)". But credit goes to Gouthami and she never objected to whatever her mother did or was upset that Chinna Babu made fun of her.

Before going out in the evening, he will call Manikyam and tell her he is going out to see a movie. His declaration would immediately start torrent of words from Manikyam about how bad it is to go for movies and how he is wasting father's money and Chinna Babu will smile and tell Manikyam, I will now enjoy the movie better otherwise there was no fun. Manikyam would complain to Father and he will tell her not to worry as he had seen this movie earlier. I also told Manikyam that this was one way Chinna Babu would kid you, but no, the same thing happened very next day they both would argue.

As a result Gouthami also became a character in his jokes. Yerakanna, a washer man in a shop next door would often come to our house requesting my father to send clothes for laundering to him and father would just smile. We had a state launderer who would come from Diwancheruvu to collect our clothes. One day, Yerakanna saw Gouthami and told my father that his daughter Nagamani looked just like her and so Chinna Babu would call Gouthami Nagamani and make her very angry. Although Yerakanna left the shop, name Nagamani remained for Gouthami for a very long time. Father did not appreciate this but he saw that everyone took it lightly and so he would chide and leave it at that. Gouthami was definitely sporting about all these jokes of Chinna Babu and laughs off when we remember them today.

Ammamma and Chinna Babu: Ammamma had very colorful language and she would express in a way that caught Chinna Babu's attention. One of her famous quotes was she would serve a small fistful of an item like pickle and calls it as small as a pearl. Chinna Babu immediately remarked "Ammamma could we get a pearl of this size in the market?" Ammamma would laugh at that. Ammamma made very good attulu, but it did not have a good geometrical shape and Chinna Babu will say "Don't look at the shape guys, look at the contents" and Ammamma would feel very happy.

Silent Death: On June 20th 2012, Chinna Babu passed away probably peacefully as he was not conscious at that time. For the past six months Chinna Babu was having periods of loss of memory and he even forgot that his second son Sriram was in the USA. One day when Sriram called him he asked when he will come back from Bangalore. Sriram became emotionally upset that his father was erratic in remembering that he even forgot that he was in US. The doctors diagnosed the cause to a tumor in the brain and advised an operation to remove the growth. Sriram asked for a transfer to India and came for the operation. I called Chinna Babu a week after the operation and he talked to me as if nothing happened and complained that he was having some pain. Soon after he relapsed and he was in a virtual coma. Pedda Babu who was there during the surgery felt Chinna Babu will recover fast as these operations are considered to be successful in many cases. He went to visit Chinna Babu on 31st May, 2012 and saw that his health was deteriorating and suggested they seek second opinion for post-operative recovery. During this period, Chinna Babu and family moved to a house near Ahobila Matham in Hyderabad close to Lakshmi's sisters and this looked like a good move since the complex had elevators for going up and down. Vikram was there giving full support to Lakshmi and Lakshminarayana and Sriram. I hoped that looking at his grandson Adi, Chinna Babu would show improvement, but that did not happen and he may not have even recognized Adi. Every time I asked Vikram if I should come to Hyderabad to see him he would say wait for some time. He believed based on his prediction that Chinna Babu would recover if he crosses 20th June date. I had complete confidence on his astrological predictions and so I told Gnanu to book our tickets for October.

Everything happened so suddenly, that even Indira did not know the details leading to his death. He died on 20th June at about 3.00 pm and they decided to cremate him the same day before sunset. In the two hours of time available, Indira contacted everyone in the family and those who were available rushed to Chinna Babu's house for final visitation. Vikram was in England where he had gone on vacation to spend time with his three sons as the doctors attending to Chinna Babu assured him there was no danger. Pedda Babu did not have time to reach Hyderabad from Bangalore and so he did not come. Bhanumati went limping and Chinna Kamala went directly to the crematorium for final view of Chinna Babu's body. There were hardly twenty persons attending the cremation process. This was the end of Chinna Babu who loved to be with many people and entertaining them making every one laugh. Today he was without a crowd of people to give him a ceremonial send off on his exit from the stage the world. He was speechless for almost three months and I am sure he did not declare his unfulfilled desires and wishes. Let us pray that his soul rests in peace.

I talked to Pedda Babu two days later and he was so distressed that if I were there in Bangalore he may have even broken down. Pedda Babu, I and Chinna Babu were inseparable when at school and he remembered all the jokes he would tell everyone. It seemed Chinna Babu lived only to make every one laugh be it a small child, grown man or even old relatives like Ammamma. Pedda Babu felt that for a person who strived to make every one laugh, he died a silent death that he did not deserve. The local TV station relayed a TV short movie he had scripted in memory of Chinna Babu. Chinna Babu wore always spotlessly white clothes and now his clothes were sullied.

CHAPTER 10

INDIRA: THE VAJRAM (LIGHTNING)

"No I will not give" declared Indira shaking her head when she was just about just six months old and was asked to give the rocking horse back to Chinna Babu. The rocking horse was purchased by father when Chinna Babu was about 5 years old and for some reason Chinna Babu was not very enthusiastic about riding the rocking horse. But the horse was his. One day when father was holding Indira in his arms and he put her on the rocking horse so that he could change his hands before he picked her up once again. He was concerned that Indira may fall from the horse as she was still not steady in sitting and once he completed his work he tried to pick her up but was surprised to see that not only she was sitting comfortably but she was not even afraid of the movement of the horse. Next to every one's surprise she began to rock on her horse fearlessly. After that she did not give the rocking horse to any one come heavens or high water. Her words were like the famous weapon of God Indra the lightening or Vajram and once she said it was final. She was firm and fearless.

Indira was born on 8th May, 1951 in Rajahmundry and mother wanted to name her after Mamma and call her Ratnamala, but Mamma would not hear anything and told my mother that she is the most unlucky person in the world and she would not like any one named after her. No one could convince Mamma so finally mother decided to name her after Akka and since her name is Mahalakshmi, Indira an alternate name for Lakshmi was selected and she was named Indira. This is the story behind her name and interestingly her name rhymes with Indra the god whose weapon is Lightening or Vajram and she shows the same strength of Vajram throughout her life. My association with Indira began from Day one as I was the only person who could be ordered around and she was my responsibility. I used to carry Indira around for many years, rather till she was independent and this was really a big responsibility for me. I have mentioned at many places that I had a great passion for outdoor activity and no one could stop me from going to the park and play. But Indira did. If I did not take her with me, I could not go to the park. So if I wanted to go out to park and since I wanted to play I must take her with me. Indira had to be carried in arms and I would carry this very fair and healthy Baby on my frail arms everywhere I went. My arms would hurt carrying her to the park, but like a good baby, she was happy if I left her in the shade of a tree and go about my play and thus she was not at all fussy. She wanted me nearby. This was a good situation for both of us as she would not move from the place where I deposited her and I would keep an eye on her without interrupting my games. Everything was going so smoothly that I thought that I was safe since at home no one knew of my arrangements. One day we were playing in the park and Pedda Babu and I were lost to the world in our games, but not Chinna Babu. Chinna Babu could not remain at one place and so he would go over to our house every now and then and come back with some piece of news. On that particular day, he came back to tell us all that the cook was making onion Pakodas which is a rarity in our house and so we ran together to the house to eat hot pakodas. Just as we reached the gate, I remembered that I left Indira in the park all alone and so I ran back to the park and carried her back to house. The day was unusually hot though I do not remember if it was a record for that year, but it was a very very hot day. Indira became red like a ripe tomato but fortunately did not show any signs of sunstroke. I was bombarded with myriads of questions for my returning late and I was trying to think a suitable answer. But Chinna Babu blurted out that I had left Indira in the park and I only remembered when we all reached at the gate. Now everyone jumped on me for being so careless and they shouted to me saying as it is I am dark and now I was trying to make my sister Indira also look dark like me and it went on and on. I felt so miserable that day.

Once Bhanumati was married in 1955, I became the real older sister or Akka to Indira and she was my playmate and companion till I got married in 1963. She would be with me all the time wherever I went and the contrast in our colors was so striking! On every festival day, I would love getting up first in the morning, light fire and heat water for my bath. I liked to be first to finish my bath, and welcome the day wearing new clothes. On our Telugu New Year day or Samvatsaradi day, I got up early as usual, lit fire and began filling the boiler by drawing water from the well. I was always the first on these occasions and even our servant maid had not come and everyone else was fast asleep. But suddenly Indira woke up and when she did not see me she came silently into the backyard where I was drawing water from our deep well and when I emptied the bucket, she pulled the rope so hard that the bucket flew from my hand and hit her on the forehead. I was so surprised that I began to call every one thinking I may have injured Indira badly, and my mother came and told me not to worry about it and began applying medicine on her head and for a very long time she carried a half lunar mark on her forehead reminding me of the incident. Even today the mark is there though it has become lighter over the years and I tell Indira jokingly that I have branded her for life. Indira was a very beautiful child and I would tell her then and even now that she is flawless in her beauty, and like moon she also has a spot on her forehead courtesy her bungling sister, me, enhancing her beauty. I called her Indirani or Queen Indira and I loved her for everything she is.

She was a beautiful child and was very much devoted to praying and worshipping. Every summer there used to be a troupe of folk singers who would sing and tell the stories of God popularly known as Hari Kathalu in a simplified language on the street between our back door and Engineer garu's backdoor. The event lasts for 40 days when the artist would tell the audience all the stories of the glory of Lord Rama and his other incarnations. Every day there would be Prasadam for all the public and on days when the organizers did not receive any confirmation from any other members, they would tell my father and father would arrange for the Prasadam. The power for lighting and mike for the function would be drawn from our house for all 40 days and father paid the bill. In addition to the lighting the Katha would be narrated over a public speaker system so that those living nearby need not come and sit at the event. There was a small stage as it was summer time and a large shamiana was enough to cover and every one would sit down and listen raptly to the artist singer known as Haridas. These artists are known to be very well trained in classical music. They would narrate stories in a very interesting manner interspersing them with small jokes to keep the interest of people alive. They rendered Hari (God) Katha (Stories) is in such a musical manner that everyone would listen intently. But the listeners have come from their work during the day and so there were more chances of their dropping off to a sleep during the story telling. So the Haridas would stop at the end of each story and chant out "Srimad Rama Raman Govindo Hari" and every one would chant collectively and call out Govinda, Goovinda!! Those who were dozing would wake up. Indira would be sleeping in my lap or mother's lap when we listened to the Hari Katha and every time Haridas would chant Govinda Goovinda, she would sit up and join the chorus. If she is sleeping inside the house and hears the chant she would sit up in the bed and sing out Govinda, Goovinda and fall asleep again till next chant. She was very much devoted to God and prayers and this has continued even today in Hyderabad where she is living.

Ours was a very busy household and there would be stream of visitors who would be coming and mostly would stay for lunch and go away by next train or by boat. So there used to be many such events where either mother or our cook had to set up plates for their meals. Indira was not very old yet probably about two years old but she ate from her plate herself. She demanded that her plate is also set up every time a meal is served to guests. This would start at 10.00 in the morning when first batch of the guests ate their meals and would be leaving for the train. This will be followed by those leaving by boat and so on and would continue like that till almost 3.00 pm when Muttayya or Veeranna who came from farm were served their meals. Indira would insist even at that time a plate would also be set up for her. It certainly looked funny to me and when I think about it or talk about it to Indira, it still sounds funny. It is not that she would eat every time; it was more a ritual to serve her than because she was hungry. My only problem was that she was heavy to my frail body otherwise we both were happy with each other. I do not remember if we ever fought.

One time Ammamma brought Punjabi dresses for me and Indira when she came from Bombay. It was black in color with gold colored dots spread over the dress and was very pretty but I was not allowed to wear as I was nearing puberty, but Indira wore the dress and she was so beautiful in that dress. I was never able to break away from traditions and I had to follow the orders from others. Indira was liked by everyone in our family and was Manikyam's favorite and so Manikyam always looked after her. On June 20, 1956 mother gave birth to Vikram and our house was full of three infants namely Vikram, Gouthami and Sekhar and mother did not get time to look after Indira and Indira became even closer to me. In just over a year after Vikram was born my mother died and for Indira this was the end of all her fun and activity. Indira became very quiet and a very lonely child. She would play with me when I returned from school but otherwise she did not have any permanent friend or someone to play during her stay in Rajahmundry. She was so lonely that she would play with young servant maids father would hire to look after Vikram or would simply wait for me and even I was not having much time myself.

My association with Indira ended in 1963 when I got married and went to Bombay. I know she had the company of Gouthami but she still did not have a companion and confidante and so Indira virtually lived a solitary life till her marriage. At the end of 1964 father closed our establishment in Rajahmundry and shifted to Kakinada and rest of her studies were completed in Kakinada. Indira was very good in maths as well as in many other subjects but she realized she did not have to excel as she won't be allowed to study more. I had Chinna Babu to challenge me but Indira was all alone. I remember that I could spend all my time with Chinna Babu and Pedda Babu playing in the house or in the park as we were so close to each other in age and activity and more importantly my mother was there for us. In those days even Babayya's children who visited us were also of our age so we played so many indoor games and the house was full of kids. Indira would sit on her bench all alone listening to radio or completing her homework. I could go and talk to my mother whenever I felt depressed or injured. But who was there for Indira to share her feelings? Manikyam loved Indira but she had her own difficulties and so Indira could share them with either father or kept it with her. She did the latter. One thing that continued with her is her devotion to God with passage of every year. She may not get up from sleep now when someone chants Govinda Goovinda, but her faith in Lord Venkateshwara remained steadfast. She would religiously get up very early in the morning every Saturday and begin chanting Venkateshwara Suprabhatam in a very melodious voice. I used to kid her that don't pray Lord Venkateshwara so much or else he might bless you with a match looking like him dark and handsome! She would get annoyed.

My father shifted to Kakinada and did not have any one to look after the children. Out of blue one of my father's cousins Rajulamma came to stay with us after her husband deserted her and went over to Benares or some such place. She was happy to be in our family and she looked after Indira in particular. She became her companion and she would see to it that she received everything she needed. Indira was looked after with great love and affection by Rajulamma. I was very happy that she was there to share the growing pangs of Indira. It is so strange that every time father needed someone to look after his children someone would come out and look after with no desire for returns. At the time of my marriage and before my father left Rajahmundry, Mavatata Garu helped father and once the work was done, he went back to Hyderabad as if he had come only for the purpose of my wedding. Similarly, Rajulamma came to stay with my father and after Indira was married she went back to her own house and interestingly her husband returned back like a counterfeit coin.

Music runs in our family and Indira was no different. Her pet singer was Leela and she would argue with everyone to convince them that there is no singer better than Leela and of course Ghantasala who is famous in every Telugu house hold even today. She learnt Violin after I stopped and she also learnt playing Veena and her knowledge of classical music is very high. She was also very good in singing movie songs and even today she has kept her interest in music and melody in her voice. Every time I visit Hyderabad now, I would sit in the adjoining room and listen to the musical singing of all prayers by Indira. My address in Hyderabad is that of Indira wherever she is staying as I would like to stay with her and spend quality time talking with her or arguing with her in fun and luckily for me even her children like me and treat me royally.

I would like to mention here that though my father was staying in Rajahmundry and did not venture out he was well known among our community and all his daughters were married without his searching that includes me too. In fact offers for marriage came from the bridegroom's side for each one of us. In Indira's case also same thing happened and father received one such proposal from the bridegroom's family for Indira.

In 1968, we all were participating in the wedding of Sethu my Doddamma Sarada's daughter in Hyderabad and there someone from Vadlamani Somesham garu's family saw Indira and they began to inquiring about her antecedents and we received a proposal for their second son Narasimha Rao who was working in TELCO at Jamshedpur. He was the second son of Vadlamani Somesham garu and was a highly qualified engineer graduated with distinction from the most prestigious institution in India, the Indian Institute of Science in Bangalore. He was selected by the famous automobile company TELCO of Jamshedpur while he was studying in the Institute and held a very high position in the company from the day he joined. My father immediately replied that he was not interested in marrying for another two years as by that time he expected Pedda Babu would be married as he wanted Pedda Babu to do the Kanya Daanam. Everyone was aghast that father was virtually rejecting such a good match and they told him and he said "if they want they will wait for two years or else Indira will get a better match. I am not worried." When nothing materialized by October, 1969, father agreed to arrange for a formal meeting of Indira with Babi who was accompanied by his uncle Tammu garu at our house. They saw Indira and both went away saying yes to marriage. No one asked Indira anything and Indira did not speak at this meeting. Marriage was then fixed for March 22nd 1970 on the day of Holi or a Full Moon day.

I was in Bombay and when I heard about the wedding and I left Bombay for the wedding. Incidentally, Chitti also received his transfer orders to Visakhapatnam and so we both came with Gnanu to attend the wedding and Chitti went back to prepare for our shifting and I stayed back with Gnanu to be with my father and Vikram. The wedding was performed in Kakinada. Somesham garu wanted it to be performed in Hyderabad but he agreed to my father's condition. Father saw to it that when they arrived they would get all the comforts they were used to in Hyderabad. After my mother's death, father had to look at someone to perform Kanya Daanam or give the bride away and for my marriage Babayya had done the task on my father's behalf. Abbulu garu volunteered saying he and Doddamma would be very happy to do so since everyone who saw Indira during their daughter Sethu's wedding asked them if she was their daughter. Father asked Abbulu garu once again and both Abbulu garu and Doddamma agreed with pleasure and this issue was settled. Father wanted Pedda Babu but he was still not married so could not perform Kanya Daanam. This probably was the start of souring of my father's relationship with Babayya.

As soon as the groom's party was settled in their house, Tammu's wife Parvati came to see us and went straight to Indira and began talking to her and came to us with her face full of smiles. We did not understand the reason for this joy or happiness on her face and so Manikyam asked her what had happened. She gave out the secret that someone was mentioning that Indira is dumb and cannot speak and during the formal visit both Babi and her husband Tammu forgot to ask Indira to talk and since she had not spoken a word at that time everyone was concerned. Somesham garu was firm that once consent has been given no matter what the marriage will take place whether Indira can talk or not. He was a man of high principles. The mistake was on their part for not clarifying in the first place and this made every one so worried. She has now confirmed that Indira can talk and talk very sweetly. She then added that it was she who had suggested the match for her brother in the first place. She was impressed with Indira during the wedding of Sethu and was keen that she became part of their family. Once she began the introduction of Indira her father Somesham garu told her he knew the family very well and he is OK with the proposal if agreed by my father. He even accepted the condition of wedding in Kakinada and quipped at the time of Pedda Babu's wedding that "for daughter's wedding he insists and gets away with it and for son's wedding also he insists and gets away with his demand?" Pedda Babu was not married in Hyderabad, Sita's fathers place but in Bhandarlanka her grandfather's place. Father thus commanded respect from our relatives.

As soon as the wedding was over, Indira was sent to Hyderabad to her in-law's place and I accompanied Manikyam along with Gnanu as an escort to Indira from our family for her first visit as per our tradition. This was the first time that I was given this responsibility and I was very much impressed by their home and their reception to us as their guests. We were treated royally by his oldest son Subba Rao garu at whose house Somesham garu was living and they gave us the respect that was due to members from a bride's side. We thought Indira was to proceed to Jamshedpur after three days with Babi, but this was changed and she was going to stay for a week instead. Tradition requires we stay there for only three days and since we had not planned a stay of six days in Hyderabad and we did not know where to go for the remaining three days! We remembered our cousin Baby, Ramam garu's second daughter and she welcomed us with open arms. Baby had shown to us a hospitality that was touching and Manikyam declared that she will never forget this hospitality of Baby as long as she lived. Baby may not shower praises or talk very nice about anyone but one thing she will always do is to help when needed and there is no one like her.

We finally said good byes to Indira and Babi for their onward journey to Jamshedpur and returned to Kakinada. Babi got Indira a passport and they both left for their honeymoon to Kathmandu in Nepal. In a manner of speaking Indira is the first person in our family who is foreign returned!!! Since her marriage, we used to meet each other for all common events like she had come to help father when Dinkar was born in Kakinada in 1971. On 4th October, 1972, Indira gave birth to Kavita and four years later on 30th November, 1976 Kalyan was born.

Our longest association was when I went to Jamshedpur with Gnanu and Dinkar in 1982 for spending Deepavali vacation and we had a good happy time. We reached Jamshedpur from Bombay by Geetanjali Express and were waiting for someone to pick us up and when I did not see any one I told Gnanu that we should pick up our bags and go outside and wait for Indira. I picked the bag and suddenly someone snatched the bag from my hand and I virtually had a shock and probably my heart missed several beats. I turned around to call police and there was Babi smiling showing all his 32 teeth in full glamour. He explained that trains do not arrive on time here in Jamshedpur and when inquired he was told the train would be late by almost an hour and so left late and the surprise was it came on time and since he too had left a bit early, he could receive me now. I boasted to Babi that trains may be coming late to Jamshedpur but when I am in the train it will come before time or on time but never late. We all laughed and that was my pleasant 15 day stay with Indira and I was so happy to see the small happy family. Next our meeting was when we all stayed with Babi when we went to show Gnanu to her would be in-laws who had not seen her which again is another interesting story but does not have a place here.

Babi occupied a very high position in TELCO but he would never show any complex about it and one would never know the value he brought to his firm unless told by his colleagues. He was so unassuming! He would be visiting various countries for acquiring knowhow and technological inputs for his company TELCO. We never knew from Indira about his importance to the management of TELCO nor would he tell us about his visits abroad. On one of the foreign trips he stopped by our house in Bombay and told us about his various trips and like what I am, I asked him why could he not take Indira with him and he promised he would take her on his next trip. He returned from his trip to Switzerland, Holland and other European countries on important conferences and when he stepped out at Jamshedpur airport he began complaining about a severe headache. He was taken to the company hospital and there they told them that he is showing signs of cerebral hemorrhage and he should be moved immediately to the famous hospital in Vellore near Madras or Chennai. TELCO arranged for his airlifting and was admitted for an immediate operation to remove the clot in his brain but even before the operation was completed he collapsed on the operation table and died on 14th October, 1995. I was in Bombay and Dinkar was leaving next morning to US on his first assignment and so I could not leave and be with Indira in her moment of grief. Like Manikyam earlier, he too was looking at Vikram as if to get the assurance that he will look after Indira and children. He was cremated in Vellore and as per the tradition, Indira's brother Vikram requested Indira to come with him to Hyderabad. He told her that he is OK with money and if required getting one more part time job was not difficult. But Kavita who was aware of their financial position told Vikram that they were very well placed financially and the company will be giving sufficient support by way of pension and other benefits.

The news of Babi's death was a big shock for me and since Dinkar was leaving for the USA, I could not even cry in front of him. When we returned from the airport, I was crying uncontrollably and wanted to leave the very next day but I could not go since Ramam garu my father-in-law was with us and he was not very healthy. Chitti and I arranged for Ramam garu to stay at a nursing home and once these arrangements were finalized we both left for Hyderabad. On 10th day Kalyan performed the rites for his father in Hyderabad and Pedda Bawa and Chitti were giving company to Kalyan. Naresh from USA had called his father Tammu garu and asked him if they had donated eyes before Babi died as that was his wish. This was a big surprise for all as Babi had not mentioned this to Indira or Kavita. Both Chitti and Pedda Bawa decided that they would tell every one that they want their bodies to be donated to a medical institution so that they can use all the organs that can be used to save a life or help in advancing the medical knowledge. At Hyderabad Chitti's sister Lakshmi came to meet us and told me to continue to give support to Indira and she went to Bombay with Chitti to look after their father. This gave me encouragement to continue to live in Hyderabad and see that Indira, Kavita and Kalyan were settled there.

It is the irony of the circumstances that Indira who once had a very high position in their society and was soaring in happiness all around, suddenly came down with a thud on this earth with a sudden new realization that Babi was not there with her any more. She became a zombie for quite a long time but once she came with Vikram, she took control of herself and in this both Kavita and Kalyan played a very significant role. They protected her from every one and saw to it that no one took advantage of her simple and trusting nature. Indira was simple but she could read people very well and she would know instantly if someone was not truthful. Next they had to go to Jamshedpur and complete all the final formalities with the company and Indira told the management that she would not like to come to Jamshedpur to sign any document and even for surrendering the company quarters, she told them her daughter Kavita will be doing on her behalf. The company management was very understanding and tried to ensure that she could complete most transactions without coming to Jamshedpur while staying at Hyderabad. She told everyone that she had come to Jamshedpur as a bride with all symbols of a married woman and now she will not visit the same place as a widow.

I accompanied both Kalyan and Kavita to Jamshedpur in her place for supervising surrendering of their company quarters to the management. We went to Jamshedpur by train and we were all in a rather sad mood with minimum discussions and the train was late as usual and since we would be passing through bandit infested area, the railway authorities stopped the train at a station during night time with instructions that we should not open windows and doors for our own safety. I was sitting there with two teens just out of their trauma and this was too much for me. I hoped and prayed that no bandit would get in the train and that I would deliver both Kavita and Kalyan to their mother safely in Hyderabad. The train started first thing in morning and we reached Jamshedpur and went to the company quarters and I could see the pain in their eyes particularly since they both lived all their lives and had so many pleasant memories. We involved ourselves in packing all items for shipping them off and disposed many others though valuable since it may not be possible for Indira to get as spacious a house as the company quarters. I was greatly touched with the support Indira's neighbors gave us and throughout our stay and we did not cook at all. Morning coffee would be sent by Sharma garu, Lunch by Banerjee family, evening meal with Rao garu and so on and on. Everything was loaded on the truck and we began our return journey. There was only one thing remaining and that was gold ornaments and Kavita and I decided to carry them with us in train but Rao garu said it was too risky since we will be passing through the bandit infested area once again and so he took all the ornaments from us and took a flight to Hyderabad and gave them to Indira safely. We came by train with other luggage and Indira rented a house close to that of Vikram's.

Indira was just 44 years five months and 5 days old on the day Babi died, Kavita was then 23 years and Kalyan not yet 19 years and for a family that had always stayed together this was a great upheaval in their life and life styles. Babi had always protected Indira from any of the household responsibilities and took care to see that she lived a very happy and care free life. Now it was the turn of Kavita who vowed that she will take all the responsibilities of running the home and see that Kalyan completes his professional career. She told her mother that she would not marry till this is completed and that Indira should also not talk about her marriage till her objectives were achieved.

She remembered her promise to her father when things were very good that she will complete her chartered accountant course (sort of CPA course in the US) and she began to study in the earnest to this goal. It is not uncommon for aspirants to fail in their goal of succeeding in the CA course and generally take more number of years to complete than prescribed but not Kavita. Without missing a single year, she become a Chartered Accountant with flying colors and was in first twenty on all India merit list and second in Hyderabad. She immediately got a position with Billimoria Accounting Services as a Chartered Accountant. She was managing all the expenses without spending beyond and within the amounts they received as pension. In 1997, Indira purchased a two bed room apartment in a very busy center in Hyderabad and they all moved there. Vikram also purchased one apartment almost diagonally opposite to theirs so as to be near to Indira if she needed. It was a short investment and they both vacated their apartments and Vikram moved to Ibrahimpatnam whereas Indira has not yet considered purchasing another house. Indira and family have been living in rental houses and are waiting for the right time and opportunity to settle down permanently. Kavita has been managing their finances in a very professional manner proving to one and all that she is a very capable person.

Kalyan got admission in Tirupati Engineering College for doing Bachelor in Computer Science and completed his course very successfully and came in the first ten in his class. He is now well qualified and has been in service for quite a number of years now and adds his support to the family finances. He is in fact the baby of the family and is so sweet and cuddly that one could carry him on her shoulders!!! Every time he is called baby I remember Amitabh Bacchan in a movie asking his grandfather to carry him like he used to in good old days. Like Amitabh he too is almost 6'3" and lanky and if I mistake not he is also an Amitabh fan.

Indira is thus set in life and everything is going so smoothly that when I visited her in India in 2010, I had a very wonderful time with her and I celebrated my 66th birthday with her and Kavita and Kalyan. It was wonderful and she gifted me with plenty of jewelry which otherwise I would never have thought buying for myself. During this pleasant visit, we discussed about her 60th birthday on 8th May 2011 and she wanted to keep it a very low key affair and warned me not to tell any of my brothers or sisters as she wanted each of them to recollect the event on their own.

I returned to the US in November, 2010 and went to Greenville in the Southern state of Mississippi. In February, Gouthami informed me of her son Vamshi's wedding on 5th May and I just thought it was a strange coincidence that that it was also Indira's 60th birthday as per Indian almanac or Panchangam. I was hoping that this day would be celebrated as her birthday in a very grand manner and I am so happy that it did happen. Since Gouthami knew about it, she with all our family members arranged a surprise birthday celebration a few hours before Vamshi's wedding reception later in the evening. Every one including Pedda Babu and Chinna Babu and Trivikram presented her with sarees. Gouthami and her sisters collectively presented her with a beautiful ring and an expensive saree. Kalyan and Kavita each presented her with gold bangles. Indira as her name symbolized looked so much like Goddess Lakshmi; serene, happy and dignified.

I was keen on presenting her with my gifts on 8th May and in a way this was also good since I virtually got a special balcony seat. Kalyan was in the USA and was leaving that week and I wanted to give something unique and one that she loves so much. Gnanu went on line and saw an offer for 6 watches and so I along with Gnanu and Dinkar sent her a gift of 6 watches each watch signifying 10 years of her life. I know everyone would ask why watches after all she has so many in her house. But only I knew her love for watches. On 8th May as promised by Kalyan and Kavita, after Indira wore a silk saree gifted by me, they gave the packet of 6 watches Kalyan brought from the US. Indira was so happy that she virtually shed tears of happiness over the phone.

Both Kalyan and Kavita are holding high positions and they look after Indira very well. There are no health issues and Indira is leading a good life mostly devoting her life to worshipping Gods and virtually every day she has a fast and even Kavita also believes in religious practices. I have had a very happy stay with them in December of 2012 when I came with Chitti to participate in Vikram's son Bhanu's wedding and we all had a wonderful time together. Indira, Kavita and Kalyan participate in most weddings but there have been no wedding bells for Kavita and Kalyan and this makes us all very unhappy. Is there no sense of justice in the realm of God that Indira who suffered so much all through her life, continues to suffer even now! When will she enjoy sharing her life with her son-in-law or daughter-in-law?

CHAPTER 11

TRIVIKRAM: RAJA VIKRAMARK

I was then 12 years old and my mother was in a family way along with my two sisters Manikyam and Bhanumati. I was very anxious to know would it be a brother or another sister. Every day as soon I came home from School, I would go around the house looking for mother to look for the new born. Before going to school, I would also look for mother, confirm and go. One morning I began to search for mother and I did not see her in her room. It was raining cats and dogs and it looked as if the city was going to see another flooding. I quietly went to Ammamma and asked her and she mischievously smiled and said are you looking for your brother or sister? I said yes and she informed me that the midwife has come home for delivery. I was thrilled and was waiting at the door just to hear anything out of ordinary and there I heard wailing of a baby boy. I was jumping with joy and this was the first time I will be holding a baby since I have grown other than my encounters with Indira. Indira was almost thrust on me at a time when I could not carry my own weight and that too denying me the freedom of playing in the park. According to my father conditions were similar to those prevailing when Lord Krishna was born. Like in those times the river Godavari would have flooded but that did not happen but the rain did not stop and the situation remained grim for three days as if it was an end of the world. Vikram was born in the morning at 7.00 on 20th June, 1956. He was a shining, bright and very fair unlike Lord Krishna who is always represented as dark. As soon as Vikram was born, mother declared that she alone was going to name this child and no one will select any names.

Once mother came into the house on 11th day after cleansing the house (punyavadinam) for naming ceremony or Namakaranam she named the child as Trivikram. Father always respected mother and so he agreed it was a good name. Once she declared that the baby boy is named "Trivikram" everyone was very pleased with this choice of a new name in our family. I sat next to mother after the function was over and when everything was relatively quiet and asked her "Why did you name him Trivikram, Amma?" My mother laughed and said I was waiting for your question as you are always inquisitive. In chanting the names of Lord Vishnu or in Sankalpam, the seventh name is "Trivikram" and he is my 7th surviving child so he is Trivikram. Mother very fondly called our jeweler and requested him to make one gold chain with a locket shaped after the famous Vishnu Chakram which he wore around his neck all the time. I began calling him Chakri short for Chakram of his locket and he would respond happily to me. However, if any one else called him Chakri he became very angry. Vikram became very close to me and I was once again very happy. It is for this reason that this chapter is very important for me.

Vikram was healthy but was afflicted with asthma that was running in our family and this made it difficult for him to sleep. Father would carry him almost throughout the night on his shoulder and he would sleep only after someone relieved him of the duty. It is no surprise that Vikram was very irritable and only father could understand his difficulty. When Gouthami and Sekhar were crawling about like any normal babies Vikram was not able to do so. Father was worried about this and asked him loudly "why can't you crawl like others Vikram?" As an answer to father's query, Vikram would go over the same distance as Gouthami and Sekhar but without crawling using his arms and rump. Believe it or not Vikram did not crawl like other children but he was not slow. Vikram was a very quiet and cuddly baby and had a rich crop of curly hair and I loved adorning his hair with red hibiscus flowers one each in every one of his curled lock. Our house had so many hibiscus plants that year and each flowered prolifically as if for Vikram. He sat patiently till I completed my task as if he too liked the attention I was giving him. Manikyam bought a pair of silver anklets for Gouthami so that they would make a musical noise when she walked, a dream of every mother. But Vikram insisted on wearing those anklets on his feet so Manikyam bought another pair for Gouthami, but Vikram would not let Gouthami wear that pair also and instead he wore on two pairs of anklets and denied Manikyam to see any anklets on Gouthami's ankles. Poor Gouthami!!

Vikram was slow in speaking and would use sign language most of the time and we were expected to understand. Father was more patient with him trying to understand him better, but he too lost patience many a times but became cool once again. My mother died just as he celebrated his first birth day and so I became sister and mother for Vikram and he very fondly called me Akka. It is to the credit of Pedda Bawa that he allowed Gouthami to remain in our house as long as we needed as company to Vikram. Even Manikyam remained at our place during the early childhood of Vikram.

My father took up the full responsibilities of infant Vikram. He could not speak and so he would only look with sad eyes. At that age it is not possible for Vikram to understand death, but he realized that he was missing his mother. He would be weeping silently every time he saw any woman wearing a nine yards saree and with spectacles like my mother and so my Doddamma stopped wearing glasses for quite some time. This was more saddening to us than any thing else. Vikram would either go to father or will come to me but no one else. It was almost impossible not to get angry with him as it was not easy to understand his sign language. Once when he was about 2 years old, he wanted another helping of brinjal chutney or pacchadi that he liked so much that day but he could not talk. So Ammamma and Mamma went on asking him all the food items and he went on nodding his head no, no, no. Father was becoming impatient but he knew that he must get an answer for Vikram's request and so he told the cook to bring all the items from the kitchen and open the dishes one by one. When the cook opened the cover of Brinjal pacchadi, Vikram's face lit up like a million candle lights and he began to smile once again. It is to my father's credit that he did not shout at Vikram even once and was patiently trying to understand the sign language. Vikram did not like mustard seeds added to every cooked item and so he would sit over his plate and search each mustard seed and put them aside. He would complain why can't you cook without mustard seeds? No one had an answer. He would indicate something and we all tried to unravel the mystery and finally one of us would succeed and there would be laughter all round. Father had utmost patience with children and he never to my knowledge had beaten a child or even scolded one and all his patience came very helpful to him when dealing with Vikram.

During day time I would go to my school and return only in the evening. So father would hire young servant girls to look after Vikram and he tried two such persons and that was the end of it. The first one was Ammani who was almost same age as Indira and so whenever she was not looking after Vikram she would play with Indira and for Indira this was a great help since she was otherwise all alone. Gouthami was still an infant and I would be away at my school. Vikram liked to be with Ammani but when I came back he would complain that she was only playing with Indira. After she left, father hired another person who was lazy unlike Ammani and for reasons known only to Vikram he refused to go to her and after some time she also left. Father looked after Vikram till I returned from school and then he would hand him over to me and say, "Amma look after Vikram now." And that would be my duty of playing with him. This was the routine till he began to talk fluently. Things become even more complicated as he expected everyone to understand him and to a fault almost everyone in our house would simply say yes to him routinely. But when they did opposite of what he said he would start crying. He would then demand if you did not understand me why did you say yes? And that would be as bad a situation as before when he was unable to speak. He believed in truth and would not tolerate if someone lied to him and for him not keeping a promise was as good as a lie. There would be a very long argument. Again father had to intervene and explain the reasons for this half-truth, but that would not convince him.

Once father and Vikram were standing at the front gate and they saw some children going to the school. He looked at Vikram and said I wonder when you will go to school like other kids. Vikram immediately replied why don't you send me to a school and I promise you I will never skip my school. Father immediately enrolled him in Sister Nivedita Kishore Vihar along with Gouthami and as per his promise he never missed his school even for one day. But this became a punishment for Gouthami who had many interests outside the school activity. He was like a dictator and he never allowed any one stop Gouthami from coming to the school with him. They were taught by one Vijaya Lakshmi teacher and they both remember her. Once Manikyam came from Anakapalle to stay with us for a few days and Gouthami was happy that this will be her best chance to skip the school. When Vikram insisted that she cannot skip the school, she immediately started crying saying she was having a stomach ache and cannot walk. Vikram immediately told Manikyam, your daughter is telling you all lies. She is complaining she has stomach ache because no one can see the pain. This is her game so don't pamper her and tell her to come to school. Poor Gouthami! She had to go with Vikram and even father could not help her.

As a child Vikram was very innocent and naive. Bhanumati was staying in our house once and we overheard a discussion going on between Vikram and Gouthami. Gouthami asked Vikram why he had no mother. Vikram immediately replied that only girls have mothers but not boys. Boys have Akka or sister. We all thought that this was the end of discussion, but Gouthami would not stop and said, then how come Sekhar has mother? Vikram paused for some time and replied "Oh that, some boys have mothers while others have Akka." I did not know what to say and kept quiet. But the real end to this tale is that everyone shouted at Gouthami for opening this topic. Poor Gouthami, every time she had to bear the brunt!! I decided at that time that I will study and become a trained nurse and look after my father and my brother Vikram, but even this I could not do as by that time there were talks about my marriage and before long I was married to Chitti leaving Vikram and father behind.

One of the most difficult things for us was to teach Vikram. He believed in precision and he expected that we should tell him exactly as his teacher told him in the class and if there was any difference then the sky would come down and he would cry till he got the answer that he wanted. Once when I returned from school, Vikram was in tantrums, raising hell with his wailing and father was already upset and became very angry. He looked at me and told me to take him away from him and not let him hear him crying. I asked Vikram what was bugging him and he told me that he was unable to write the number '8' and no one explained him how to write. I told him to sit next to me and drew two circles one above the other and told him this is '8' he looked at it and said it is so simple, why could others not tell him. It was so simple, draw two circles the lower circle bigger than the upper one! He was so happy that he began to laugh and father asked me what I did and told him he now knows how to write '8' and told him the whole story and father said what I would do without you.

Vikram was not a pampered child since he lost his mother by the time he was one and every one including my father were upset with him if he began his tantrums. His two playmates were Gouthami and Sekhar and both received lots of love and gifts from their parents. Two very important characteristics of Vikram are: one is punctuality and second is his profound intelligence.

Punctuality: If someone says he will come back after 5 minutes, he wanted to know how to count it was five minutes and so slowly he began to read the clock and he became expert in reading the time and that became another very big problem for all of us as we could not fool him. Father would take Vikram to our family doctor Sambhayya garu, a homeopathic doctor for his medicines. He would announce that today we are going to see Sambhayya garu at 10.00 am and Vikram will be waiting from 9.00 onwards and if father is not ready by 10.00 Vikram became very angry. If he is given a time he would be ready one hour before the schedule time and no power on earth could make him late. He maintains the same time consciousness even now. So what! One may say. But that awareness of time and being punctual all the time is very difficult. At one time or other one would like to give some excuse for late coming and Vikram would never give such an excuse. I am reminded about a small couplet of a joke about punctuality.

'Do tomorrow what you need to do today

What you plan to do tomorrow do it day after!!

After all you have such a long life to live

Does it matter whether you do it now or later?'

But this is not true for Vikram as he would rather do it yesterday than be five minutes late or postpone it to tomorrow.

Memory: A second characteristic was he could remember things in such minute details that it would be regarded as miraculous for anyone else. We had a large collection of gramophone records and Vikram listened to all those records when I was in school. All the records in those days were made by the same company 'His

Master's Voice' popularly known as HMV so the labels were same. Every day when I returned from School, Vikram would call me in and pick up and ask me to play a particular record even though he did not know how to read or write he was correct. If he wanted to listen to the devotional song by Ghantasala, it would be the only record he would pick up. He never made mistakes. How he did this I could not say, but he always selected the record of his choice and this was a big mystery to us. It is not that he would only call me but he would call any one during the day time whether it was Muttayya, Mamma or Indira and he would give them the record that he wanted to listen. I wanted to test him and so I changed the order of records in the box but yet when he wanted a particular song he picked up the correct one from the box and hand over to play the record. We have not unraveled the mystery even today and probably Vikram may not remember any of this. But looking at his brilliance in the later years, I think that he showed the sparks of his brilliance even at that formative age. I know this looks like I am making him look like a superman, but then he did have some characteristics that certainly were unusual.

Of course this is all true. He also had an extraordinary sense of smell and may be that is precursor to his profession of chemistry. As soon as he entered a room, he will twitch his nose and immediately pick up any unusual smell. He would enter the kitchen trying to smell anything and everything and this is where his career in chemistry began. He studied in Rajahmundry for the first two grades before Father decided to move to Kakinada and support Pedda Babu and Chinna Babu in their higher studies. I do not think this made any difference to Vikram since he had not lived the way we lived in Rajahmundry. When we were growing up, we were all a close knit family of almost similar in ages. This began to change with Indira who did not have company and for Vikram the only company he had was that of Gouthami. Both Pedda Babu and Chinna Babu were busy with their higher studies, their own friends and activities. I asked Vikram recently if this sudden change of place affected his life and he told me that he did not feel any dramatic difference in his change of environment.

Father moved to Kakinada and settled in Vignana Bhavan in Srinagar Colony near Kakinada railway station as this house was closer to both Kakinada Engineering College and the Medical College so that both Chinna Babu and Pedda Babu would save time on travel and can come for their meals if they wanted. Father requested one of our distant relations Ganti Narasimha Murty to enroll Vikram in a primary school and enroll Indira in high school. Vikram could not adjust to the changed life style. He came from a household where his word was a command for everyone, now in Kakinada he did not have any one to command. He was generally left alone in his school at Rajahmundry because of his tantrums but the same tantrums in Kakinada brought punishment and he began to realize that life is different now and he will have to make drastic changes in his thought processes. The first school he joined was Kondayya Palem School but he studied there for less than three months as he was unable to cope with the conditions.

He was enrolled in Basic School in Srinagar nearer to our house. He became friends with Sitaram and other kids in the school and he began to understand that things are different now and began to adjust with everyone in the class. Once he knew the how he could interact with other students, he became very comfortable and he picked up his education from where he left in Rajahmundry. He completed his primary schooling there and to his surprise and that of every one, this cranky child of the yesteryears had become a very friendly kid finally growing into a responsible teen. He participated in many school activities and both Gouthami and Vikram played a mythological play with Gouthami playing the role of Dhritarashtra and Vikram that of Duryodhana and it was interesting to see both Vikram and Gouthami in one single scene with no tantrums from Vikram! This was the most enjoyable time for Vikram. He not only participated but showed his aptitude for music and mimicry by singing songs in the same tone as the famous singer Ghantasala just as Chinna Babu did earlier.

He was extremely good in mimicry and could imitate any character both on screen and on the radio. One of the most famous radio topics is a Question and Answer session or "Dharma Sandehalu" meaning religious doubts in Telugu by an authority on social issues named Ushasree. Every Sunday this famous Telugu writer would answer questions from the listeners on Vijayawada Radio Station. Ushasree had a very distinctive voice not nasal yet different and a distinctive style of reading letters and giving answers. All of us listened to this program most Sundays and Vikram would mimic soon after and make us all laugh. He once began his own original version of the Q and A and would take examples of each of the children and gave answers in Ushasree style. "This question is from one Yagneshwar of Anakapalle and he is asking our cow has just delivered a calf in our farm so what should we do? Dear Yagneshwar, leave the farm problems and that of the cow and calf to you father and you concentrate more on your maths and social studies." It is not that Manikyam's son Yagneshwar was fond of farm or of farm animals, but he was the correct choice for this question. Yagneshwar, Manikyam and Pedda Bawa laughed every time they heard this piece of the audio tape and Yagneshwar did not take any offence. I do not know where this memorable piece of Vikram's audio is now and since we did not make copies in those days we may have lost this piece of history forever.

The life in the rented home in Kakinada began very happily similar to the one we were used to having in Danavaya Peta house in Rajahmundry, I missed all this fun since I was already away in Bombay. Indira, Vikram, Gouthami, Rajulamma and father had a very entertaining time. If Chinna Babu was there he too would add to the fun with his funny stories. Pedda Babu was generally busy with his studies or his music practices and did not take part in the fun. There was fun all around and this showed how Vikram changed from what he was in Rajahmundry. He became friendly and fun loving person and began to understand others who did not meet his standards of punctuality and precision. He still believes in discipline but he will not insist that Gouthami should be the scapegoat. Indira was in her high school and she was about to complete her graduation from the school when her marriage was fixed. Before we realized three weddings took place in a span of 18 months and the house became smaller.

Vikram moved to Oriental Zilla Parishad high school in Ramarao Peta where he completed his matriculation. His cultural activities continued, he played his cricket and continued to score high marks in his annual exams and generally remained at the top of the class. He passed his matriculation with high percentage of marks and joined Intermediate course in Ideal Junior College. He then joined the famous PR College of Kakinada for his graduation studies. He selected Maths, Physics and Chemistry, a group which was common for those aspiring to become an engineer or a doctor but Vikram did not compete for either and completed his Bachelor's in Science. After graduation, he joined Andhra University in Visakhapatnam and completed his Masters in Chemistry. I was there in Visakhapatnam during 1970 to 1975 when Chinna Babu was with us for completing his engineering, but when Vikram came to Visakhapatnam I was back in Bombay. I went to visit him in his hostel during my visit to Visakhapatnam in 1976 and we went to his hostel. First time we went Vikram was not in his room but we were surprised to see a row of buckets and mugs arranged neatly. I did not know why in this small room Vikram needed so many buckets and Agrawal or Agrawal kaka Chitti's very close friend who had come with us laughed and told us that Vikram had 7 roommates and that is why there are so many buckets. Vikram studied in these cramped conditions, away from home and successfully completed his Masters in Analytical Chemistry. I do not know why Father did not admit him in engineering college or medicine as he did for his older sons, but I presume this may be because father could not afford expensive studies anymore. After all father was supporting all his sons and two of them were married. Pedda Babu used to work small supporting jobs but none that would help the large household.

Vikram realized the situation early in his age and was very careful about his expenses. Once when his bicycle was stolen from our house he did not ask or demand for a replacement with a motorcycle or a scooter fitting for the son of a landlord instead he either travelled in buses or often went walking. The story of his bicycle is so strange that it is difficult to mention here as it is also unbelievable. Thus he became very responsible after graduation, Father decided to move to Hyderabad where both his older sons were living now and set up a joint family and Vikram can also join the work force. Slowly it was clear to Father that this was not possible now since both Pedda Babu and Chinna Babu had set their own individual families and both Vikram and he had no place there. This was no time for a joint family. He realized he will be more comfortable living with Vikram and he did so till the day he died. Vikram loved him dearly and was fully aware of the reality and knew that Father has place in his house only. He began to look for some opportunities in Hyderabad and he became a lecturer at New Science College (Nuisance College for us) near Ameerpeta, a local college in Hyderabad. In India, salary of teachers was always very poor and this salary was not enough to maintain an independent family. So he and his friend Subrahmanyam began teaching in a tutorial college. Vikram would work day and night to make both ends meet and support our father. In 1982 Vikram decided to marry my sister Bhanumati's daughter Durgasree an important decision and one that did not receive support from many of our close family members including father. Father was against marriages among close relations. Vikram married Durga in the evening whereas Sekhar, her brother was married on the same day in the morning. Bhanumati was very happy that both son and daughter were married. Thus began a very long and tortuous journey of Vikram and Durga.

Agastyeswar Bhanu (Babloo): One and half years later on 7th December, 1983, Bhanu was born in Hyderabad and Vikram had just started his professional career. Father and Vikram rented a small apartment just in front of the Vijayanagar Municipal Park a few blocks away from Chinna Babu and close to Bhanumati who also lived in the same Vijayanagar Colony. Agastya was a most unusual baby for the world and was fondly called Babloo. Vikram and Durga had to face the sniggering and taunts of every one about his size all by themselves. Surprisingly father also joined the chorus and I was surprised that father did not realize that Vikram needed his support. He had no one to share his difficulties and everyone who looked at infant Bhanu would make some funny comments that hurt both Vikram and Durga and they now moved away from the society. Though he shunned the society, he did not avoid his own responsibilities towards Babloo and looked after him with greatest love and affection any parent can give. But the biggest gift he gave Bhanu is his younger brother Nannu or Lakshmi Narasimha Murty who was younger by one year and of normal height. It is said that history repeats itself, so also here. I was enrolled in the same class as Chinna Babu so that he could study with focus and here Babloo had to join the same class as his younger brother so that they both support each other. Babloo had to defend himself at every stage of his life and he needed this support from his brother.

The schooling of the two went very well except that everyone was making fun of his small size. The credit for his upbringing goes to Vikram who impressed upon him not to care for these remarks and like a dutiful son he followed his father's suggestions. He faced jokes not only by children of his age in school and outside but he also had to face the same treatment by his close relatives. This would make him frustrated very often and was at war with the whole world. How could he fight with every one? Vikram knew what was passing through his mind and so he devoted more time to him and also keep Nannu with him for support and without Nannu feeling neglected. It was a delicate balance. He advised Babloo not to be angry or violent with those who made fun of him and this was very difficult for Babloo. Babloo not only studied well in his school, but he succeeded in the competitive entrance examination and joined Engineering College. Even before we realized Babloo graduated from the engineering college with good grades and he went to London for his Master's in Business Administration and is now a very responsible professional and probably not at war with the world.

When I asked Babloo how he felt about his father, Babloo's eyes lit up and said Sammamma you do not realize how much I have gone through in my short life. I had to bear the insults thrown at me by bullies in my class and I was never sure if I can go to any of our relative's homes with a guarantee that they will not tell something bad about me and my size. I was afraid of meeting any guests in our house and when I was hurt by their taunts all I could do was to cry silently. I have suffered a lot to reach to this level and every step of the way I have suffered injustices. You may not believe but everything that is bad happened only to me. It has never happened to Nannu or Bannu. Nannu was more than welcome in every house and he was also given special treatment in front of my very own eyes. Mind you Sammamma Nannu did not allow this to go to his head and behaved so nicely with me.

I am not saying that my father Vikram did not give me support at every stage of my life. If it was not for his encouragement, I probably would not be playing cricket at club level in this country of cricket England. My father inculcated sportsmanship in all my brothers and we participated in our favorite sport cricket. Our house in Ibrahimpatnam was like Oval in London for us all. We had our own cricket ground and come Sunday and father and every visitor in our house would don white track suits and play cricket and my father saw to it that we all played a professional game. He came to London in the summer of 2010 and he was welcomed by all the members of our club and he played some competitive cricket and I looked at his image as a bowler and felt as if Dennis Lillee the cricket legend has come to play with us. I know without him I probably would have ended my life long time back and would not be the confident person living independently in a foreign land.

In 2012, Vikram began planning (Upanayanam) thread ceremony for Bhanu, but the hitch was that though Nannu received his work permit, Bhanu did not. He did not know what was delaying since every document was properly presented, but Nannu got it but not Bhanu. No one knows how stressful it was for him, but luckily all the three brothers were staying together and that made things easier. Vikram has great confidence in his predictions and accordingly he selected May 31st as the auspicious date for the event and not only Babloo came to India but the function was also completed to the satisfaction of both Bhanu and Vikram. This function of Upanayanam was a precursor to the wedding that would follow. Vikram had selected a bride for Bhanu through online after screening several matches since Bhanu in particular needed a close review of the proposals. Parul Malviya daughter of Bharat and Kiran Malviya was found acceptable to all of them.

Pedda Babu came from Bangalore for the Upanayanam to bless Bhanu and so also Chinna Babu's wife Lakshmi came with her daughter-in-law Sudhira. Indira, Gouthami, Lakshmi Kasi and Kamala also came for the occasion. Chinna Babu was still recuperating after his brain surgery and I was in the US while Bhanumati could not come as travelling long distances was difficult for her due to her arthritic pains and so we were the main absentees. Bhanumati's son Sekhar came with his wife Bala. It was a small family event with little fanfare. Vikram, Durga and Bhanu later went over to Tirupati for seeking blessings of Lord Venkateshwara before leaving for England. The doctors attending Chinna Babu had indicated good progress after the surgery and this helped Vikram to decide to go over to England with Bhanu. The doctors were wrong and Chinna Babu did not recover and succumbed to brain tumor on 20th June, 2012. Vikram broke down uncontrollably when I spoke to him when I heard the news. He said even a slight hint given either by Lakshminarayana or Sriram he would have returned by the very next available flight. He was very close to Chinna Babu during all these years in Hyderabad and there was a great degree of rapport between these two brothers.

Vikram and Durga have proved to be excellent parents and they have shown a great responsibility in bringing up all his children. They gave everything to their children and they received best training. Life in general had been difficult for Bhanu, but Vikram has given him the best. Vikram and Durga accompanied Bhanu to England after telling Mr. Bharat Malviya that they have accepted Parul whole heartedly and the final decision rested with the bride's parents. Both Bharat and his wife Kiran Malviya visited Vikram in Hyderabad and were happy with the family and Bhanu. This was first experience for them in venturing to south for a match and they were skeptical and their visit to Hyderabad helped alleviate their fears. They agreed for a wedding date as early as was feasible looking at the distances from Bhopal to Hyderabad to England.

Vikram consulted the astrological chart and his three sons in England and decided that 15th December, 2012 was the most suitable date for the wedding as not only the stars were favorable but his three sons also got their leave for the occasion. The wedding was scheduled in Bhopal and the entire bridegroom's party began preparation for the event. The wedding was to be performed in both their style and our style and so Vikram also took a priest to perform the same as per our traditions. Bhanu and his two brothers returned to India again for his wedding to Parul on 15th December, 2012 and I came to participate in the same marriage at Parul's house in Bhopal. The marriage party had to leave for Bhopal by air as the time was short and the train services were not convenient. The party was received by Paras Malviya, brother of Parul.

During our trip to Bhopal everyone was remembering Chinna Babu. Earlier in 2011 a similar party of the Upadhyayula family was going to Aduru for attending Chy. Siddhu's Upanayanam ceremony and he said, it would be real fun if we all go in plane to Bhanu's wedding. No one took him seriously then as it was wishful thinking, but when it actually happened we all felt his absence. Pedda Babu came with Sita, Aparna came with Prasad and her two sons, Sriram came with his wife Sudhira and son Adi and so on. This was probably a second occasion when we all got together and for me this was of special significance since this time I too came with Chitti.

Nannu: Narasimha Murty was born on 19th July, 1985 in Hyderabad and he was a normal child and so everyone in our family began comparing him with Bhanu and this was more painful to Durga and Vikram. They too loved Nannu, but they needed to give more attention to Babloo and also treat both brothers equal. They both grew up together and studied in the same class. I must credit both these boys and their parents that they did not allow any sibling rivalry at any time. I do not know if Vikram knew any child psychology, but he certainly practiced as if he knew every thing about in bringing them together and keeping them united all the time. This was the best option available to Vikram and with Nannu's help he was able to support the education of Bhanu. Together, they saw to it that Bhanu was not left unprotected, not because he was weak, but because he looked different from others.

Nannu followed the footsteps of his father and he never liked to quarrel with anyone and believed in a very quiet life and thus he became a very good partner for Bhanu and this may be the main reason for Nannu playing a supportive role for Babloo. He was a gifted artist and like his grandmother Bhanumati or Chinna Babu or Pedda Babu he could draw and paint in a very professional manner. He was invited by his school for any painting and drawing assignments just like his uncle Chinna Babu in his school when young. Nannu along with Babloo successfully competed in the entrance examination for engineering and he gave company to Babloo in Engineering College and studied in the same class as Babloo and after graduating he too went to London along with

Bhanu and completed his Masters there. Vikram and Durga went for the graduation ceremony and for them it was always two in one graduation and so the costs were half. He was life of Bhanu's wedding party and became an instant hit with his dance on the wedding night with the members of the bride's side. The trip to Bhopal is thus memorable for Narasimha Murty too.

Srinath: On December, 11 1987 Vikram was blessed with one more son and he was named as Srinath and that was one more addition to Vikram's family and this completed his family of five or the famous five of Upadhyayula that loved each other and became a very close knit group. Although everyone had their own names they became known by their pet names as Babloo, Nannu and Bannu. Bannu was again of a slight build and as a child he hated going to school. He found that the writing assignments in the school were so many that his hands would pain and he could not complete the assignments every day. He would cry with pain and Vikram would cajole him to complete the home work slowly. Each member including Chinna Bawa helped Srinath in completing his assignments. Even in examinations he was unable to complete his answer papers as he could not write fast. Srinath is the example of the faulty education system in our country where emphasis is given only to writing home works and many children fail because they could not complete their answers in the limited time as their hands were paining. Anup, Baby's grandson also complained of hurt in his arms due to writing homework and was reluctant going to school. Hopefully things will change and children in India will not have to do so much of homework.

Once again the child psychologist in Vikram realized the difficulty of Bannu and he was taken off the school and he tutored him privately and enrolled him for private matriculation examination which he successfully completed. Once he completed his matriculation, he joined the college and he never looked back. He too like his brothers graduated in engineering and he joined his brothers in London in 2010 for his post graduate studies. With all the brothers together in London, Vikram and Durga felt that part of their responsibilities have been completed.

Kaliyuga Bharat: Vikram is the character of the current centuries and so one would expect him to be like every modern growing person. But though he was born in twentieth century, his upbringing was that of a character from Ramayana. He believed in the principles of Rama like his father and always obeyed his father and showed utmost respect for him but he represented by his position Rama's youngest brother Bharat. He is the modern Bharat who was supportive of his entire family. He did not expect his two older brothers to share his responsibilities towards our father. In Kakinada, he would bring medicines for him; do the errands for him always with a smile. He became the additional right hand of father and became indispensable for my father. He would hand over any amount of money to Vikram like he did earlier with Muttayya and did not worry about completion of the job. He knew money was safe in Vikram's hand. He selected disciplines in education that would not tax my father and his meager income in his later years of life. He did not demand that he also is educated to the same professional courses as his two brothers and knowing my father, he was aware father would have borrowed or mortgaged his land to fulfill this desire. Vikram knew this so well! He chose to do B. Sc and do his post graduate studies in Chemistry in public schools where the cost of tuition was not very high. He probably realized that the doctoral degree was less important than his duty to his father. Once father realized that he cannot stay alone in Kakinada, he called him and Vikram halted his studies and came to Hyderabad with my father.

Father still received good revenues from Diwancheruvu but now he was an absentee landlord and he had to wait for Muttayya or Muttayya's son Satyanarayana to do all the contracting work which otherwise he used to attend in Rajahmundry. The income dropped and there was no other source of income for them. Chinna Babu always lived independently but he still did not have a permanent position so depended on father's income from Diwancheruvu. Pedda Babu completed his Masters and went over to Bangalore to settle there permanently. Father loved Pedda Babu more than any one else and he fondly hoped that he will be near him giving support but this never happened. Father realized that he could only depend on Vikram for the rest of his life. Vikram's marriage to Durga was not appreciated by my father as he did not want marriages between close relatives and this may have made him unpleasant towards Durga but again the psychologist in Vikram prevailed and harmony was maintained in the house.

Vikram rented an apartment in front of a park in Vijayanagar Colony which was a cramped three room tenement and father occupied the front room and kept all his medicines and drugs for his chronic Asthma. Our father died in 1984 and Vikram began to seek more opportunities to supplement his meager income and support his growing family. Death of our father was a blow to us all daughters and we thought we lost a strong support, but Vikram took over these responsibilities of our father without any second thought as if it was natural. For us Vikram's house became almost like our father's house.

When Manikyam died in 1985 she was seeking a promise from Vikram to support and educate her only son Yagneshwar. Vikram made this promise on 10th day after Manikyam's death and made her soul to rest in peace as signified by the hovering of crows considered as the medium between the departed soul and this world. He lived up to his promise and tutored Yagneshwar to get admission in an engineering college and thus fulfilled his promise given to Manikyam. Vikram moved into Bhanumati's house at 7/2RT in Vijayanagar Colony as it was vacant for some time since Chinna Bawa was posted in places interior in Andhra Pradesh. Both Sekhar and Murty were living independently in Sanatnagar closer to their work place and this is where Vikram and his small family began to enjoy and this is where his children began to love cricket in their very small front yard. The house was a two room tenement and so the space was limited. Vikram began a comfortable and a peaceful life there and he took additional responsibilities of earning additional income by teaching in a tutorial college and so he was away in the evenings. He did not have to worry as this was a familiar house very much part of their family history. My son Dinkar came to Hyderabad from Bombay in 1988 and he was tutored by Vikram in the same house.

Next Vikram became mentor to Chinna Babu's son Lakshminarayana and since Chinna Babu lived in a rental house just a few blocks away from Vikram's, Lakshminarayana dropped in the house for tutoring whenever Vikram returned from his tutorial college in the night or when free. The house was full of cries and fights with Babloo crying for attention from Vikram who was not at home to listen to his complaints of the day, baby Bannu trying to grab attention of his tired father and Durga practicing her Veena now that Vikram was home. Everyone wanted his undivided attention and this was the only time when even Lakshminarayana could get his school problems solved by Vikram. But he never expressed annoyance to any one and gave full attention to all. I do not know when he slept but if any of us sisters were there he would talk to us till late in the night. We would never know when he had gone to his work next morning. I do not know how many hours a day he worked but he became very comfortable with money through his hard work and good management of finances. In the matter of money Vikram became more like my father and everyone in the family came to him for help. Chinna Babu was always short of cash and Vikram became his private bank and Vikram never asked for return of the money. I know Vikram must be having his own accounting system and he must be keeping a record of all the money he has given to us. I know that every one of us has taken help from him at one time or other including his older brothers and that is why I am calling his story 'A Kaliyuga Ramayana'. Like Bharat he too went to voluntary exile when he saw that his children were being mistreated. He just did not want any occasion for his children to be slighted by any one and what better method than by keeping away from the curious crowd!

He not only stayed away from public gaze, but began to study if he could find out how Bhanu can be treated and so he also became a practicing doctor in Homeopathy like our grandfather Abbayi Tata Garu. He would go over to many medical colleges, meet doctors and look for answers for his queries but everyone was intent in using Babloo as their experimental material. Vikram began studying all books on the subject and also followed up with few tests advised by Pedda Babu as we all trusted his professional expertise and his diagnosis. But he had to depend on his own personal judgment. He even went over to nature cure clinics in Hyderabad and went through all the rigors of dietary disciplines.

I cannot list all the things he did to find a cure for Bhanu and that too without hurting his feeling since Bhanu was becoming sensitive to every little thing. I remember a time when Durga bought a full piece of cloth and then made pants and shirts from that for every one including Vikram to save the costs. It was always a sight and fun to watch and mind you every one made fun of Vikram. But Vikram did not mind it because he could see that his children felt very happy when they saw their father also wearing the same clothes as they did. He would search the entire market to buy shoes for his children and finally found a shop in Charminar and he would then take time out to go over that particular shop and buy their shoes every time they needed.

Accident: Hyderabad became a center where most of us began to settle. Babu Rao was posted in Hyderabad from Bhadrachalam and he bought an apartment in Habsiguda a long way from Vijayanagar Colony and Gouthami became a frequent visitor. Chinna Bawa had retired and so he came back to the house and began to watch over the three kids and Vikram now had a solid support both from his sister and Chinna Bawa. He now concentrated on his additional tutorial activities particularly since his tutorial institute became very famous. His working habits also became very long and once in 1994 when he was returning late in the evening on his scooter, he fell off the scooter. The effect of the accident was not small for Vikram. He became virtually blind and was rushed to an eye doctor. Babloo became so emotional that he was crying and saying all this is happening to his father because he was worried about me all the twenty four hours in a day and I caused this accident. I was in US visiting Gnanu so did not know much about it till later when Chitti wrote to me. Dr. Reddy examined him and confirmed that the retina in his right eye had ruptured and this required an eye operation performed only at the famous eye hospital Shankar Netralaya in Vellore and nowhere else. Immediately Chinna Bawa and Bhanumati packed their bags and went to Vellore along with Vikram and took him to the surgeon who confirmed the earlier diagnosis and told Vikram that he will be scheduling his operation for a later date as there was a very long queue and he will have to return back later. Pedda Babu came to see him from Bangalore.

Operation was successful at the eye hospital and Vikram was recovering well. Durga was alone in Hyderabad with three kids and was very much worried. She had no one to give support and none to talk to her. One day, Babu Rao phoned Durga for the latest information from Vikram but she could not talk and was just crying on the phone. Baburao sent Gouthami who came late in the night and stayed with Durga till Vikram returned. Babloo and Nannu received tutoring from a neighboring student who was close to Durga and so their studies were not interrupted. The staff at the Tutorial College was very helpful and his salary was not stopped and so there was no stress about the money. As soon as, Vikram returned, the entire family moved to their another house in Mianpur so that Bhanumati could take proper care for Vikram during recuperation and this helped Vikram to the road of recovery. Once his eye sight was restored, Vikram began to go to his Tutorial College, as his service at New Science College was terminated after a lengthy litigation and so his only occupation was the Tutorial College. This must have been the most difficult period for Vikram and his family and it made us very happy that Vikram came out of the situation and regained his eye sight as before.

The Big Brother: On October 14th, 1995, Indira's husband Babi died at Vellore hospital after a massive cerebral hemorrhage at the age of fifty three. Indira was totally devastated and did not know what to do; for her all this looked like a bad dream that would go away when she woke. But this was no dream. Indira was invited to their home by Babi's sister Isola Parvati garu. Indira was in such a dilemma and she wanted someone from our family to invite her and that was not happening. Bhanumati and Vikram were standing there and overheard this conversation and immediately told Parvati that Indira is coming with us to stay in Hyderabad. Indira became very happy that Vikram found a solution to her immediate problem. Vikram thus took the place of Big Brother to Indira though he was five years younger to her.

Vikram did not know the financial position of Indira when he invited her to stay with him, so Kavita took time to explain the entire position to Vikram and assured him that they will not be dependent on him for long. But Vikram said he was not worried. They needed a shelter for a very short time till they tied the loose ends at Jamshedpur and once they vacate the company quarters they needed a roof for a very short time. Once the material from Jamshedpur came, Indira rented a house behind his house and began to search for buying a house in Hyderabad. She confided to Vikram and he immediately said "let us look for a house together and stay near to each other. I too need to move out of Bhanumati's house so that they can stay there." Both took apartments in a new apartment complex called Shubham Arcade in Ameerpeta. Indira settled in Apartment No. 206 and Vikram took a smaller apartment No. 203 almost diagonally opposite to Indira. Chitti had retired so we too came to Hyderabad and stayed with Indira and her family till we migrated to the US in 1998. This is where I had occasion of greater interaction with Babloo, Nannu and Bannu. We were living in an apartment complex so it was not difficult for Babloo to realize that they were viewed differently by neighbors. They became recluse and began to play among themselves and creating a very strong bond among the three brothers. One of their main pastimes was to watch wrestling shows and they knew names of all world champs on their fingertips. Their fascination with WWF only indicated how helpless they felt in the normal world and so they created their own strengths. Cricket still remained their passion.

All the three of them watched the same cartoon shows, same movies and had same favorite movie hero. In fact one would say the entire Vikram family became fan of the superstar of Telugu movies Chiranjivi. Children would watch his movies tirelessly and when Vikram returned from his myriads of activities in the night he would also watch the same movies. Once Vikram and the entire family went over to Kodaikanal along with other faculty members of their tutorial college for a vacation who else would they meet but Chiranjivi! He had also come with his family for a film shooting there and Babloo, Nannu and Bannu took their photographs with their superstar. These kids were thrilled that they could meet their idol in flesh. They lived in a different world for many days after their return from Kodaikanal. Every year Vikram and family went to vacations along with other staff members of his institute and children learned to live with normal people and so also many normal people accepted them in their company. But still they did not find life in the apartment very enjoyable.

Vikram felt the need for looking a good place for settling and one that would be near to an education institution where his children can go for higher studies. Vikram and Indira thus began living at two different locations. Vikram took a plot in Ibrahimpatnam away from the city. The house in Ibrahimpatnam became a most enjoyable period for everyone.

Bhanumati and Chinna Bawa decided to live with Vikram since they sold their house in Vijayanagar Colony and Vikram had a nice area with a large space for gardening. Vikram virtually went on exile again and let me say in our family everyone had to move away from social activities at one time or other. Pedda Babu had to do it once; Chinna Babu also went away almost for one year and now Vikram. Only in the case of Vikram these periods of exile came twice to my knowledge but it may be even more than two but I am not aware about the others. It is difficult to fight the society, so it is best to leave the society alone. His move to Ibrahimpatnam certainly was not an exile in a real sense but a sacrifice for his children. Both Bhanu and Narasimha Murty joined the engineering college that was just at a stone's throw from their house in Ibrahimpatnam. It was almost 2 hours travel for Vikram to his tutorial college. Durga would drop him at the bus station at 4.00 am and after almost 2 hours travel by bus Vikram would reach his destination at 6.00 for his first class. By the time he returned, it would be near midnight and after 4 hours sleep he was ready to leave again. He made use of travel time and slept in the bus most of the time.

Vikram slowly became the God Father of the Upadhyayula Empire but that did not last for long as brothers sold the land in Diwancheruvu. Vikram may independently start his own empire later but then that would be a different story altogether.

His philosophy was that you should forgive and try to forget all harm that has been done to you and he is a living example. As a youngest offspring he single handedly helped all his siblings and their children whenever he could. Would anyone benefited from Vikram remember these incidents or they will be forgotten like everything else?

Durga: After marriage with Vikram Durga did not have a wonderful married life since all those who were dear to her did not appreciate the wedding and she had to live among those like my father. But she did not utter a word about her difficulties and assumed a supporting role for Vikram. If my father spoke some harsh words to Durga she would receive solace from Vikram.

His income was modest and so Durga lived very frugally and economically and tried to save money where possible. She found that buying cloth in bulk was cheaper and so she bought full lengths of cloth and made dresses for every one including Vikram and no one complained. Vikram when asked would laugh it out and say Durga likes to economize and I do not care what I wear and nor do my students in college. They are made for each other.

Durga was a very brilliant person adept in sports, studies and music. She had a special love for classical music and played Veena. She did not get time in the day to join any class but she would practice her Veena whenever she was free and especially when Vikram was at home. She attended Veena classes once children began their schooling and by virtue of her hard work she became very proficient in Veena. She successfully completed her audition with the All India Radio. Durga received intimation while in London in 2012 that the national radio All India Radio has selected her as an artist to play Veena in their music department. Now Durga can be invited by the radio for giving classical performances in Veena. The greatest thing about Durga is she even completed MA in music from Osmania University. She is a 'sarathi' to Vikram and drives him to his Institute in the morning if needed or when he did not get the bus. Now she also conducts music classes to teach Veena to aspiring students. In addition to her activities, Durga is an excellent cook and prepares a wonderful meal any time of the day. She even trained Babloo, Nannu and Bannu cooking and now that they are living in England, they are cooking all vegetarian dishes on their own and each has divided their work.

She faced so many hurdles in her married life that only a strong woman could remain sane. Without Durga's active support probably even Vikram would not have remained so strong and philosophical. Both of them together made a life wonderful for their children. I wish their family remains so close knit and loving forever.

EPILOGUE

THE BANYAN TREE OF DANAVAYA PETA

Father told me that his grandfather Upadhyayula Narasimham garu was like a benevolent patriarch who was kind to all and helped everyone around him. My grandfather Abbayi Tata Garu went one step further and looked for ways to support the community and help those who need them. He started what is known as "Chalivendra" or free water camp near Diwancheruvu.

Chalivendra: Diwancheruvu is located on a highway earlier known as Grand Trunk Road that connected Delhi with Calcutta. Common mode of transportation was walking, bicycling or traveling on a bullock cart. It would be so hot during summer months that people died of dehydration. Some benevolent members set up small huts along the roadside filled with water in an earthen pot and covered with wet cloth to keep water cool periodically. My grandfather Abbayi Tata garu used to walk to Diwancheruvu and knew the difficulties of the farmers and other poor people walking along the road and so he maintained a Chalivendra below a banyan tree. One person was employed to see that the earthen pot is refilled every time it is empty. Sometimes my grandfather also served dilute butter milk (mazziga teta) at his Chalivendra along with plain drinking water thus providing some salts for the dehydrating body. He continued this practice as long as he lived. My father then continued even after his death again till his death in 1984. By that time even the practice of people walking on the road became less common and practice of Chalivendra may be unnecessary.

Banyan Tree: My father, the lion king of Danavaya Peta was like a huge banyan tree that gave shelter to everyone. He gave support to his family members and his house became a stepping stone for many for greater independence. He did not reap any fruits in return. Babayya lived with us for a large number of years till he became independent and could afford to live independently. Once he got his wings he just left without looking back at this tree. But father never stopped loving him. Every year the best crop of mango fruits would be packed and shipped to Babayya and he never heard a word about how good they were! In 1955, Babayya demanded that the property should be divided and his share should be given to him. My father suggested that they should sit down together and look over the account books to finalize the accounts. He was least interested and said accounts can be manipulated. As far as I remember Babayya never sat down to discuss the modalities of partition with my father. Finally father told Ramam Mavayya, his sister's husband to work out a deal and partition the property. Babayya demanded the property in Gurraja Peta completely for him and not divide both the pieces of properties equally and father agreed without any argument. Rajananna, who was in Rajahmundry at that time, was furious with this decision of my father. He told him once again that he was making a serious mistake. But my father the follower of Lord Rama decided to sacrifice his right for his younger brother.

Next to go was Pedda Babu who too left Father after completing his medical studies and moved to Hyderabad for his betterment. This was a second blow to father as he had planned a very successful practice for Pedda Babu in Diwancheruvu or Rajahmundry. His dream of having a doctor in the family doing service to poor in the area was shattered. My father was always looking for opportunities of giving back to the poor people of Diwancheruvu by providing medical service but the call of city was greater than service. This happened with Rajananna also when his two sons settled in Bombay and never to return back.

Once he sold the house in Rajahmundry father did not have any permanent place of residence and moved to Kakinada temporarily till the education of his three sons was completed. Poet Vemanna has beautifully described the strength of a person within his own environment by describing as "Sthana Balamu" and this is what my father lost. He was a lion of Danavaya Peta, a land lord in Danavaya Peta and every one respected him, but when he decided first to move the family to Kakinada, he lost his power and strength with this one single stroke. In poet Vemanna's words he was like an alligator out of water hounded by even street dogs. In Kakinada he was supporting professional education of both Pedda Babu and Chinna Babu and enrolled Indira and Vikram in local schools. This was the most important decision father had taken and he hoped that this would help him augment the resources for educating these two sons and bring the family closer. Vikram was still very young and he could adjust in any situation. Pedda Babu graduated as Bachelor of Medicine and Surgery (MBBS) and he began to work in local dispensary. In 1974, Kamala was born and she became my father's pet and he was feeling very happy. Indira was married and was well set in Jamshedpur, Chinna Babu was also married and yet to settle and Vikram was chugging along with his studies. They were all living in Ramarao Peta when Pedda Babu suddenly decided that he will move to Hyderabad and do post graduate studies. Father became very disheartened by this decision as he felt he should have been consulted before he moved to Hyderabad.

He was helpless as Chinna Babu has not yet completed his studies and Vikram was still doing his matriculation. He did not have to worry about his daughters, except Manikyam who would come to Kakinada often as Gouthami was still staying with Father giving company to Vikram. Manikyam's life was also not very smooth and she looked forward to these visits. Although Chinna Babu was married he had not yet settled in life and his wife Lakshmi would stay both at her parent's place and with Father in Ramarao Peta and Chinna Babu was happy to stay at both the places as they were in the same city and in walking distance. Father was always worried about Chinna Babu and he kept a watchful eye on him so that he does not stray. Life was becoming more complex for my father as he had nowhere to go except remain in Kakinada. I was staying in Visakhapatnam as Chitti was posted there from 1970 to 1975 and I was a frequent visitor, but the house was not as spacious as earlier houses. Chinna Babu came with me to Visakhapatnam in 1974 and gave me company when Dinkar was a baby and also connect the loose ends of his professional studies and I enjoyed his company with us. Vikram was in a degree college in Kakinada and was doing well in his studies and so father and Vikram stayed in Kakinada even after Pedda Babu left for Hyderabad. This was probably the loneliest time for Father. Both his sons were all grown up and married but they did not stay with him. Two more residents of the big banyan tree deserted him. Now he was not a banyan tree any more. He became the famed old lion who had lost all teeth and power and was helpless as he could not even do his own hunting.

Chinna Babu completed his studies and he was posted to Ramagundem as Assistant Electrical Engineer and thus he began his professional career that was short-lived. Soon Chinna Babu moved away from Kakinada along with Lakshmi. Vikram completed his Bachelors in Chemistry and was admitted to Andhra University and father had no other course left but to move to Hyderabad and join Pedda Babu. Once he left his own place he lost all his individuality and the independence. He did not get the same respect but he began to live in an accommodative manner. Both Pedda Babu and Chinna Babu did not live up to father's expectation and he did not find his self-respect till Vikram set up his own family in a very tiny apartment after his marriage, a life style my father was hardly used to. But he made most of his discomforts and lived as happily as possible.

Deshamu, Kaalamu and Paristhiti: In a way my father was a philosopher and he would always quote that "Deshamu, Kaalamu and Paristhiti" meaning Time, Place and circumstances governed actions of every human being. I was more likely to be angry whenever I saw injustice to any one and particularly when I saw father becoming a victim. Throughout his life he helped everyone and people took his hospitality when they stopped at his house for their meals or extended stay. He gave shelter to many people during the famous flooding in Godavari River in 1953 and I did not even know many of the people who stayed with us. I have not heard any one mentioning this occasion and I would feel so upset and father would then say "Amma, every action of man depends on 'Deshamu, Kaalamu and Paristhiti' or people change because of their going away to another country, or the time may have changed their outlook or the circumstances would not let them remember things that happened in the past. Let us not judge them but try to understand them and not blame anyone for their faults." He had indeed a very short temper and he remembered all the details and injustices that were heaped on him but he tried to maintain a composed nature avoiding hurting anyone. He was immersed in his Ramakoti or Shivakoti whenever he thought ill of others.

Today when I see Vikram, I feel he has inherited the philosophical nature of my father. His life had been one of a struggle from year one. There are many instances where he did not receive what is due to him but he does not harbor ill will for any one. As usual I complain to him about what people talk about him and his children he would laugh it off and say "Akka, if they did not tell to me directly, that means it does not concern me and if they tell anything behind my back why should I care. One must have the ability of forgiving or Kshama Gunam." There was one more comment by him and he always wanted us to view from the other's point of view or 'Aa konam' or from that angle. I would get angry and tell him that it not 'Aa konam' or third konam, you must look from my konam (angle) always and he will laugh it out. Even though he is so much younger to me I still go to him for any advice for my problems.

In a way marriage with Durga was necessary for Vikram to look after our father since anyone from outside the family may not have looked after him well and this must have been the main motivating factor for Vikram. Father began to realize that he could not expect anything from his other two sons and Vikram will have to support him all his life and he wanted to do something correct for him. Once when we came to Hyderabad, father asked Chitti to accompany him and took him to the local registrar's office near Nampalle station and asked him to sign as a witness to his will that he later registered with the registrar. He explained to Chitti that since Vikram will be having the responsibility till his death, his part of the property should go only to Vikram. He also told Chitti that he spent more money to educate his two older sons, but gave nothing to his youngest son who was looking after him. Chitti did not dissuade him. He died in 1984 and one year later on his death anniversary day that was celebrated in Rajahmundry Chitti asked Vikram to look for father's last will and there it was nicely kept in his small trunk in an envelope boldly written on top as Last Will in his own neat handwriting.

Reaction to the final will was something I could not understand. Pedda Babu and Chinna Babu were totally upset with the content of the will and they were convinced father wrote this will under the advice of Chitti and they were all against Chitti for that reason. Vikram saw that this was beginning to break their relationship if he insisted on the will and so the next best thing he did was to compromise and agreed that the property should be divided into four parts as per the final wishes of father and father's share of property was equally distributed among all the seven siblings. This brings me to the end of my memoirs as it started with my story of my father and mother and the seven siblings.

The big banyan tree is no more. He left behind a small tree we all know as Vikram who continued father's tradition of providing shelter and help to father's large family. He would send money to Mamma for support on behalf his brothers when needed. He supported his sister Indira in times of need; he directed his nephews to professional courses and saw them reach greater heights. Today all of us look towards this youngest brother in our family for any type of support including financial, medical or in any other form. He is following the ideal of Rama even today by his devotion to his two older brothers and also to us sisters. I feel my father still lives in him.